going social

excite customers, generate
buzz, and energize your brand
with the power of social media

JEREMY GOLDMAN

AMACOM AMERICAN MANAGEMENT ASSOCIATION
New York · Atlanta · Brussels · Chicago · Mexico City
San Francisco · Shanghai · Tokyo · Toronto · Washington D.C.

Bulk discounts available. For details visit:
www.amacombooks.org/go/specialsales
Or contact special sales:
Phone: 800-250-5308 / E-mail: specialsls@amanet.org
View all the AMACOM titles at: www.amacombooks.org
American Management Association: www.amanet.org

This publication is designed to provide accurate and authoritative information in regard to the subject matter covered. It is sold with the understanding that the publisher is not engaged in rendering legal, accounting, or other professional service. If legal advice or other expert assistance is required, the services of a competent professional person should be sought.

Library of Congress Cataloging-in-Publication Data

Goldman, Jeremy.
Going social : excite customers, generate buzz, and energize your brand with the power of social media / Jeremy Goldman.
      p. cm.
Includes bibliographical references and index.
ISBN-13: 978-0-8144-3255-6
ISBN-10: 0-8144-3255-7
1. Internet marketing. 2. Social media. 3. Social marketing. 4. Online social networks. 5. Customer relations. I. Title.
HF5415.1265.G644 2013
658.8'72—dc23

                                                                                        2012019622

About AMA
American Management Association (www.amanet.org) is a world leader in talent development, advancing the skills of individuals to drive business success. Our mission is to support the goals of individuals and organizations through a complete range of products and services, including classroom and virtual seminars, webcasts, webinars, podcasts, conferences, corporate and government solutions, business books, and research. AMA's approach to improving performance combines experiential learning—learning through doing—with opportunities for ongoing professional growth at every step of one's career journey.

Printing number
10 9 8 7 6 5 4 3 2 1

CONTENTS

ACKNOWLEDGMENTS

This book wouldn't be in front of you right now if not for a number of great people:

The good folks at my startup, iluminage, who have supported me during this entire process—especially my terrific friend Niña Montelibano (@ninamontelibano), who has been a phenomenal help and source of great advice.

Lara Eurdolian (@PrettyConnected), who came up with the initial book concept with me, and is one of the more supportive people I've ever met.

Paula Gantz of the Paula Gantz Publishing Consultancy, for her sage advice from decades in the publishing world.

My amazing Consulting Editor Alison Butterfass (@one-toughcookie), who (along with Ilana Garon) helped me whip my manuscript into shape pre-acquisition.

The A+ team of interns and associates that have helped me develop a platform, including (but not limited to!) Casey Yee (@beauty101blog), Tayler Bartman (@taylietot), Nina Bahadur (@nbahadur), and Stephanie Leon (@nbahadur).

Melanie Notkin (@SavvyAuntie), who (in addition to serving as a case study in going social) served as the tipping point in convincing me to find a publisher I admired.

The talented people at AMACOM, including superstar editor Ellen Kadin, Andy Ambraziejus, Michael Sivilli, Barry Richardson, Kama Timbrell, Jenny Wesselmann Schwartz, William Helms, and many others.

My incredibly helpful family—Sam, Susan, Jonathan, Elizabeth, and Schil.

My beautiful wife Victoria (@VSGoldman), who is so much more than anyone could ever reasonably ask for in a spouse.

Thank you all, and thanks to everyone else who helped in bringing this book to life. I greatly appreciate you all.

INTRODUCTION

Why read this book? After all, to be completely candid, a number of books touch on the same subjects I talk about here. My editors probably don't want me to admit that, but it's true. Sorry, Ellen and Michael!

Unlike many books covering social media engagement, however, this one is written by someone who has spent the better part of the last decade on what I call the social marketing front lines. Many social media books are written by theorists who are much more professorial than I am. Some authors in this field come from gigantic consulting firms. Others come from an agency background, where they serve as social media evangelists, while a junior employee's typically handling the engagement.

My experience is different: I've been the one doing the direct social media engagement with my brands' audiences, and I've been doing it for some time. During that time, I've also managed my brands' e-commerce presence and often the customer service and online PR functions as well. Because of that, I have a pretty good understanding of how these functions work, and I can share with you actual lessons learned on the social marketing front lines. Tapping into my diverse set of experiences, I can look at these functions holistically, as opposed to viewing them as siloed parts of a business.

Another thing: A good number of consultants use their books to increase their business leads, so the books serve as customer acquisition tools. I'm not that interested in speaking engagements or drumming up consulting gigs. I want to spend most of my time building a new brand I'm helping to found—*iluminage*, launching in 2013—and spending my few remaining hours with my wife and six pets (yes, really). My only motive for writing this book is to help you succeed in building your businesses by going social.

Before continuing, let me say that my comments about consultants and theorists don't mean I wish to denigrate those thought leaders in any way. Far from it. I have learned a great deal from authors like David Meerman Scott, Brian Solis, C. C. Chapman, Mari Smith, Olivier Blanchard, Jay Baer, and many others. I'm truly in awe of some of these folks, and I don't want to come across as disparaging. I do, however, want to explain why my points of view on some topics are different from others'.

I never want to presume that my experiences on the social marketing front lines are the same ones that anyone else would have. To provide you with the best chances to succeed, I'm sharing a number of stories and lessons learned by others in my social circles: entrepreneurs like Laurie Davis of eFlirt Expert, community managers like Maria Ogneva of Yammer, bloggers like Koren Zander of EnKore Makeup, social media directors of large businesses like Scott Monty of Ford, and human behavior experts like Umberto Castiello of the University of Padova. In this way, I can share a wide range of experiences with you, giving you a more well-rounded approach to developing your own presence on social marketing channels.

This book is about social marketing. That doesn't mean socially conscious marketing or socializing for the sake of socializing. I'm talking about marketing to your customers in a truly social way. That's my overarching approach, regardless of the channel.

True social marketing is about developing ongoing relationships with your customers, rather than optimizing around a small specific campaign. Your goal should be to win loyalty from your customers and judge that growth by your increase in Facebook fans, Twitter followers, and brand mentions.

You can find plenty of lists out there with names like "The Five Essential Rules of Social Media Marketing" and "The Ten Laws of Social Marketing." But they are simply lists, and they will rapidly need updating. There really aren't immutable rules or laws. Not yet, anyway. If you knew a rule that might change at any moment, would you really consider it a rule? Probably not. Too much is changing in the social marketing world from month to month to set down any strict laws about social media marketing. However, some general guidelines will probably not change much over time. This book isn't about rules; it's about suggestions. That's because I trust you, my capable and intelligent reader, to make the right decisions when it comes to your own business. It's just a matter of presenting you with the decisions that have to be made. So, it's time to start making decisions. You ready?

social marketing: even more important than you think

AVINASH KAUSHIK, Analytics Evangelist at Google, famously said: "Social media is like teen sex. Everyone wants to do it. Nobody knows how. When it's finally done there is surprise it's not better."[1] In a similar vein, many business owners see social marketing as something that will change their businesses fortunes forever and perhaps overnight. However, they don't know what they're doing, and they don't get the results they expected.

If you're reading this book, you've most likely realized how important it is for your business to use social marketing effectively. You're probably also aware of how much the Internet is used for socializing and sharing information. To drive that point home, the story of a solitary man walking on the side of a highway off-ramp in central Ohio offers a good example of how quickly things spread on the Internet.

The man is named Ted Williams, and, for quite some time now, he's been panhandling by the exit of I-71 that leads onto Hudson Street in Columbus. Thousands of people drive past him each day, presumably paying him no attention. True, data aren't available on this, but it seems unlikely that many people mention to their friends that they saw a panhandler as they exited the highway.

All of that changed in the first week of 2011. *The Columbus Dispatch* posted a short video of an interview with Williams, dubbing his voice "golden" for its perfect, radio-quality pitch. The video was ripped from the newspaper's website and posted on YouTube by a Good Samaritan, along with the following brief message: "Throwing this video from *The Columbus Dispatch* out there, hoping we can find this talent a place to call home."[2]

Soon the sheer oddity of a bedraggled man speaking in such a clear, voiceover-quality tone touched a nerve with a number of people, who forwarded it to their social networks. Within hours, Williams had job offers. Mind you, he hadn't applied for these jobs through LinkedIn or CareerBuilder; these employers contacted him after hearing his voice via YouTube forwarding. They also weren't mom-and-pop businesses; some of these offers came from the Cleveland Cavaliers and the National Football League. Williams ultimately accepted an offer to be the new voice of Kraft Macaroni & Cheese.

Humans Beings Are Social

Within just a few hours of birth, newborns try to imitate the facial gestures of the first people they meet—an early attempt to socially interact. Humans have such a need to be social that we're social even when we're still inside our mothers' wombs. Researchers recently used ultrasound to record the interactions of twins and found that the twosomes were reaching out for one another at 14 weeks of age. That means people have a propensity toward social action, which is already present before birth. "These findings force us to predate the emergence of social behavior," says Umberto Castiello of the University of Padova, one of the researchers who led the study. "When the context enables it, as in the case of twin pregnancies, social movements, i.e., movements specifically aimed at another individual, are observed well before birth."[3]

Given how social we are, it makes sense that people will find ways to "bake" social features into new technologies. In fact, there's been a tremendous paradigm shift in the last few years, in that the fastest growing and most influential digital companies are the ones that create websites and applications that are more people-centric, such as Facebook, rather than technology-centric or algorithm-centric, such as Google. As a matter of fact, companies like Google are moving more toward people-centric models with social channels like Google+, as we'll discuss later. We are moving into a world where we will be able to bring our online identities and networks with us wherever we go.

The human need for social interaction is more important than the need for material goods and monetary wealth. Don't believe that? Think about the foundation on which a site like Facebook is built. On social networking sites, the users create the vast majority of content, which in turn is monetized by the company owning the social network. The hottest web properties are nearly entirely comprised of things that users contribute for free. Take YouTube as an example: On average, 60 hours of video are uploaded every minute; every week, users upload the equivalent of 240,000 feature-length films. It would take you approximately eight years to view all the content that gets uploaded on any given day.[4]

Facebook, Twitter, YouTube, and similar sites are social hubs, and our need to be social runs pretty deep. To survive, people require food, shelter, and clothing at a minimum. Once people have those things, the next thing they typically desire is to be able to socially connect with others. Paul Cohen, founder of Cognection, has built a business around human social behavior, and he has found that humans are hardwired to be social: It's helpful for us to keep track of whom we're indebted to and whom we should probably delete from our iPhone's address book. "If you look at social networking based on its ability to enable reciprocity, it makes complete sense that we want to engage in prosocial behaviors," Paul explains. "It makes it easier for us to transmit social signals that allow us to reciprocate."

People want a place to hang out virtually and interact much more than they want to make a quick buck. Does that statement sound outrageous? Consider the following: In an effort to attract users away from Google and Yahoo, Microsoft offered cash rewards so that customers would run searches on its Bing search engine. When users shopped online using Bing, Microsoft sent users refunds of as much as 50 percent of their purchase.[5] When Bing started aggressively offering this feature, its market share was 8 percent, compared with Yahoo's 20 percent and Google's 65 percent.[6] By most accounts, Bing Rewards helped contribute to Bing's growth; it reached 12 percent of the U.S. market by December 2010. Yet during that time, its growth was far outpaced by the top social networks. In 2010, Facebook grew 48 percent in the United States, with many emerging countries growing at even faster rates.[7] In 2010 alone, Twitter opened up more than 100 million accounts.[8] The desire to socialize and make meaningful connections with friends and strangers online is outpacing the need to search, even when incentives such as refunds are thrown in. People are apparently more interested in socializing than in making a dollar for searching for fleece penguin pajamas on Bing.

Maslow and Starbucks

Maslow's Hierarchy of Needs is a theory in psychology developed by Abraham Maslow in 1943. It's usually defined as a pyramid, with the most fundamental needs at the very bottom and the desire for self-actualization at the very top. The most fundamental needs are physiological, such as breathing, food, water, and sex. Next up on the pyramid is the need for the safety and security of the individual, the family, and property. After that come love and belonging: friendship and family. Once an individual's physiological and safety needs are met, the remaining layers of needs are all related to social well-being.

The basic principles behind online socialization are the same as those behind socializing in so-called real life. As I write this, for example, I'm sitting in a Starbucks on 75th Street and 1st Avenue in Manhattan. It's 7:30 on a Sunday night, and I can count 18 people sitting alone. Most are on their laptops; a few are reading from piles of newspapers in front of them. Oddly enough, at this time, not a single person seems to be sitting with someone they know; everyone is reading or working. All of these people seem to have coffee next to them, but they're not really here for the coffee. The coffee is serving, essentially, as an admission pass. It entitles these people to sit in Starbucks and read or write for as long as they please. The benefit of sitting in Starbucks, as opposed to working at home, is the availability of company, of human companionship. Even though no conversations are going on between patrons at the moment, all these people would rather spend $3 for a cup of coffee from which they'll only drink a few sips so that they can work in a big room surrounded by other people. When we go online, why would we lose our overriding urge to be sociable? It's deeply embedded in all of us.

Increasingly, customers want to be reached on social platforms, such as Facebook, Twitter, Pinterest, and the like, by companies with which they choose to interact online. When Facebook first launched its news feed in 2006, it was a game-changing feature that allowed individuals to stay in touch with their "real connections"—that is, their friends and family. Now, however, an individual consumer's friends and the businesses they love are lumped together in the same feed. When customers become fans of a business on Facebook, they are opening the door to communicating with that brand. People want to feel as though they belong and are accepted by a larger whole. Your organization can tap into people's innate need for love and belonging.

Old Paradigm, Meet the New Paradigm

Even if your job involves working with social media channels at a business that has its own Facebook page and Twitter presence, the process of communicating directly with your customers can still seem confusing and fraught with complications. The old model of doing business was that you developed your product, found people to sell it for you (be they your own sales staff or a wholesale distribution partner), and then received feedback from the people responsible for selling the product. Most of the time, you didn't receive feedback directly from the customer; if you were lucky, you received feedback through an intermediary. In the new model, if your company has a presence on social media, your most important feedback will come straight from your customers—the people who actually use or consume your product.

If you're one of those people who find the idea of going social directly with your customers to be nerve-racking, keep in mind we live in a world where having an online relationship with customers is rapidly becoming the norm. At one point, even having a website was a scary proposition for a company. Today, if your CEO were to say that having a website is just too much effort, he might have to update his LinkedIn profile and start looking for a company based out of, say, 1996.

The Rise of Social Media Has Transformed Society

People are arguably becoming more social as a result of social media. Think about how costly it would have been a generation ago for me to have over 900 friends. It would be just about impossible to call everybody, send people snail mail, and keep in touch with all of them. However, I have 900 friends on Facebook and follow many more people on Twitter. The cost of staying in touch has gone down dramatically, and so has the cost of marketing directly to a customer. Of course, as a result of costs going down, you need to break through much more noise in the marketplace in order to be heard. After all, just as it's really easy for a customer to like your Facebook page or start following you on Twitter, it's just as easy for them to stop following you.

Each day, over 20 billion minutes are spent on Facebook.[9] Not only is a high percentage of the world's population on Facebook, but over half of its registrants log onto the site at least once a day. In many cases, rather than beginning a web-browsing session with the static old media properties like *The New York Times*, people are using social networks as an entry point of sorts to the Internet. They will follow recommended content from Facebook or Twitter and then follow links off-site. This isn't all that different from the dawn of the Internet, when people started their web browsing from the AOL start-up screen. The only difference is that now people are going where they want to go based on recommendations from their network, rather than where a single corporation has decided to send them. Your company can still affect what content people read, but first your firm has to build trustworthiness in the eyes of your audience.

This makes sense, right? You want to be where your customers are. Let's say you're opening a day care center for children between six months and three years old. Presumably, when you're scouting for locations, you're not going to consider the part of town that is filled with retirement communities and has very few young couples needing your services. It's the same thing online: Just as you wouldn't set up your business far away from your customers in the physical world, so too, online, you have to be where your customers are. And your customers are spending more of their time on social networking sites. This isn't just if your customers are young: The fastest growing segment of social networking users is between 35 and 49 years of age.

The emergence of social marketing has coincided with a new-found lack of reluctance to post personal data online. At one time, if you wanted to figure out people's political affiliations, you might have to have many discussions with them around the watercooler at work before you could finally figure out that they were diehard libertarians. Now, there is a pretty good chance you can find this out from a colleague's social profile.

Social Recommendations

Users of the social web watched the video of former panhandler Ted Williams because their peers recommended it to them. Social recommendations occur every second online, and, with the rise of new social media, the pace at which these recommendations occur continues to grow exponentially. In 2010, Josh Bernoff, coauthor of the bestseller *Groundswell*, analyzed a 10,000-person survey studying online influence that was conducted by Forester Research. He found that, between social networks and posts on blogs and forums, there are more than 500 billion recorded social impressions about products and services a year (opening up any webpage with a product or service opinion counts as one impression), with the number undoubtedly growing since the study. As a point of reference, Nielson estimated that for a 12-month period, there were about 1.974 trillion advertising impressions (including all types of paid media, factoring in text, images, and video), compared to those 500 billion influence impressions (including any peer-to-peer recommendations). Of course, not all impressions are created equal. Although there are still many more advertising impressions than influence impressions—four times as many—the latter hold more value. In fact, each online impression is up to 50 times more likely to trigger a purchase compared to another kind of recommendation.[10]

Who among us is more likely to spend time focusing on an online ad rather than a comment from a friend about the new pizza place down the block? Think about your recent web browsing: Off the top of your head, can you list some advertisements you've seen today? Yes, maybe some particularly clever ones have embedded themselves in your conscious mind, but a much larger number of these are valueless impressions that made no impact on you whatsoever.

Now imagine logging in to Facebook and seeing a stream of status updates and pictures shared by friends and influences. In the not-so-distant past, if you wanted to recommend something to others online, you sent them a link. That has quickly been replaced by the social recommendation or social action. Whenever sharing their activities online, people are engaging in an implied recommendation for something. When beauty and makeup guru Michelle Phan listens to "Crazy in Love" by Beyoncé using Spotify and that action is syndicated across Facebook, it essentially serves as a social recommendation. It is an implied endorsement from Michelle to her 250,000-plus Facebook subscribers that she's a fan of the song.

This phenomenon isn't limited to celebrities, of course. How much more of an impact do you think the average status update posted by your second cousin from Kentucky has on you than a 120×600-pixel ad for a brand you couldn't care less about running along the side of an article on ESPN.com this morning? There's a good chance Cousin Billy's review of *The Twilight Saga: Breaking Dawn Part 2* is going to get more of your attention and could have 10 or 20 times more impact than that 120×600-pixel ad. So the fact that influence impressions represent only one-quarter of the total of advertising impressions doesn't tell the true story when it comes to social influence online.[11]

In the world of 2013, the web's social platforms are filled with many examples of innovative ways in which companies are successfully getting to know their audiences so that they can better market and sell to them. In a matter of years, the term social web might not even exist, with nearly all websites being social in one form or another. Websites that aren't social will be few and far between, and they will need a very compelling reason not to be.

E-Commerce Makes Going Social Even More Important

Social recommendations are likely going to grow in importance as time passes, because e-commerce already is growing at a rate that no other channel can match. This means that the time between a social recommendation from one customer to another and an eventual purchase has never been more compact. Under the old paradigm, if a friend recommended a CD (remember those?) or a book, you'd weigh the recommendation and then maybe go into a store to buy the product. But a lot could happen in the interim. You could get distracted en route to the store or not find the product when you got to the store. Today, word-of-mouth recommendations are so important because people can read a friend's recommendation and then immediately act on it.

MP3s are a great example of this phenomenon: Instead of going into a store to buy the CD, you can download a few tracks on iTunes or Amazon in the first minute or two after hearing a band. As a result, artists aspiring to be the next Nicki Minaj or Bruno Mars simply have to be going social in order to succeed.

The same principle applies to authors, given that e-books are one of the fastest growth categories in e-commerce. Random House, the largest publisher of trade books, had their two biggest days for e-book sales on December 25 and 26, 2010. This new sales figure was 300 percent that of the same two-day period in 2009, which had been Random House's previous two-day best.[12] According to the AAP (Association of American Publishers), e-book sales more than doubled in January 2011 from the January prior, going from $32.4 million to $69.9 million. This growth rate will only keep picking up steam, as young readers will soon start having some of their first reading experiences on e-readers. During that two-day sales blitz in late 2010, Random House saw large sales increases for children's picture books available in e-book format, such as *GO, DOG, GO*, the P. D. Eastman classic from 1961.[13] Pretty soon, the e-book format is going to be the default format for people first learning to read, which makes it more and more likely that this format is going to start taking over—increasing the influence of social channels on the purchase decision.

Virtual goods, such as music tracks and e-books, are hot, but let's not forget about app purchases. In the final days of 2011, more apps were downloaded than any previous week ever.[14]

Of course, "traditional" online retail spending for physical goods is strong as well. U.S. retail e-commerce hit $43.4 billion in the fourth quarter (Q4) of 2010, an 11 percent increase from the same quarter the year prior. Moreover, the season featured the first-ever billion-dollar day in e-commerce history.[15] In the third quarter of 2011, online retail spending in the United States surpassed $36 billion, up 13 percent from the third quarter of 2010, and making it the eighth straight quarter of year-over-year growth and four straight quarters of double-digit e-commerce growth. This growth in spending is due in part to more e-commerce shoppers in general: 22 percent more, to be precise. In fact, 74 percent of all U.S. Internet users made at least one e-commerce transaction during the third quarter of 2011.[16] Overall, 2011 ended well for e-commerce, with U.S. retail e-commerce spending totaling $161.5 billion, an increase of 13 percent over the previous year. Moreover, the overall percentage of holiday shoppers who engaged in e-commerce more than doubled that same number from 2010.[17] A hot category for e-commerce is technology (such as computer software, consumer electronics, computers, and tech peripherals), although toys and books are examples of other strong categories.

Regardless of whether your business is small or large, it's fast becoming commonplace to have e-commerce contribute a significant percentage of your sales. In the last quarter of 2010, 68.4 percent of all e-commerce sales went to the top 25 Internet retailers, which would at first indicate that they have a stranglehold on e-commerce. If you're a smaller player, you might wonder why even try to compete? Well, the percentage that the larger corporations control hasn't been consistently growing; in a few quarters, it has even contracted! This means there is ample opportunity for the smaller players to carve out a profitable niche.

All of this e-commerce growth means that social marketing is even more important than before: Social recommendations are not only likely to lead to a long-term sale in traditional retail but are increasingly leading to immediate and long-term growth in online sales.

No E-Commerce? No Problem!

Even if your business has no e-commerce component, social marketing can still be critical to your success. For example, 2010 was the year of the location-based check-in, thanks to fast-growing services such as Foursquare, Yelp, Google Places, and many others. Consumers use these services to publicly broadcast the businesses they've visited, often syndicating check-ins to their Facebook and Twitter feeds. Patrons can also add comments and tips (recommendations) to their check-ins. On Foursquare, mayorships are awarded to consumers who have checked into a venue the most number of days out of the last 60, and friendly competitions exist for these coveted positions. Businesses are encouraged to, and often do, offer rewards to crowned mayors. Rewards for check-ins are a great mechanism for companies to attract loyalty; they're also becoming a great way to get some free PR. When Umpf, the British social media agency, moved into a larger headquarters, they celebrated the move with perhaps the most extravagant Foursquare check-in reward ever: a voucher for £1000 (US$1500) in free social media services. All anyone had to do to be eligible for the voucher was to check into Umpf's new office and then tweet that check-in to Twitter.[18] With repeated check-ins implying a strong social endorsement, these location-based services can be very powerful tools for a brick-and-mortar business.

Social Marketing: Less Marketing, More Social!

Social marketing is more about the social component and less about the marketing. Conversations and collaboration come first. Instead of just talking about your company and its products, why not share industry trends and other things that are both interesting to your customers and relevant to your company? Temptu (the airbrush makeup company where I managed digital marketing) prides itself on being at the forefront of beauty innovation. Given the company's relatively Lilliputian size in relation to huge conglomerates like L'Oreal and Estee Lauder, and with far fewer products in the Temptu catalogue, we decided to open an online dialogue with our customers about trends and new innovations within the beauty industry. Sharing these trends helped establish Temptu as an authority on beauty innovation. What's great about this discussion is that it engages the audience more than just talking about the company itself all the time. As a result, when the company does talk about its own beauty innovations, customers are more likely to pay attention because, by then, Temptu has already established its credibility.

Enhancing your company's aptitude at going social will only become more important as time passes. Customers are online and connected for a greater percentage of their waking hours every year, and that trend isn't going to go reverse itself anytime soon. The result is that your business has the ability to interact with customers as never before.

Remember some of the old-school ways of getting customer feedback? We've all gone to a restaurant and received one of those little surveys that ask, "Tell us how we're doing?" Simple mechanisms like that used to be one of the best ways to get feedback from customers. Besides their inefficiency, these old-school types of feedback tend to be organized and structured by one side: the brand itself. The problem is that they're not a good way to be a true friend to your customers. With online communities on the rise, brands can hear from their customers outside of the old, structured methods. Customers provide feedback in creative ways when they weren't even asked, and how companies respond to this feedback is crucial.

You can't get much more creative feedback than the city of Cleveland received from Mike Polk. The Cleveland-area comedian launched the comically critical, "Hastily Made Cleveland Tourism Video," on YouTube in April 2009 to viral success. (If you haven't ever seen it, feel free to take a break and watch it. I'll wait!) Despite my close relationship with the city (my wife is originally from the suburbs of Cleveland), I couldn't help but crack up and share the video with everyone I know who still lives in the city, as well as all of its escapees. Although the video was undoubtedly a success for Polk, Cleveland's tourism bureau, Positively Cleveland, was able to respond to the criticism in a constructive way—and within just a few days, as a result of its social marketing. Positively Cleveland encouraged Clevelanders to upload their own videos in response to Polk's work at positivelycleveland.com/hastilymade, with contest winners receiving a deluxe hotel and entertainment package.

Improving Marketing Efficiency Through Social Media

An added benefit to social marketing is that, when it's done well, it can be very cost-efficient. Instead of signing an advertising contract with a one- to five-year commitment, you can start and stop spending on a minute's notice. Instead of placing television advertisements, which aren't particularly good at targeting the specific consumers you want to reach, social marketing allows you to reach out to the right people with the right messages and not pay for access to everybody else.

Social marketing can also allow you to refine your marketing in real time. Launch a Facebook or Twitter advertising campaign, and, if you don't like the results, you can change your spending, your ad copy, and other elements almost instantly. If your retail chain posts industry news to its blog and generates little engagement, but your Product

Spotlight posts generate significant engagement, you have the opportunity to immediately refine your strategy to focus on what's working.

What's great about getting fans to click on the like button to join your page on Facebook or to start following you on Facebook is that it essentially replaces the snail-mail or e-mail signup. For a lot of businesses, the default for getting people onto your marketing list is to get them to give up their e-mail addresses. Now, customers don't even need to give their e-mail addresses to businesses; they just need to click one button to confirm subscriptions—be it on Facebook, Twitter, YouTube—or to subscribe to your blog and opt in to your communications. As a brand marketer, you can get opt-ins directly from customers more efficiently than ever before.

Just a few years ago, building real relationships with your customers online was a competitive advantage against other brands in your category. Now, it's a requirement for doing successful business. If your brand isn't participating in these conversations and monitoring social interaction, you'll be at a competitive disadvantage when pitted against socially adept competitors.

Luckily, plenty of companies still aren't doing it particularly well, and we'll show you how to grab market share away from them.

going further · · · · · · · · · · · · · · ·

For bonus materials and updates pertaining to this chapter's topics, please visit: *http://goingsocial.jeremygoldman.com/ch1*.

devising your strategy
and getting started

IF YOU PICKED up or downloaded this book, you probably
already understand that social marketing has to become part of your
business. After all, saying you have nothing to gain from social marketing is akin to saying ten years ago that there was no value in having a website. The odds are high that your business will be able to
use social marketing for consumer research, customer service, campaign management, and any number of other areas. If your business
has a B2B model, social marketing can be a key component of it.
Even if your business is in an "unsexy" category, such as college
textbook distribution or printer paper, social marketing can still fit

into its processes. There are plenty of strong examples of B2B social marketing out there.

Is Social Marketing Right for Your Business?

Although going social is important, your business model and product will determine whether it's right for you and how big a factor it should be. Even if some of your colleagues at other companies are engaging at a certain level, that level is not necessarily the right one for your business. Certain types of brands do better via online social marketing initiatives than others. If you're selling a new innovation that serves as an early detection device for Herpes outbreaks or a pill geared to lessen flatulence, chances are that most of your customers aren't posting their affiliation with your product onto their Facebook timeline or Pinterest.

Likewise, even if your chief competitor is spending half the marketing budget on social engagement, you do not have to do the same. Your organization doesn't have to turn overnight into the kind of social media powerhouse that social marketing case studies are written about. In fact, if you don't have the resources to engage properly, you'd be smart to wade into the social marketing waters bit by bit. Don't promise your customers more than you can deliver. I've seen brands that post questions on their social media presences to encourage customer participation, only to find themselves unable to respond meaningfully to the feedback they receive. Don't bite off more than you can chew. Before jumping in, make sure to figure out how social marketing can add value to your business with the understanding that, as time goes on, the percentage of companies that should not invest in this area is shrinking dramatically.

A Pew Research Center survey released in late August 2011 found that half of all U.S. adults say that they use social networking sites. Social marketing naysayers might point out that this means half of all adults do not use such sites, and they'd be right. Bear in mind, however, that this figure was just 5 percent of all U.S. adults in 2005. That's pretty dramatic growth in six years.

While the number of younger users continues to consistently grow, the gains made by baby boomers and older seniors were of particular interest to the researchers. "The graying of social networking sites continues," said Mary Madden, coauthor of the report, "Half of U.S. Use Social Networks, Older Population Catching Up." "While seniors are testing the waters, many baby boomers are beginning to make a trip to the social media pool part of their daily routine."[1] So if your product's audience tends to skew a bit older, don't assume social marketing can't be a fit for your business. Although companies with younger demographics have tended to embrace social marketing more quickly than those with older customers, social channels may be right for your business even if your demographics tend to be older. According to eMarketer, there are 206.2 million U.S. Internet users as of 2011, with 71.2 percent of the U.S. web population on Facebook. Baby boomers are joining social sites faster than ever: Usage of social sites among people 65 years old and above doubled last year. As a result, 26 percent of the people within that age group are now logging onto sites like Facebook and Twitter at least semiregularly. Younger boomers are interacting with brands online at an even higher clip: 47 percent of Internet users between ages 50 and 64 now utilize social media. That's up nearly 90 percent from the prior year. According to iStrategy.com, between early 2009 and 2010, the number of Facebook users aged 55 and up went from 1 million to 10 million— a shocking rate of growth.

Pretty quickly, the question has gone from, "Should my company have a presence in social media?" to *"What kind of presence* should my company have in social media?" Let's take a look at devising a strategy.

Strategy First, Tools Second

Before getting into the specifics of the tools and platforms you should be investigating, let's be clear that your strategy comes first, and tools should come second. Social marketing platforms keep sprouting up all the time, but they can't transform businesses simply by existing. If you want these tools to transform your business, you need a clear, well-developed strategy, and you have to make sure that your market is ready for this type of technology. Bloomingdale's, for example, doesn't sell exactly the same assortment of items on their website as they do in their department store. They started out with their e-commerce essentially mimicking their print catalog; the results were unsuccessful to say the least. They learned over time that creating a dynamic property that took advantage of the new technology and didn't simply try to mimic the old would be a lot more successful. It's the same thing with your online social presence: Even though you can't yet segment your in-store promotional signage, you should segment online and try to show customers the messages to which they are most likely to respond.

When I was at Temptu, we were always asked whether and when we would make eye products. Given that many companies don't want to reveal details of their product launches until the right moment—Apple, for one, typically officially unveils products such as its latest iPad iteration less than two weeks before their release—we had to develop an internal playbook for how to respond to customers when they asked these types of questions. Your company has to do the same, so your online community manager and employees know what they can and cannot say, as well as when and how they should say it.

Monique Elwell manages the social media agency Conversify, which caters to a client base across the United States and the United Kingdom. One of Conversify's primary offerings to its clientele is to create a social marketing guidebook. If your company advises others on social strategy, that's something you should be doing for your clients on Facebook and Twitter, so that there will be a level of trust with the brand. Much like a font guide or print style guide, you absolutely need this social marketing guidebook in order to engage as a brand.

Some of the questions your brand may want to include in such a playbook are:

- What types of outside brands and personalities is the brand allowed to retweet?

- What brands and industry keywords are permissible to be mentioned publicly? For example: In the beauty industry, we'll use the phrases "packette" and "window animation" in our everyday conversations, but this is internal verbiage we wouldn't necessarily include in an external communication.

- Are brand representatives allowed to publicly discuss the company's upcoming product offerings?

Start from this short list and build an extensive list that is appropriate for your business.

Lucy Swope, an online community manager working at digital advertising agency R/GA, knows firsthand the benefits of clearly articulating a client's social marketing objectives. A social strategy plan is always drawn up for each client, including carefully crafted brand guidelines, the tone of voice outline, moderation guidelines, escalation process, stakeholder contact information—"the whole 9 yards," as Lucy puts it. Having this kind of working document available to both the client and agency is incredibly helpful because it lets the community managers do their job with a minimalist approval process, and it helps promote consistency regardless of who is handling the account.

Creating a Conversation with a Point

My wife doesn't like it when I open my mouth without having anything productive to say. Although I'm admittedly not good at following this advice, I try to use that general concept to make me a better social marketer. If a brand I represent is going to be present on social channels, it has to serve a business purpose: It has to have something productive to say.

Social marketing has to be embedded into your company and integrated into your processes. It should not be in a silo, cut off from everything else you are doing. If your company treats its social marketing strategy as a disconnected and unimportant part of the organization, you are not going to get far in building relationships with your customers and improving the bottom line.

The whole point of Web 2.0, or the social web, is to facilitate communication between brand and customer, and you should take advantage of this opportunity. The place to start is by posing questions to your customers. If you work at a company that makes organic baby diapers and you're not sure whether to launch new diaper colors or larger diapers, simply ask your customers what they think. It doesn't have to be any more complicated than that. There is always a chance that, with certain questions, people won't be 100 percent honest in their responses. But for the most part, if you ask for feedback that makes clear your desire to improve the customer's experience with your product or service, you'll get honest answers. If you're not confident you'll get enough responses to develop an actionable plan, consider offering a minor incentive, such as a small discount or token of appreciation. The trick is to offer something that will encourage an influx of responses, but not such a juicy incentive that you lead people into giving answers that don't reflect their true points of view or that encourage those who'd never try your product into giving their opinions. Create the proper incentive for your customers to give you valuable feedback, and you will not only gain their respect, but your company will be able to improve its offerings and sell more to them.

Facebook likes and comments, Twitter tweets and retweets— all these indicate customer engagement, which is what you're going for. But that doesn't mean all engagement is created equal. One tried-and-true method for generating interactions is to post provocative content, but you have to make sure there is a purpose behind the content! The Facebook posts of one company in the fashion/lifestyle space often have virtually nothing to do with their brand or what they sell; the posts are made just to get reactions from fans. If you're the online community manager at that brand, the method you use to track ROI (return on investment) might indicate that you're doing well because you're creating so many conversations, but you're really just encouraging mindless chatter that's not relevant to your brand. On the other hand, if you're a brand trying to make product development decisions for the next year, and you post questions that get to the heart of what your customers are looking for in terms of future products, you will receive the kind of feedback that will propel your company forward.

Who's My Audience Again?

Now that you're in the process of figuring out exactly what type of investment your organization ought to make in its social channels, make sure you know who your audience is. I'm putting this even ahead of determining strategic objectives because knowing your audience should help you determine what your objectives should be. The audience should not, under any circumstances, be an afterthought.

Mark Nebesky is cofounder and Director of Marketing and Business Development of Goozex, the popular video game and movie trading community. For Mark, social marketing is rooted in understanding your audience. "The basis for social marketing is a clear understanding of who your customers are, the experience you deliver to them, and why they choose to associate with you," Mark explains. To best socialize with your audience, Mark has found, you have to know them very well. "The core Goozex customer is what many would classify as a hardcore gamer—someone who spends a lot of time and entertainment budget on video games. Two important values that Goozex delivers to our members are saving money and a sense of community."

Not knowing your exact audience is no longer a valid excuse. Before online social marketing took over, marketers didn't know much about the prospects they were engaging in an attempt to convert them into paying customers. Now, however, the first interaction with a prospect looks very different than it did in the old days. Not only can you look at somebody's profile before ever talking to them, you can also see their activities (assuming, of course, their privacy settings allow you to). If you were reaching out to a prospect a decade or two ago, you would probably know the prospect's name, title, and company (assuming, of course, that the list of leads you had bought from a direct marketing company was up-to-date). Today, when you are looking to engage prospects and customers, you have a wide array of information at your fingertips.

Maria Ogneva, Head of Community at enterprise social platform Yammer, feels that a brand really has to know its customers to know what types of messages will be appropriate for them. "What are your customer demographics? What age brackets do they fall into? What do they value? Examine what product category you're in as well: a candy brand is a little more playful than anti-virus software." Like any good marketer, Maria knows that defining your social message in relation to your customer is not a one-shot deal; there should be a consistent feedback loop as to what your customers think about your message. "Take a look at how your customers are talking to each other, and talking about you. Listen to how your employees and other stakeholders in the ecosystem—press, bloggers, and influencers—are talking about you."

People make decisions about what brands they should publicly interact with because of what it communicates about them to their networks. Interacting with your brand should say something about those customers—something positive. If your brand is an adult entertainment site, customers will understandably be reluctant to interact publicly with you online.

CASE IN POINT: Savvy Auntie
Finds Its Lucrative Niche

Some people consider "niche" to be a dirty word when it comes to describing a business. Not Melanie Notkin, who founded the Savvy Auntie community for aunts to "exchange ideas, get advice, find gifts and connect" with other aunts. "Carving out a niche can absolutely be a positive," Melanie proudly asserts. Indeed, one of the reasons why Savvy Auntie resonates is that it has a clearly defined audience: Instead of creating a website and a brand as a retread of something already out there in the marketplace, Melanie found a way to add to the conversation and create something unique.

Melanie's content is designed with a specific audience in mind: aunts, especially aunts who are secondary caretakers, whether by relation or choice. Melanie describes her brand as "playful luxury" because her audience is typically shopping at Target rather than Walmart. These women might be in a "luxury" class relative to the typical mom because they may have more time and discretionary income than some moms.

One of the most powerful things one can do when developing a tribe—a community of women who identify with one another and support one another—is to use unique language. Melanie's community, affectionately dubbed the Auntourage, is united by its own terminology: a secret handshake of sorts that helps the members of the community identify one another. Whenever Savvy Auntie posts an Auntie Up! discussion topic on Facebook or an Auntieversary (the anniversary of the day a woman first became an aunt), it reinforces community bonds.

"All these words empower the tribe to feel connected," Melanie explains. "So not only did I do my best to define a niche but I also keep working at it in a very organic way to lead the tribe." Melanie's tribal leadership has not only resulted in a very engaged audience but has also led to a book deal, columns in the *Huffington Post* and *Psychology*

Today, numerous television appearances, and a thriving business. Still think niche is a dirty word?

Focusing on Where Your Audience Is

When you go to a buffet, do you put a little bit of everything on your plate? Then, after your fourth trip up to the buffet table to gorge yourself, do you realize that you might have been better off having had more of one specific dish rather than trying everything? It's the same way with social marketing platforms. There are so many social networks and apps to investigate, you run the risk of trying to do a little bit with everything, rather than engaging in fewer places more effectively.

I've seen some brands get into a firefight trying to prove how Web 2.0 they are. One brand in particular has icons for Facebook, Twitter, MySpace, LinkedIn, Flickr, YouTube, Wordpress, Vimeo, and Bebo (a platform that's fallen completely off the map) on their website's footer. Apparently not everyone gets the old less-is-more adage. It's not necessarily a bad thing to engage on multiple platforms—in fact, it's a bit odd to engage on only one—but don't spread yourself too thin as a brand either. If you think only 5 percent of your customers ever go to a particular social media site, such as Vimeo, don't spend time there. Focus is a good thing. Spend your time where your customers are.

Different demographic groups tend to spend more time on one social platform versus another. For example, baby boomers make up a bigger percentage of Twitter's users than Facebook's: About 15 percent of Twitter's users are 55 or older, whereas Facebook's 55 and older population is only 10 percent of its total.

Although it's still maturing, Pinterest users tend to be well off, with nearly 30 percent having annual household incomes of more than $100,000. They're also more likely to be female, with roughly 6.5 women for every 3.5 men on the site; the most common age range is 25–34, clocking in at nearly 28 percent of the total.[2]

If you're interested in running a social campaign with a significant Foursquare component, bear in mind that the platform appeals to men more than women. Although the company doesn't release much demographic data, it's possible to look at the high volume of social activity that takes on Foursquare Day (4sq Day for short), the annual April 16 holiday celebrating the check-in platform and observed by many brands and social media junkies. This past year, over 62 percent of mentions of 4sq Day were made by males. The 25–34 demographic is very strong on Foursquare, accounting for 48.1 percent of 4sq Day mentions. That's nearly twice as much as the next-closest age group, 35–44 year olds, with 24.2 percent.[3]

Because many of the social platforms you'll be engaging on are just a few years old, there's a good chance their demographics will shift over time, so be sure to do some research before jumping in.

Geography affects participation as well. In Brazil, it took until the very end of 2011 for Facebook to overcome Orkut as the most popular social platform. Orkut has 60 percent of its users living in Brazil. After Brazil's defection to Facebook, there are only six remaining countries where Facebook is not the dominant social platform: Poland, Russia, Vietnam, South Korea, Japan, and China. If you're operating in these markets, it's absolutely essential you focus on where your audience is spending its time. Direct your efforts to where your customers and prospects are, so you don't spend time talking to yourself.

"Channel is very important," agrees Maria Ogneva of Yammer, which creates private social networks for enterprise use. "If your customers are expecting you to be on Pinterest because that's where they are, you should go there. If not, then don't get on Pinterest just because it's a 'shiny new object.'" Dee Nuncio, a community manager at SapientNitro, agrees: "Brands need to figure out the personality behind the voice, then decide which social channels allow that voice to be heard as clearly as possible. They don't need to be on every single social network—they need to be on the ones that will strengthen their overall personality and voice the most. Being among those who will find their content the most relevant is key when it comes time to having people share the messaging."

Likewise, even if a site is more niche than mainstream, or even declining in market share, you shouldn't automatically exclude it from your social marketing efforts. For instance, Flickr, the Yahoo-managed photo-sharing site, has been declining moderately in the last few years. However, even as visually driven platforms such as Instagram and Pinterest have risen, Flickr remains somewhat popular with more visual niches such as photographers and makeup artists. Even if a platform isn't a priority for most people, don't rule it out as an opportunity for you.

Not sure where your audience is? Not a problem. It doesn't cost much for you to run searches and see how much of your prospective audience is on a particular social channel. For example, when first wading into the waters of engagement, environmental technology start-up Ecycler looked to Twitter. "We were looking for tweets like 'I just recycled' or 'I just got this much money for cans,'" cofounder Craig Robertson explains. "Then we would just enter into a conversation with those people, and maybe tweet to try to get them to come to our site." With solid results from its initial foray into Twitter, Ecycler recognized that Twitter would be a channel it should focus on.

When researching where your audience is, it's a pretty safe assumption that, in some way or another, they are on Facebook. After all, Facebook is the premier social platform in terms of time spent, and as such is a place where much of online engagement occurs. That said, Facebook and LinkedIn's Ads tools are also invaluable for understanding how many people are in any specific group. If your brand operates only in the U.S., Canada, and Brazil, and your audience consists of senior managers who are 35 and older, it takes just a minute or two using LinkedIn's Ads tool to see you have an estimated target audience of over 7 million LinkedIn members.

CASE IN POINT: Word Balloon Finds Its Audience—Literally

Message boards and forums have been a major factor in the success of *Word Balloon*, the comic book interview podcast developed and managed by John Siuntres. John regularly appears on prolific comic book writer Brian Michael Bendis's message board, Jinxworld, where he solicits questions from his audience in The Bendis Tapes. In 2005, before Facebook's dominance and Twitter's arrival, it occurred to John to actively go to message board communities where he knew people were talking about comic books and let that community know that he had interviewed a comic creator. At this early stage, comic creators such as Bendis and Colleen Doran (one of John's first interviews) were online, developing followings on MySpace, and had already started developing independent communities. Pretty soon, even though he didn't know it at the time, John was becoming a social marketer, appearing online wherever his potential audience might be. "You go to the creator's site and let them know, because they are already built-in fans of the subject of your interview, so I would say, 'Hey, I know you guys like Colleen. I do this interview show.' I would explain my background in radio and say 'Hey, I did this interview;

you may want to listen to it.'" John continued to tap into creators' communities, letting comic fans know about his product. The result? A devoted, captivated audience.

Buying Real Estate

If you're going to build a house, buying the supplies is well and good, but wouldn't you make sure you had land to build on? The same principle applies to social marketing. Make sure to park, or reserve, your brand name across the social channels you think you'll be most active on. Platforms like Facebook, Twitter, and YouTube let you create accounts for free, so you ought to take advantage and reserve the land you'll be building on eventually. Besides focusing on major social networks, you should also focus on emerging platforms that you think might become big, as well as niche platforms that aren't that big but that are significant for your audience. Keep in mind that many of these sites tend to rank very highly in Google, so if you can park these names across multiple networks and platforms, you will likely have more control over your Google rankings.

If your company is named something relatively generic—say, Cats, Inc.—you might have a difficult time parking the same account name across multiple channels. I could tell you that consistency isn't so important, but I don't want to lie: I strongly recommend getting an account name that can be consistent across as many channels as possible. If you're in the process of starting your business, I'd even recommend checking to see whether your potential brand name is available across all the social platforms you're looking to engage on.

Parking your brand name whenever possible on emerging platforms is also a good way to save money having to pry it away from someone else a few years down the line. After all, you never know which social channels will expand as time goes on. When Twitter launched, I was quick to grab @jeremygoldman (and later gave it up in a moment of silliness). I applied the same principle to the microblogging service Posterous: When it launched, I grabbed the http://jeremygoldman.posterous.com URL as soon as I could. I didn't wind up using the service for anything for some time, but, considering that parking a name on new services typically costs you nothing and will take up all of five minutes of your time, it's a great habit to get into.

Speaking of things that are easy to do: Make sure your Facebook URL is formatted in a reader-friendly way. As of press time, by default, your Facebook page URL could very well be given an automatic URL such as http://www.Facebook.com/pages/not-so-user-friendly/5758787367. Facebook lets you set this URL to something much more user friendly, such as Facebook.com/BrandName.

While you're standardizing your username across all channels, make sure your visual identity is consistent across all social channels as well. Having a few standard touches across all your social channels will help your brand look like a serious business venture that your audience can trust.

Coca-Cola is a brand that standardizes its social channels particularly well. You can find their Facebook presence at https://facebook.com/cocacola and their Pinterest page at http://pinterest.com/cocacola. If you're looking for them on Twitter, simply go to http://twitter.com/cocacola. See a pattern? What's more, they use the same identity elements, such as their iconic bottle silhouette, across all their channels. Although it's great for a well-established brand like Coca-Cola to standardize its social channels in order to establish trust, bear in mind that the smaller you are, the more important this step becomes.

How to Get Buy-In for Your Program

Depending on what type of management your company has, you might have a hard time convincing leadership that you need a social marketing program. This is less prevalent today than in the past, but it can still happen. One of the most common concerns management has is that, if you begin a social marketing program, people are going to start saying negative things online about the company. If that's the case, it's important to gently let them know that people are already saying negative things about your company, but the brand isn't there to hear about it or to deal with it. It is important to sell upper management on the ability to see and respond to negative feedback in real time.

Business justification for any program is always a necessity, but this may become even more difficult depending on the politics of your organization. Typically, at any given moment, companies have their entire budget already allocated to projects that are ostensibly making the company money. So if you're going to lobby for a social marketing budget, you're going to have to prove a positive ROI. Otherwise, you will just be taking money away from a program that has already proved its value to the organization. Your company is not going to put resources behind something they can do without; therefore, you have to prove that your social marketing program is something your company cannot live without or should not have to live without.

If you are in charge of marketing for your organization and have to decide what to cut, your mind will instinctively move toward trying to decide what initiatives are less beneficial to the organization. The sad truth is that, for your program to get budgeted, somebody else's program has to be cut or somebody else is not going to get the resources they need for their program. This is reality, and the sooner you can accept this the sooner you will understand what you are up against.

You will always come across naysayers within your organization who decry your social marketing efforts. For example, your company might have a head of sales who believes in the popular misconception that being social with your customers is "wishy-washy" and never actually leads to increasing sales. Even though opinions like these are a bit out there, they still hold water in some organizations, so you will have to address being challenged on this front.

· · · · · · · **GUEST POST** · · · · · · · ·

Doug Straton, Director of Global Ecommerce Innovation at Unilever, on:
How to Get Buy-In

In the next ten years, we will witness one of the great channel upheavals of the past 100 years. The rise of social and mobile technologies, their acceptance in developing and emerging markets, and the importance of user-generated content means that online marketing is critical.

The key issues that many organizations face arise from the relative size of online revenue versus traditional channels. That revenue can be, depending on market's development online, very small. Typical share measures cannot accurately record the offline impact of a given online initiative. Therefore, organizations may deprioritize online activities based on short-term realities without regard to long-term trends.

As a result and depending on the size of the organization, it may be difficult to socialize the reasons to invest in robust online marketing programs or to execute them with excellence. Incentives—with good reason—are typically tied to short-term performance. Therefore, it is crucial to get upper management to drive long-term strategy. By validating trends with research and modeling, one can gain an understanding of the importance of online presence among executive leadership, followed by a commitment to address it. Only then will organizational resource and focus follow.

This backing needs to be visibly driven by leadership. The rest of the organization needs to understand the reasons for the strategy and reallocated resources. Processes to protect these resources may be needed to ensure that business silos are not able to dilute online efforts in the face of near-term business realities. At this point, the organization can move from strategic intent to tactical reality.

Sprucing It Up

Most brands trying to stand out online recognized long ago that their website needed to have a unique, engaging homepage; the same thing goes for your presence on the social web. It's a good idea to brand your page with graphics and its own design. Ever since FBML—Facebook Markup Language, now defunct—and free or nearly free Facebook customization providers have been around, brands have had the opportunity to spice up their Facebook presence. Increasingly, having a well-designed, branded Facebook presence has become an imperative to building your brand online. After all, whatever your audience sees when they visit your page for the first time is their doorway to your brand. If you want people to take your brick-and-mortar business seriously, you spruce up the entrance to your location; the same principle applies online.

Facebook has eliminated the ability to set a default welcome tab for display to visitors. Instead of landing on a placeholder asking them to like the page, they will go straight into brand posts on Timeline. That content has to convince visitors to become fans of the page. Brands can still create a page for newcomers versus fans/subscribers; visitor traffic can be directed to that tab from a link in a post, an ad, a newsletter, or something else. Although many considered welcome tabs obnoxious, plenty of brands relied on them to build up a following in a short period of time. However, building up an audience by trading a coupon for a like doesn't typically lead to long-term relationships. Gimmicks tend to create spikes, as opposed to ongoing engagement. So, in many ways, the death of welcome tabs is a blessing in disguise for many brands that relied on them too much as a crutch.

If you own a neighborhood business and your neighborhood changes, wouldn't you take a look at your storefront and optimize it to reflect your new reality? Like it or not, you need to do the same thing when Facebook changes its layout, as it did recently when it switched to its Timeline format. When it comes to cover photos, keep in mind that you have an 851×315-pixel banner to evoke your brand. You can't include contact information, pricing or discount codes, or arrows encouraging people to like your page. But you can post a memorable image that will intrigue casual viewers into sticking around and seeing what you are all about.

Underneath your brand's profile picture, the Timeline layout has an area where you can provide information about your brand and include links. You have only a small amount of space (roughly 160 characters for pages that are not listings for a physical location) to attract someone's attention here. So it's a good idea to keep this brand information succinct and avoid industry jargon. For a physical location, this is where—shocker—your address and hours of operation are featured.

To the right of this area, you can do as you wish with four spaces. Here you can include Facebook applications that are installed by default, such as Photos, Videos, and Events. You can also display the number of likes that your page has garnered and install third-party apps and let them take up real estate here. It's a good idea to add a custom thumbnail to any third-party app that you use on your page, so that you can better brand yourself. If you can't pick just four things that you want to feature, not to worry; you can include up to 12. However, keep in mind that all but the first four are typically hidden and likely won't be interacted with as much, so put your top four apps in the first row for maximum visibility.

Whereas your brand posts are generally displayed from newest to oldest, you do have the ability to pin a post so that it shows up at the top of your page. You can also highlight a post so that it occupies both columns of your Timeline simultaneously, giving it more importance.

Another nice feature of Facebook's Timeline layout is the ability to add a brand milestone, which allows you emphasize important things that have happened to your brand over time, such as bringing on a new team member or opening up a new retail location. All you need to do is name the milestone, indicate when and where it happened, include a description and a photo, and you are set. Brands with storied histories such as *The New York Times* do a great job leveraging their history by sharing compelling milestones, but young brands can also get creative with their milestones as well.

Keep in mind that you don't really know how much each one of these like-ers actually *likes* you. Nor, for that matter, do you know exactly why they've stopped by your page in the first place. As a result, it's a good idea to diversify the content that you have on this page so that you don't risk alienating anyone who happens upon your brand's page. This principle is no different from talking to a friend in real life: Nobody wants to talk to somebody who's focused on the same subject all the time.

When you are crafting the content for your page, above everything else, try to make sure that it is consistently engaging. You don't have to be over-the-top with silly catch phrases, but it should be interesting and intriguing. Ever watch a few minutes of C-SPAN and catch footage of a member of Congress sleeping in the background while a colleague is making a speech? This isn't entirely the snoozer's fault. It's not that the dozing legislator doesn't want to hear what is being said; it's just that the colleague isn't presenting in an appealing enough way to actually keep the audience's attention. Even if you're not on television, you don't want that feeling of ennui happening to your fan base, do you? Make sure to present your content in a consistently engaging fashion.

Of course, all of this basic setup won't mean a thing if you're not able to easily communicate your brand and don't know how to resonate with your audience in a crowded marketplace. Determining your social voice and personality is probably going to be the most critical factor in your success. Good thing we're covering those in the next chapter.

going further · · · · · · · · · · · · ·

For bonus materials and updates pertaining to this chapter's topics, please visit: *http://goingsocial.jeremygoldman.com/ch2.*

engagement 101: determine your voice and personality

ONE OF THE first steps you have to take when getting started in social marketing is to establish a basic framework for who your organization is: your voice, your personality, and your approach to interacting with customers. All these things will significantly impact how you become known online. In essence, how you engage will determine your social brand.

Given the importance of communicating your brand, it is imperative that you refine it before communicating it to the outside world. Clearly identify your mission, along with the brand's values. Once your brand has a clear identity, improve the odds that your audience will recognize you and see your cohesion by choosing the same or similar profile pictures, headlines, and descriptive texts for your brand across all platforms.

Many social media experts out there will tell you the right way or the wrong way to talk to your customers. I'm not going to do that. To quote the theme of one of my favorite 1980s sitcoms, *Diff'rent Strokes*: "What may be right for you may not be right for some."

Now, you may be asking, "What'choo talkin' 'bout, Jeremy?" I'll explain.

Defining Your Brand and Corporate Culture

Hopefully you know who your company is by the time you decide to start engaging with customers online, but, if you don't yet know, it's time to ask yourself this all-important question:

WHO ARE WE?

What does your brand believe in? What will your brand avoid at all costs? What does your brand feel passionately about? What is your brand selling? I'll give you the answer to this last one: It's not your product. It's the *value* the customer gets from your product. This is an incredibly important distinction because it will impact the types of online engagement. Not all of your engagement can be about selling a particular product directly, but it can tie back to the value created by the product. Donna Karan New York (DKNY) sells clothing, sure, but it's selling the good feeling that well-designed fashion can evoke. Snack company popchips sells healthy chips, but it's actually selling the happiness a customer feels while snacking and guilt is taken out of the equation. Make sure that most of your engagement with your customers ties back to the value you're creating for them.

Ultimately, your company's social voice should reflect your organization's corporate culture, so that the way you "sound" when reaching out to customers mirrors the way the organization "feels" on the inside. If your organization tries to have a social voice that is different from how the organization truly feels, you run the risk of coming across as inauthentic.

Before Randall Weinberg founded Giantnerd, he saw an opportunity. There are plenty of places for outdoor enthusiasts to spend their money, but there wasn't an e-commerce site that truly resonated with these shoppers. So Randall and his team looked at what they did and didn't like in the industry.

In creating Giantnerd, the founders asked themselves what they cared most about. Brad Fredricks, Vice President of e-commerce for the company, shared their conclusions: "We cared about treating people with kindness and love and respect, so we looked at the values that had been missing in online retail: What did we feel like we would be good at? How do we as customers want to be treated?" Giantnerd is really an accumulation of the things the team knew they liked and a rejection of all the things the founders never liked about other sites. "We've built this business according to these core values," says Brad. "What really helps you keep going is sharing values with the people on your team."

Your social voice needs to reflect not only your corporate culture but also your own team's experiences. Tripping, a service that connects travelers with locals, looked for what set it apart from other companies to inform its approach to social engagement. The company's executives and board members (more on them later) all travel extensively, have lived abroad, and speak multiple languages. That diverse set of experiences and international perspective has shaped the personality and voice of the

Tripping brand. If your team has a set of experiences that sets it apart, make sure that your strategy is built with this distinctiveness in mind.

Defining Your Voice and Knowing Your Identity

If your social voice is well defined, your content will be more likely to stand out from the crowd and less likely to be skipped over by potential fans experiencing information overload.

For example, Gregg Spiridellis, cofounder of digital entertainment studio JibJab, describes the company's voice as "whimsically irreverent—we try not to take ourselves too seriously." The head of Social Media for Ford, Scott Monty, says their brand is "quietly confident, using innovative technology to advance on our fuel efficient, safety, smart design and quality efforts, and ultimately human and relatable." Aliza Licht, DKNY's Senior Vice President of Global Communications, describes the brand's social voice as "friendly, eclectic, and fun." Being able to describe your brand's voice in such a concise manner can pay huge dividends for your brand because you can go back and see if the way you're speaking is truly the way you wish to be perceived.

Snack maker popchips describes its social voice as "conversational, casual, and witty," which helps it build a more personal relationship between the brand and its consumers. "We do our best to keep that voice consistent across all platforms," says Brian Pope, popchips' Vice President of Marketing. Brian isn't kidding: All emails I've received from the popchips team—even out-of-office messages—have had the same stylistic discipline of being 100 percent lowercase. Part of popchips' success has been its consistency across all channels, from Facebook to Twitter to e-mail to conversations occurring at "real-life" sampling events.

For Scott Monty of Ford, the key to success has been striking the right balance between humanity and brand consistency. "It really comes down to being present and understanding the platforms on which we're active," he explained. "We follow the mantra 'If you wish to persuade me, you must think my thoughts, feel my feelings and speak my words,' as Cicero said over 2,000 years ago. We're not afraid to be human, but we also need to be consistent with our overall brand. It's a fine line to walk, and one that comes with practice."

Laurie Davis founded eFlirt Expert, a company that provides online dating coaching (you'll hear more about eFlirt later). "We want our voice to be flirty and fun so it resonates with daters and speaks to our brand," shares Laurie. For example, rather than writing "thanks," eFlirt Expert will frequently write "blushing." It's a small detail, for sure, but all those small details add up to a brand that resonates. Because dating can be difficult, eFlirt Expert also tries to encourage singles with an upbeat approach by being "110 percent positive." Above all, eFlirt Expert's persona strives to be "knowledge squared," as Laurie puts it. "We want to educate singles through actionable tips and fresh perspectives. We're not too authoritative about it, and that's been a strength of ours. Striking the balance with advice has been integral to our marketing success."

While you have to know what you are, it's just as important to know what you are not. To that end, make sure you adopt a voice that reflects your brand's values and attributes rather than someone else's. A brand like Barneys New York would sound pretty awkward if it communicated to its audience on social channels using the same tone Forever 21 evokes, wouldn't it? This might be obvious to you, and, if it is, I'm happy. Unfortunately, some companies out there have an identity crisis and "feel" completely different in social channels than they do in their traditional channels. Avoid this misstep, and you'll be taking one giant step in the right direction.

· · · · · · · **GUEST POST** · · · · · · · ·

Lynn Teo, Chief Experience Officer at McCann Erickson, on:
Why an Identifiable Social Voice Is Important

A unique social voice makes every interaction that a brand has with its consumer memorable, and that's part and parcel of brand building. In some ways, I would argue that having an *identifiable* social voice is more important. We identify uniqueness all around us, but an identifiable uniqueness is what brands should strive for. Subtleties in tone, attitude, and disposition all come across in a social voice. Those elements, together with all the brand cues surrounding the brand—typeface, color palette, shapes, and brandmark—work together to further its personality. Customers who respond to this identifiable social voice will likely share the brand's values, tastes, and preferences. As with all other forms of communication, like attracts like. Adopting a uniquely identifiable voice helps a business strike up engagement online with the "right" target audience.

Engage. Then Understand. Then Engage Better.

Playwright Samuel Beckett once wrote this famous phrase: "Ever tried. Ever failed. No matter. Try again. Fail again. Fail better." Beckett's quote is particularly true when it comes to engaging your audience on social channels. If you try to engage on social channels and do something that you consider a failure, so what? Try again, and if you're paying attention to lessons learned from your first failure, your second attempt at engagement may not be perfect, but it will definitely be better. Still, if you're after the goal of perfection (as any good marketer ought to be), you're technically failing. That doesn't matter, though, because every time you fail is an opportunity to get better. Fail again and fail better. Rinse, repeat.

One of the primary reasons a brand fails when it comes to engaging its audience is by not thinking enough about consumer behavior and customers' needs. Consumer behavior should never be an afterthought when it comes to your social marketing approach. If anything, it should be one of the first things you think about when developing your social marketing strategy. After all, consumer behavior is inherently the basis that drives purchasing decisions. Paul Cohen, CEO of product recommendation firm Cognection, agrees. "Assumptions about how consumers will respond to incentives, such as price discounts or coupons, or even new product lines, aren't meaningful unless they are actually true," says Paul. "A true understanding of actual consumer behavior, the factors that drive consumers to purchase products, and the psychological aspects behind a decision-making process, is absolutely one of the most important components of the business that a proprietor must understand."

If you don't understand your customers, how can you engage effectively? The question is rhetorical: You can't.

CASE IN POINT: ModCloth's Social Voice Becomes the Fabric of Its Success

Founded by husband-and-wife team Eric Koger and Susan Gregg Koger in 2002, ModCloth sells affordable wares from independent designers, with women's fashion its primary focus. The retailer has attracted a strong, loyal audience through its selection of indie clothing and engaging content across its social channels and blog.

With approximately 90,000 Twitter followers, ModCloth opts to use its Twitter bio URL to build its community rather than sell directly. Instead of linking users to its homepage or a specific shopping promotion, the e-tailer links to the "Social Butterflies" page on their site, which introduces the team behind the company's social marketing. "Hi there!," begins the copy on the Social Butterflies page. "You must have come across a tweet so fantastic or an update so enticing, that you just had to know more about the fabulous brains behind it! . . . We aim to be the front-runners of what's fresh in the world of fashion, culture, and social media—and provide a dose of good ol' fun!" Copy like this is just one more way ModCloth aims to share its personality and quirkiness with its audience.

The voice ModCloth uses across all its social platforms originates from the tone it takes in its product descriptions. It can best be described as friendly and approachable, fitting in with the company's overarching mission to "democratize fashion," explains Natalie Brova, ModCloth's Marketing Writing Manager. "We don't want fashion to be viewed as something scary or unattainable. We like to say we're 'the fashion company that you're friends with.'"

In Natalie's mind, authenticity is one of the reasons ModCloth clearly resonates with its customer base. "Consumers are getting more and more savvy, and they can tell when you're just putting on a shtick to take a particular action. We *are* our customers. We're not just a bunch of marketers trying out all of the latest ploys that we can. We know what they're doing because we're doing it, too . . . we love the things that they love. Because it's always been an authentic voice, it's something that has resonated and allows us to continue to grow."

ModCloth has been able to have an authentic, consistent voice in part because the company does all of its graphic design and copy in house. The creative team is the gate-keeper of the brand. The Social Butterflies work very closely with the graphic design team to make sure every-thing is in sync. The internal team holds "vision meet-ings" before they even create a single one-off newsletter to make sure everyone is on the same page. "We're all working to tell one story. It's never fragmented," says Natalie. "If everything was more fragmented, I don't think we'd be nearly as successful."

Modcloth's ModDogs Facebook page, with 3,500 Likes, launched out of the company's love affair with its mascot, Susan and Eric's pug Winston. Does the ModDogs page directly lead to any sales? Not really. But, is it part of a strategy that builds community and foster customer loy-alty? Very much so. ModCloth's business model and mar-ket segment could be copied, but the intensely devoted community it has created is much harder to replicate.

Modcloth works hard to cultivate this sense of commu-nity. When speaking to its social audience, ModCloth uses "we."

Modcloth also tweaks its voice based on the social plat-form, noticing that its Twitter and Facebook audiences were different from that on, for instance, Pinterest. When ModCloth initially got on Pinterest, they knew their audience was a little older and a little more mature. Internally, the ModCloth team discussed whether they would post a cocktail recipe on Pinterest, which is something they wouldn't have done on Facebook since their demographics there are younger. But they determined it was appropriate for a Pinterest audience.

It would be easy for ModCloth to simply pin its product imagery to Pinterest, and call it a day. However, ModCloth doesn't even directly pin its products! Instead, the brand pins beautiful imagery that appeals to its demographics, and reinforces its quirkiness. Arts and crafts, style inspiration, and cute animals are all focuses of their pinboards. ModCloth also includes a "Guest Pinner Gallery," which showcases inspiration from the brand's social audience.

While many brands use contests to drive short-term awareness and social media statistics, ModCloth uses them to reinforce its brand. "Name It & Win It" is an ongoing contest in which customers are allowed three chances to give a quirky name to a specific product being featured. Offer up a winning name, and you'll win the product. In this way, ModCloth lets its audience join in on the fun.

The end result of all of these efforts is striking: By August 2012, Modcloth's Facebook page was about to break 600,000 Likes. One of the fastest-growing Internet-only retailers, activity around the brand grew at such a breakneck pace that ModCloth grew from just over/nearly 100 employees in mid-2010 to almost/more than 350 by Q3 2012.

Be Inviting

It's very important to interact with fans in the way that they want to be interacted with. This might seem obvious, but a lot of brands communicate with text that is uninviting and that sounds like a prose-heavy, snooze-worthy press release.

Even an aspirational brand—one that a sizable segment of its audience wishes to possess but simply can't for economic reasons—knows that they will have to employ new tactics when it comes to going social. After all, going social was typically never a part of an aspirational brand's DNA. Whether it's through a brand's social channels or brand "remixes" on social "mood boards," such as Polyvore and Pinterest, a luxury brand's audience members want to engage with the brand. If you're a luxury brand and your audience wants to engage with you, why wouldn't you encourage that desire? Isn't serving the customer part of why you exist?

"Gone are the days when luxury brands were thought of as being distant and unattainable," voices Lynn Teo, Chief Experience Officer at McCann Erickson. "Being approachable is an attribute of every good business. Why would luxury brands adopt a different approach?"

Luxury brand Bergdorf Goodman embraces this new paradigm by tweeting about beauty, fashion, and quick slices of life that are of interest to the brand's audience. This makes the 110-year-old department store feel more approachable, helping it to achieve its (somewhat surprising) position as a social media powerhouse. Bergdorf has such a strong interaction with its followers that, when it created a Twitter contest to put together an outfit for Linda Fargo, Bergdorf's fashion director, the contest drew over 5,300 entries—approximately one for every seven followers, a staggering level of engagement.[1] If you want to foster the type of engagement

Bergdorf Goodman does, it's important to be approachable. This isn't that different from what you'd do if you were a CEO who wanted the firm's employees to feel more comfortable suggesting ways the company can improve, is it? Being approachable encourages engagement; being unattainable and elusive discourages it.

Brands can increase the feeling of approachability by making sure their tone does not come across as impersonal or by letting a spokesperson speak on the brand's behalf in order to come across as more relatable. DKNY (which we'll talk about in more detail later) does this to great effect with its DKNY PR Girl persona, which is the alter ego of Donna Karan International's SVP of Global Communications, Aliza Licht. Ski resort Whistler Blackcomb, in its Twitter profile, clearly indicates that Twitter users @amberturnau and @LaurenAEverest provide its tweets. While these Twitter accounts contain mainly their own thoughts and content sharing, this type of loose affiliation lets Whistler Blackcomb's followers know who's behind their engagement, thus increasing openness and transparency.

Differentiating Yourself and Being Unique

It is also important to find a tone for communicating with customers that will distinguish your brand from your competitors. Remember, the less distinct you are, the more likely you are to be overlooked or forgotten. Being an interesting brand makes you less replaceable. Of course, people need to actually desire or have a true need for what you are selling; apart from that, however, it will be a major boon to your business if your customers actually like hearing from you.

When in doubt, make your content fun, attention grabbing, and even inspired. While you don't want to go over the top as a brand

and have to deal with backlash, you run a much greater risk of failing by being too boring than failing due to offending one or two people. I'm not saying that your brand should make light of fragile political situations; Kenneth Cole did this to great uproar (and we'll cover that later). But I am saying that, even if you were to misstep in your attempt to be witty and interesting, you'll most likely survive. It's much better to err on the side of being "too exciting" than "too safe." Starbucks, for example, has weighed in on divisive topics such as health care reform, same-sex marriage, and Occupy Wall Street. It's not uncommon for the company's Facebook page to contain discussions of the company's positions. Starbucks doesn't fear courting a bit of controversy because it knows the benefits of being engaging outweigh the potential cons.

Speaking of being too safe: It's not only okay to be contrarian in your views; it's encouraged! I'm not suggesting being provocative for its own sake, but if you have an opposing point of view, why not share it? If everyone is arguing that your industry needs less regulation and you put together an article about why your industry actually needs more of it, your content has a better chance of standing out. To offer a differing point of view, just monitor trending topics at sources like Twitter and Google News, or look to see what questions are being asked at sites like Quora or LinkedIn. This way, you'll know what's hot right now, allowing you to express a differing opinion on the topic. You earn bonus points if you can find an interesting way to write about a current event or trends that are seemingly unrelated to your business and then turn it into a relevant article. Being a bit off center can also help you succeed when you're developing an article post made up of different bullet points. The world has enough top-ten lists; your top-11 list might be more noticeable. Heck, instead of a top-five list, why not a top-4.5 list while you're at it?

Just as your format ought to be interesting, it's important to bring up the unique aspects of your brand rather than focusing on the same elements as everyone else. In real life, you make connections by sharing what's noteworthy about yourself and by letting that feature help define you as you interact with others. If you're single and speaking with someone attractive to you, do you mention that you're a trained classical pianist or that you have ten toes and ten fingers? When you're defining what your organization's social voice and approach ought to be, think of what makes you stand out from other firms.

Being a Good Friend to Your Customers

If you're trying to be a good friend to your customers, which is part of what social marketing is all about, you need to be thinking about what you can offer your audience that is relevant to them and that will help them in some way. If your audience can get something from you that they cannot get anywhere else—and this can be a feeling or a physical reward of some sort—then you have a good chance of winning customer loyalty.

Do you have a friend who talks and talks and yet has nothing to say? I might not be exactly like that, but I'm considerably closer to that archetype than my wife. Victoria barely speaks. In fact, I've driven to a party with friends and forgotten she's in the car. However, when she does speak, she can be counted on pretty consistently to say something witty or thought provoking. I envy and admire that about her, just as I admire brands that consistently communicate in ways that don't waste my time as a consumer. The important thing to think about when someone likes your brand's page is that you know nothing about them; all you know is that they liked you in some small way for at least one moment in time.

With that in mind, it is imperative not to communicate too often or to be too self-aggrandizing or promotional. Sure, a few super fans out there might want to consume each and every piece of content your brand has to deliver. But, if people are feeling overloaded with your communications, they are going to un-like your page, unfollow you, and find other ways to tune you out. Facebook, in particular, has made it easier than ever for users to decide the types of updates they see from their connections and how often. If your messaging doesn't reflect that you're a good friend, you can easily be put on mute forever.

This is not to suggest that you should wait to engage with people until they like you on Facebook. In real life, if someone says "Give me a call" or "Keep in touch," you don't make them wait a long time to hear from you. Engaging with customers while you are still in the forefront of their minds is key. Once you get people to engage with you more often and draw frequent commenters on your Facebook page, you should then respond frequently to posts. Engaging with people who are engaging with you turns your brand into a social one.

Going social is so much more about the soft sell than the hard sell. "Buy this now; it's 30 percent off!" doesn't work nearly as well as "Have some questions? We'd love to help you out." Customers don't want to feel as though they are being sold to or that they are part of your business plan; they want to feel that they are empowered to decide whether, when, and how to begin a sales cycle. Assuming that people are looking for your product, having your brand be a "friend" to your customers and prospects will lead to a sale. If people are not looking for the product but they tell you what they are looking for, active listening will let you create the product that will sell.

Peer-to-Peer Recommendations

Just as in other areas of life, one of the top social person-to-person interactions pertains to recommending venues, products, or services. Because peer-to-peer recommendations are typically the most trusted kind of recommendation—much more than a brand's direct recommendation to its customers—it makes sense to influence people's opinions. The 2009 Nielsen global online consumer survey indicated that 90 percent of consumers trust recommendations from people they know and that 70 percent trust consumer opinions posted online, such as Amazon product reviews.[2] A June 2010 eMarketer study revealed that 26 percent of respondents "trust completely" blog posts by people they know, with 38 percent saying they "trust somewhat" that content. When asked how much they trusted a blog post by a brand, product, or company, only 11 percent said that they trust the content completely, and only 25 percent indicated that they trust the content somewhat. In the eMarketer study, the same pattern holds true for posts on social media sites. In one particularly telling example, 23 percent said that they completely trust their friends' Facebook posts, with only 9 percent saying the same thing about a brand's Facebook posts—even when it's a brand they are actively following.[3]

> **CASE IN POINT: Giantnerd's Crowdsourced Curation**
> Giantnerd set out to be "the web's best social shopping community"—an ambitious goal, to be sure. But what's amazing is that plenty of people would agree that they've succeeded. The site gives outdoor enthusiasts social technologies to communicate and collaborate with other site users, all to support the goal of having happier customers make more educated purchases. The company has

embraced being social in a way most brands have yet to do: In fact, the <TITLE> tag of their page (which contains the text displayed above the Internet browser when a page is loaded) is Giantnerd Social Shopping.

Giantnerd's homepage has standard e-commerce trappings, but it also has a news feed of social activity taking place on the site. The brand has a clear focus on giving customers a robust shopping experience, while actively socializing with them. Nerds, which Giantnerd affectionately dubs its customers, have the opportunity to share their opinions and product feedback with other Nerds. Giantnerd is, as it states wherever appropriate, "powered by love™."

Although powered by love, it is also powered by people. Giantnerd leverages peer recommendations to build a strong e-commerce business in a number of ways. One method is the organic "pure play," where someone makes a recommendation or otherwise contributes to the community and then shares that message. Giantnerd provides the capabilities and functions for consumers to share or message out their actions within the community. By contributing and sharing, community members actually drive traffic and awareness back to the brand—standard social strategy but something that Giantnerd executes flawlessly. "It's far more engaging for somebody to see that his friend purchased something, made a comment on something, or likes/wants something versus us soliciting, either through Facebook ads or any kind of advertising mechanism," says Brad Fredricks, Giantnerd's Vice President of Ecommerce.

Giantnerd users are incentivized to share their recommendations via the brand's loyalty system. In addition to earning Nerd points for purchases, Nerds earn additional points every time they interact with the site, including reviewing products, answering other Nerds' questions, commenting on discussions, making product lists, editing Wikinerdia (a Wiki on giantnerd.com managed by the company's audience), or sharing content with their friends.

Sharing Giantnerd content outside the site is particularly effective for brand awareness, with one Nerd having the potential to reach out to 50—or 500—individuals who have never heard of Giantnerd. It's also effective for actually selling products: The company typically sees an incremental 2 percent jump in conversion rate when Love It, Want It, and Own It votes are attached to a product, a pretty significant impact considering most e-commerce sites convert at a 2–5 percent conversion rate.

Of course, turning the community over to the users is not a uniformly positive experience. On occasion, users pan one of Giantnerd's products. In one case, only 20 percent of users loved a product, with 60 percent of users disliking it. "That was a little scary," Brad admits, "but at the same time, Giantnerd realized that it was much more authentic to people than us just saying this is great, you want to buy this."

Rather than patting itself on the back, Giantnerd is looking to find the next frontier for social shopping. The company is considering letting the community write the content and copy pertaining to individual products. "You go to a website, and you always read what they're telling you about a product," laments Brad. "And then you have to scroll down to get the reviews, even with our site. What if we could change the funnel on that process where the review and the product description [are] the site review?" Giantnerd is trying to bring crowdsourcing to new heights, all in the name of servicing the customer better.

going further . . . .

For bonus materials and updates pertaining to this chapter's topics, please visit: *http://goingsocial.jeremygoldman.com/ch3*.

how to develop content that promotes engagement

MOST EXPERTS WILL tell you that using social media is all about content. Although there's a good deal of truth in that, that's not the whole story. It's kind of like the old philosophical question: If a tree falls in the forest, and no one is there to hear it, does it make a sound? At Temptu, we created a one-minute video teaser for the temporary tattoos we developed in conjunction with Tina Knowles' fashion line, *Deréon*, featuring Beyoncé on the cover. Although the content was all right, what made the video a success was where it was placed and the social activity surrounding it. The placement was key in that it was the featured content on Beyoncé's official Facebook page. As a result, it generated over 8,100 likes and 1,200 comments. This amount of social activity inspires others to join the conversation. So, while your social media content is certainly important, equally important is that the users comment on and share your content with their networks. In other words, your content must not only be good, it must encourage interaction as well. After all, most sane people don't want to be the only person participating in the conversation!

Here is an example from the physical world: When I was working at the Australian skin care company Jurlique, a few other people from the corporate team and I occasionally visited our smaller concept stores. Foot traffic was typically light for these stores. However, we noticed that whenever a few of us from the corporate office were in the store at the same time, suddenly the traffic would pick up, and more people would walk in the door. No one wanted to walk into a store with no customers inside. The same principle applies to interacting with content online: No one wants to be the only person commenting on the thread. Although it's hard to get the first person to interact with you, a snowball effect follows: It's easier to get the second person to engage, even easier to get a third participant, and so on, until you have a pretty impressive snowball.

To elicit initial responses on your content, it's very important that you post at the most opportune time. Use a tool like PageLever, which offers advanced Facebook analytics, or Crowdbooster, which can let you know when your audience is typically tuned in, to ensure that you're posting when people are most likely to see your post. Your audience is less likely to engage if they see a post has been sitting there for 10 hours without being commented on. If you have close relationships within your community, you can reach out directly to alert them that you've posted a new piece of content with which you'd like them to engage. Getting some of your closer contacts to engage with your content encourages others in your audience to jump in right afterward. Of course, be sure not to call in this favor too often, or your closest supporters might tune you out.

If you're looking to increase engagement, I'd recommend encouraging your audience to comment on your brand content rather than to simply like it. Most people view the act of hitting the like button as an easy way to say they enjoyed a piece of content. After all, our society is so fast paced that saving the four seconds it takes to write "Nice post!" is worth something to the average consumer. Thus, ask questions in your posts that implicitly encourage more specific feedback. The downside of this technique is the potential embarrassment of posting a question and receiving no responses. If you're not getting the amount of feedback you're expecting, either you're asking the wrong questions or your fan base isn't as engaged as you thought.

Ford Motor Company is a brand that gets social marketing right. Part of the reason why Ford is so successful is that it lets its audience lead in the partnership with the brand. As a testament to its openness, Ford displays reader comments prominently on each of the company's articles placed on its social site, The Ford Story. More than just a blog, The Ford Story is divided into a few key sections: Our Articles, Your Stories, and Your Ideas. Notice the one instance of our and the two instances of *your*. That's a clear indication that Ford is building a two-directional conversation. Users not only have the ability to respond to Ford articles, they can also submit their own Ford stories (which other users can comment on) or ideas to improve Ford and its products (which other users can vote on). The Ford Story site is a pure vehicle for engagement.

If you're going to let your audience participate in content generation, however, bear in mind that one of the biggest mistakes a brand can make is trying to control the conversation in connected media in the same way it would in traditional media. "If you put your brand out there, you'd better be prepared to talk about whatever the audience wants to talk about," voices Gregg Spiridellis of JibJab. "After all, you handed them the mic." Gregg's right: Once you realize you've relinquished some control to your customer, you won't feel as stressed about trying to control something you can't really control.

Reworking Content to Make It Social Friendly

Ever see a novel adapted into a movie that doesn't work because it is a little too faithful to the source material? What works well in one media channel has to be translated and optimized to succeed in another. The same principle has to be applied when you're developing your brand's social content. You can't just post your press releases on social platforms. Think about it for a moment: Press releases are literally *releases* meant for the *press*. Will some media outlets pick up your press release verbatim and regurgitate it on the Internet? Absolutely. However, while most press releases are written in a somewhat standardized business tone, your social marketing content should have a voice unique to your brand or unique to a brand representative. Just posting a cold, clinical press release won't do much for you, and it certainly won't encourage your fans and followers to engage you in a conversation.

The beautiful thing about social marketing is that it can be incorporated into any of your company's existing activities. For example, does the concept of a FAQ (frequently asked questions) sound boring to you? It doesn't have to be. There's no reason your FAQ has to be a static, less engaging part of your marketing collateral. Creating a social FAQ has a much better chance of attracting your audience's attention. Invite customers to make it better! Ask your audience if they don't see any questions addressed in the FAQ, and be sure to answer those questions. I've seen brands add a social component into just about every facet of their business with great success. Maybe you don't want to crowdsource your legal department, but you get the point: Try to think of creative ways where you can add a layer of engagement in an unexpected manner, and your audience will typically reward you for your efforts.

There are plenty of effective ways to add unexpected, inventive layers of engagement. For example, Sonic Drive-In makes its homepage social by letting users upload pictures of their Sonic experience that fill the entire homepage canvas. The Vaccines, an indie rock band, used Instagram to ask their fans to share photos of themselves at different festivals using the hashtag #vaccinesvideo. The band sorted through over 3,000 submissions and used the most appropriate ones for their upcoming music video, *Wetsuit*. Another brand, Olla Condoms, sent Facebook users surprising friend requests from their hypothetical unborn children. The company took a male Facebook user's name, created an account with that name plus *Jr.*, and sent the friend request along with the message, "Avoid surprises like this one." When Sr. clicked on the friend request, he saw an ad from Olla. Although technically a clear violation of Facebook policy, the campaign generated tons of buzz as a completely unexpected way of promoting social engagement. I'm not encouraging anyone to break the rules, but there's no denying the inventive nature of Olla's campaign. If you can achieve that unexpectedness, your brand will have a better chance at standing out from the pack.

Customers as Content

Featuring customer testimonials is a great way to show how much your brand stands behind your products or services. If you want, you can give your customers very basic guidelines on what you're looking for and then let them give product feedback completely unedited. Although the kind of feedback generated this way tends to be a bit rough around the edges, that's completely alright. Just make sure your audience knows that customers are giving uncensored points of view so that you get brownie points for authenticity!

If you're going to interview customers with the intent of having a copywriter or videographer develop a polished piece of content, that's fine too. If you take this approach, though, make your brand's case studies and customer testimonials human and emotional. Don't focus just on your product or service, even though that has to be a major component of your content. Get users to care about the person or organization that your product or service has served, and your audience will be considerably more engaged.

Zappos encourages fans to send in photos, allows other fans to vote on the best picture, and then proclaims the winner the Fan of the Week. Zappos features this customer on their Facebook wall, costing the brand nothing apart from management costs, but engendering intense loyalty from the fan base. People love adulation and being fussed over, and that holds true for your online friends. Make your fans the stars of your social marketing campaign, and they'll likely become brand advocates. Best of all, this is a virtuous cycle: The more you turn your fans into stars, the more loyal followers you will have to love your brand. And the more beloved your brand is, the more fans will appreciate being featured. Your brand doesn't have to be the size of Zappos to engender this kind of loyalty: At one point Zappos was a tiny, struggling shoe e-tailer. Over time, it grew by building goodwill among its customers and by treating them well with free shipping and returns, strong customer service, and consistent respect. Zappos' success is built squarely on the basis of this tremendous goodwill. If your brand follows their best practices, you'll have a shot at being similarly successful.

· · · · · · · **GUEST POST** · · · · · · ·

Making It Interesting

C. C. Chapman is the author of the book Content Rules *(Wiley, 2010) and the founder of Digital Dads, "Where a dad can be a guy." As a consultant, C. C. helps a variety of clients embrace all forms of new media and online marketing to take their campaigns to the next level. His work has won awards, and his clients have included HBO, American Eagle Outfitters, Verizon FiOS, and The Coca-Cola Company.*

The truth is that, if they are not already creating and sharing content, your competitors will be doing it shortly. The web is the first place your customers and potential customers go to find information, and you want to get on their radar as quickly as possible.

As the cost of making content continues to fall and the ease of making it increases, you must do something different, unexpected, and interesting to stand out from everyone else.

Take a moment and think about the standard answer, pitch, or way of showing your product or service. Once you have the obvious ways, try to think of how to do it in a way that would catch people off guard. You don't want to offend or upset anyone, but you want to spark an emotional response from them that will make them remember you and share your content with others.

My favorite example is how a small camera store in Calgary showcased that they were passionate about photography. Even if you are not personally into photography, you can surely think of several ways they could have done this. But their amazing solution grew out of their deep love of photography: They staged a battle, complete with sound effects, using nothing but camera equipment. As soon as you can, take a moment and watch the video "Battle at F-Stop Ridge" (http://youtube/awq90 APEVgw).

Anyone can do standard and boring. Be the one who gains attention by making your content as engaging as possible!

Relevant and Compelling Content

As a customer, the content that shows up in your social feeds has to be relevant to you; otherwise, you're going to jump ship. This principle applies in real life: Suppose you always go to a bar where you know everyone. One by one, over time, your friends move away until the only ones left are strangers. After a while, there's a good chance you will stop going there. It's the same thing on your Facebook page, your Twitter presence, or your private standalone social network or blog: It pays to build a sense of community. The more relevant a site or social hub is, the more likely people are to interact with it.

Most Facebook users log in to see new comments on their status updates, to share photos, to see whether they've been tagged in any friends' photos, play social games, and to see whether they've been invited to any new events. Generally speaking, people don't go on Facebook with a specific idea in mind about how to spend their time. This tendency gives you an opportunity as a marketer: Customers and prospects can be distracted into looking at your content if it is compelling enough.

For example, suppose your brand posts a question of the day and it gets 11 responses, three of which are from Jessica's friends. There's a strong possibility that the post will show up prominently in Jessica's feed, increasing the odds that she will notice the question and even like or comment on it herself. If you have engaging content, you have a good chance of being rewarded with high levels of engagement from your audience. This lets you turn the prospects in your audience—those who are intrigued by your product but who haven't made a financial commitment—into customers. It also lets you loyalize the paying customers in your audience into buying more and spreading positive word of mouth about your brand.

There is some danger in pandering to your audience too much. For example, you run a flower delivery service, and on the morning you've scheduled a new Facebook post, nude pictures of the latest pop sensation crop up on the Internet. You probably *don't* want to post that content as part of your company's communications (even if it's fascinating to all your fans) because it has absolutely nothing to do with your brand, your audience, and your social approach. It doesn't make sense to post sensationalist material purely because of the large number of clicks and shares it will receive. Posting irrelevant material, no matter how attention grabbing, pushes your business in a different direction and ultimately blurs the focus on your product.

CASE IN POINT: Martell Home Builders Wins with Relevancy

Martell Home Builders is a company that has demonstrated it knows how to succeed at social marketing, in large part due to its relevant and engaging content. The Atlantic Canadian builder of custom homes, founded by Pierre Martell, had a business model that typically heavily relied on realtors to get the word out about their services. A home builder such as Martell essentially delegated its brand to a real estate agency. But Pierre Martell wanted to do something different. "We wanted to create a brand ourselves," Pierre explained to me. "We had no budget. But we had time. We started engaging in social media because it was an efficient use of our time, coupled with a lack of budget. In hindsight, it's the best decision we could have made." The company jumped into developing a conversation directly between themselves and their potential customers. This allowed their business to cut out the realtor middleman and reach people they hadn't been able to reach previously.

The key to a strong social marketing plan, for Martell, was a robust content creation strategy. Pierre focused on topics his customers would genuinely care about. Soon, the company's blog was teeming with entries such as "Eco-Friendly Homes with Uber-Cool Designs," "Home Staging Tips & Techniques," and "14 Must-Have Tools for New Homeowners." For the first three years, the company developed all its content internally, with Pierre eventually stepping away from the day-to-day content creation when things became too busy. Eventually, he hired an assistant to collect links the brand might want to share and to develop longer-form content, which Pierre approves before publishing.

Not every social channel will wind up paying equal dividends. In the case of Martell Home Builders, Pierre found Twitter to be the most productive channel, despite an earlier start with Facebook. While some Twitter marketers focus on quantity, intent on amassing tens of thousands of followers who aren't true sales leads, Pierre estimates that over 50 percent of the followers of their @martellhomes Twitter handle are in the immediate geographical vicinity. He thinks @martellhomes has succeeded on Twitter in part due to the informal communication ratio he tries to adhere to: eight value tweets for every one personal tweet.

Pierre also started creating some YouTube videos, linking them to the company blog, which helped increase traffic. Although Pierre doesn't think his company has utilized any channel to 100 percent of its potential, he thinks the pros of experimenting across a number of channels outweigh the cons. To Pierre, finding the company's niche was key. "I always tell everybody, do the things you'd like to do," he explained. "If you don't like to write, you should get on Twitter. If you're personable, do YouTube videos. Find whatever you're best at, and that's the way you're going to succeed."

Martell Home Builders gives all its clients access to their own secure microsites, where all of the decisions and options associated with the build are loaded, so that the client can be part of the building process on a virtual basis. The company also puts up wireless solar webcams so clients can remotely monitor progress.

To encourage social sharing, the project manager in charge of the home build will take extensive photographs of the build, which then go to Martell's virtual assistant, who watermarks them all. There is no click-to-share functionality associated with these watermarked pictures yet (Martell's working on it). Despite this limitation, customers tend to be so excited about their homes' progress that the watermarked photos are shared via social channels on an incredibly frequent basis.

Before Martell's social marketing programs took off, Pierre used to spend eight hours in a sales cycle. With the efficiency of social marketing, the typical sales cycle is now about 1 hour and 40 minutes. "Customers get to know us and like us and trust us much quicker than before," explained Pierre. "Our ROI is huge in terms of time saved. We sold four homes via Twitter in 2010, and in 2011 we're at 6, with two months to go." Today, close to 9 in 10 new customers come directly as a result of positive word of mouth.[1]

To Pierre, *word of mouth* is a nice phrase, but *word of click* is even better—and has turned into a monster advertising vehicle for Martell Home Builders. "In year one, we had zero word of mouth," Pierre shared with me. "Year two, we had maybe one or two referrals. Year three, maybe 30 percent of our business came from direct referrals. This year [year four], it's 65 percent walking in, ready to purchase a home because they've researched us online, or they've been engaging with us already online."

In Pierre's opinion, the secret sauce is pretty simple: "Don't sell. Just try to help. Social media simply builds on what you're already doing, and amplifies it."

Breaking Out of the Pack

A lot of people will tell you to stay away from the shiny new object in the social marketing world. I'm not going to tell you that because—let's face it—the shiny object that catches your attention as a marketer has a decent chance at catching your customers' eyes as well.

Ford Motor Company has excelled at building content in new places to break out of the pack. Early on in the lifetime of Google+, Ford created two accounts: Ford Motor Company and Ford Europe. On its first day, Ford Europe held a contest for captioning an image, with a prize for the Google+ user with the most popular comment. Ford Motor Company chose to test the Hangouts feature, creating a so-called Huddle, where up to 10 consumers could talk with Ford execs regarding future innovations. "The Huddle chat capability has potential for webinars, analyst calls, even customer service [uses] for people to have a face-to-face experience of the brand," said Scott Monty, head of social media for Ford.[2]

Ford is leading the way when it comes to innovative uses of Google+, creatively stretching the platform's limits. The automotive company held a media forum on Marketing to Millennials. "We piped in a few millennial marketers via a Google+ hangout and made them part of the forum, then we livestreamed the whole thing," Scott explains. "We united online and offline participants and opened it up to more than just the select few who were in the room or in the Hangout." If your brand can take a page from Ford's playbook, you'll be in a good position to stand out.

Knowing Your Strengths

As a society, we're fascinated by celebrities trying to do things they're not known for. Seeing celebs like Sugar Ray Leonard and Florence Henderson on a show like *Dancing with the Stars* is a perfect example. It's interesting to watch because these people are doing what they're not necessarily any good at. When it comes to your social engagement, however, it's better to be safe and do what you're good at rather than risk a fascinating train wreck.

A perfect example: While most social content creators focus on text, images, and video, most of *Word Balloon*'s content is audio. On one hand, it might seem a bit odd to create audio content around such a highly visual medium as comic books. However, *Word Balloon* founder John Siuntres is just playing to his strong suits. *Word Balloon* isn't a blog about comics; John would see running a blog as a chore because he doesn't really like writing. With a background of 25-plus years in radio, it's easier for John to broadcast as opposed to writing something down. Even though online video content is clearly on the rise, John jokes that he has a face and a body perfect for radio, so he'll likely stick with his audio podcasting. And that's fine. Knowing your strengths and delivering content you're good at creating is far superior to creating content in a format you're not passionate about and not particularly good at.

Different Social Platforms, Different Content Strategies

When you're going social, it's important to understand what types of content and messaging will work in each of your social channels. One of the key considerations should be any one individual's signal-to-noise ratio. This ratio is a measure often used in science and engineering to compare the level of a desired signal to the level of background noise, but it's applicable to social marketing as well. You want as good of a signal as possible and as little noise as possible.

Giantnerd is an example of a brand that understands this point well. It doesn't think Twitter is always the most appropriate place to broadcast sales messages because Twitter doesn't have the strongest signal, and there's a lot of noise out there. "We don't want to be a commerce company that still thinks it's appropriate to sell everything on Twitter. That's not Twitter—Twitter is really a content media broadcast mechanism," says Brad Fredricks, Giantnerd's Vice President of Ecommerce. Twitter is great, however, for sharing what Giantnerd finds inspiring and for starting conversations. As for Facebook, Giantnerd has found that it's a great channel for communicating deals, offers, and special promotions and incentives to its audience.

Ski resort Whistler Blackcomb has found that different types of engagement work on each of its social channels. For instance, the resort relies on Twitter to offer real-time updates to questions such as whether a particular lift is open today and other quick service inquiries, in addition to marketing messages and live event coverage. On Facebook, Whistler tends to post content that doesn't have to be real time to have impact, such as beautiful photos, great videos, and event recaps. One of Whistler's Facebook albums is chock-full of photos of audience members. As soon as Whistler adds new photos to the album, it's reshared in the feeds of anyone who's liked Whistler's page, leading to a slew of audience members' adding their photos to the album.

Travel service Tripping is another company that engages differently according to the channel. On Twitter, it's all about reciprocation: thank-yous, shout-outs, and retweets go a long way toward keeping the audience engaged. Facebook, on the other hand, has been about providing the audience with content that interests them and pulls them into the conversation.

As we all know, some of our colleagues are missing the best opportunities. For some reason, many companies aren't seeing the value in social marketing through LinkedIn. In fact, only 61 percent of companies plan to increase their social marketing through LinkedIn. Although this may seem like a lot, the numbers for Facebook, Twitter, blogs, and YouTube all fall between 73 and 77 percent.[3] What this means is that, if your brand can find a compelling way to engage with your audience on LinkedIn, there's a good chance you will be engaging on a less cluttered playing field. In addition, LinkedIn users tend to be considerably better educated than the users of other social networks. A Pew study conducted in late 2010, for example, found that 38 percent of LinkedIn users had completed graduate school, compared to just 18 percent for Twitter and 15 percent for Facebook.[4]

It's very important you understand which social channels are good for which types of messaging. If you and your team aren't personally using Facebook, LinkedIn, Pinterest, Twitter, Instagram, Google+, Foursquare, and others, you won't understand how each of those channels is developing and evolving what's appropriate and what isn't on each channel.

Creating (and Curating) Engaging Images and Photographs

If you're looking to develop a strategy related to photographs and other static visual content, a social channel like Instagram is a good bet. A few brands, including such luxury brands as Gucci, Marc Jacobs, Oscar De La Renta, Burberry, and Bergdorf Goodman, have begun developing social marketing platforms around Instagram. Burberry is among the largest, with 265,000 followers as of April 2012, largely due to sharing visuals from its latest marketing campaigns. Gucci posts events that provide a look behind the scenes of a glamorous brand, sharing pictures from exclusive events its insiders have attended, as well as old archival pictures of employees from way back when.

One of the reasons brands are flocking to Instagram is the ability to crowdsource by encouraging creative submissions from their fans. As mentioned previously, the U.K. rock group The Vaccines crowdsourced the entirety of the video for the single *Wetsuit* from fans' Instagram submissions.

In addition to its ease of use and relatively robust functionality, Instagram hooks seamlessly into Facebook (which acquired the mobile photo-sharing platform in 2012) and Twitter. Instagram users typically share their Instagram photos in their feeds. For example, Oscar de la Renta's company persona, Oscar PR Girl, has 8,300 Instagram followers, but her true reach is considerably greater, considering she consistently posts her Instagram content to the 100,000+ followers of her @OscarPRgirl Twitter account.

If you're a brand looking to leverage Instagram, consider taking advantage of the mapping function of the app that allows you to pinpoint where a specific photo was taken to take pictures of all of your brick-and-mortar retail stores. Encourage audience members to like the photos of their favorite locations, thus expanding these locations' visibility. Bergdorf has used the app to reinforce its New York City heritage, posting pics of the city's hotspots and using the mapping function of the app to link to the exact location where each picture was taken. These pictures are typically shared from the @Bergdorfs Twitter account, with a following approaching 150,000 users.

Another highly visual platform to take notice of is Pinterest, which for many brands is the platform du jour. To say Pinterest's popularity has exploded over the last year might not be giving the social platform its due. In case you're not familiar, Pinterest is essentially a big virtual pinboard. Users take content they have found across the social web and "pin" it to different collections, or boards. There's no limit to the number of diverse boards a user can create, from Pets to Great Marketing Campaigns to Inspiration and so forth. In addition to finding content all over the web, users can browse other users' boards and repin another's content to their own boards.

Like many similar social services, Pinterest has a pin-it bookmarklet that users can add to their browser toolbars, making pinning images (and making them social) incredibly easy for many users. While a lot of early users focused their pins on arts and crafts, there's no right or wrong way to use Pinterest. As more users sign up, the type of content being pinned becomes increasingly diverse.

A brand can interact with the Pinterest audience in many ways. You can tag other users in your posts, repin other users' content, comment on their posts, or just like their pins as a nod of approval. If you find things that will be useful to a member of your audience, you can use an @mention in the caption for your pin, which will notify the other user that they've been mentioned, building your reputation with the community.

All of this interaction makes it relatively easy to make connections with Pinterest users who may be interested in your products or services. Once you build those connections with the Pinterest community, pinning to a board doesn't have to be a solitary activity. Boards can be set up to be collaborative, so that you can collaborate with your customers on a specific contest, product development crowdsourcing initiative, and more. Pinterest is even a great tool for collecting competitive intelligence: I've teamed up with collaborators to pin inspiration advertisements.

I've seen a number of successful strategies employed on Pinterest. Luxurious retail giant Bergdorf Goodman has boards that are organized around fashion trends for the current season. Each board's description allows interested users to learn about current fashion trends. *Real Simple* magazine publishes boards with tips that tie in to its brand ethos, with subjects like New Uses for Old Things and Problem-Solving Products. Whole Foods not only pins foods that it sells and recipes that tie in to those products but also includes boards dedicated to ecofriendly living, including recycling and gardening. Handmade and vintage marketplace Etsy features items from its many storefronts organized into neatly curated boards such as DIY Projects, Gift Ideas, Stuff We Love, and even locale-specific boards such as EtsyFR for France and EtsyAU for Australia.

When images are pinned to Pinterest, they are automatically linked back to their original source, so Pinterest is capable of driving considerable referral traffic to your website. In fact, by some accounts, it drives more traffic than Google+, YouTube, and LinkedIn combined.[5] However, remember always to work on your soft sell. Don't come across as too pushy in getting people to buy your products. Think about the kinds of things that will help your audience before you think about what you want from them, and you'll have a chance of winning their loyalty.

CASE IN POINT: The Viral Growth
of a Photodocumentary

Although many fun brands are profiled in this book, remember that going social can be incredibly rewarding for a more serious-minded venture as well. That's exactly what Angelo and Jennifer Merendino discovered with "My Wife's Fight with Breast Cancer," a Facebook page and website Angelo set up to document Jennifer's struggle with the illness.

In September 2007, Angelo and Jennifer married, but their honeymoon period was cut short when Jennifer received a diagnosis of stage 3B breast cancer shortly thereafter. After a double mastectomy, months of chemotherapy followed by over a month of daily radiation, and reconstructive surgery, doctors thought Jennifer to be cancer-free.

Over two years after Jennifer's first cancer diagnosis, the couple received word that her cancer had returned. While Angelo and Jennifer had a strong support group of friends, it was hard for most people to truly understand the daily struggles the couple was encountering, from chronic pain to dealing with endless treatments and medications to battles with insurance companies. Angelo, an accomplished photographer, began documenting this daily life, humanizing the face of cancer to those who had a hard time imagining its human toll. Through engaging photographs posted on his website in a photodocumentary, Angelo documented the couple's struggle through Jennifer's treatments. "Initially, the photos were only supposed to be for our close family and friends, so they could understand what we were going through," shared Angelo. "But we had no idea the kind of interest total strangers would have."

In July 2011 Angelo created "My Wife's Fight with Breast Cancer" as a Facebook page to promote his photodocumentary, which he had entered in a worldwide competition. "Once Ange posted the link to the photos onto Facebook, people began to respond with more love and support than he imagined," Jennifer wrote on her blog, sharing that women "from around the world who are currently fighting or who have fought cancer have contacted Ange telling him that his photos and my fight have encouraged and inspired them in their own journey."

By December 19, 2011, the page had 2,814 likes, jumping to 3,080 just two days later. On December 22, Jennifer passed away, just a year and a half after this second diagnosis, and just a few months after the couple celebrated their fourth wedding anniversary. Her passing sent shockwaves around the Internet: When Angelo announced her passing in a post on the Facebook page, it received 855 likes of recognition, 586 comments, and 233 shares, gargantuan numbers for a Facebook post, demonstrating how powerful the photos had been to so many people. The caring didn't stop after Jennifer's passing, as Angelo continued to share heartfelt photos from Jennifer's journey. "I think we all want a little more honesty in our lives," Angelo shared, trying to explain why the pictures continue to resonate. Purely through grassroots efforts, the photodocumentary wound up being featured on CNN'S photo blog. Though bittersweet, Angelo's photos have led to book offers and a successful string of exhibits featuring his photographs.

Creating Engaging Video Content

If a picture tells a thousand words, imagine how many words a video can convey. To say that video should be an important piece of your content pie would be an understatement for most businesses. Online video content is not a television commercial. As a marketer, you need to understand the difference between video that customers have decided to watch and video that has been foisted upon them.

Producing online video content can result in many benefits for your brand. It's not only a great way to engage more deeply with your existing audience; it can also help you reach new audiences and build buzz around your brand. Video content can also increase SEO (search engine optimization) for your brand's website. Best of all, your video content can be used to populate your other social channels, such as Facebook and Twitter. Video content is a great way to test your audience's sentiment toward a particular product. It's easier for brands to put out several unique messages and approaches to test and see which gain the most traction. Yet another virtue is the freedom that online video gives you: Unlike a television spot, you're not limited to 30 seconds to make your pitch. If your online video needs to be three minutes to tell its story properly, that's no problem. As long as the content is of high quality and is compelling, you can theoretically have as much time as you need.

If you don't know how big a place video will occupy in your content mix, start small. Spend the right amount on your video content, but that doesn't mean you need to spend too much. If you're a larger company or blog network, shooting on a video camera purchased for under $100 may leave your video underwhelming. At the same time, you hardly need to rent a complete studio for a video that will be generally shown at a 640×480 resolution.

Be practical. When you're purchasing equipment, try to have a sense of where you're most likely going to use your equipment.

Portability is nice, but keep in mind it's significantly more difficult to get good audio quality outside. When it comes to production, the bare essentials—such as lighting, sound, and competent camera work—should be handled with love. If you don't make the most of your production capabilities, the audience can tell, and it will be harder for your content to resonate. As for postproduction, a good edit is essential. I've seen video shoots where a number of critical elements went wrong, but a strong editor nevertheless helped me develop a strong final product. The opposite isn't true: An amazing shoot followed by a lackluster editing job can often underwhelm.

"The biggest mistake brands make when posting video content online is that they post a commercial to the web and expect the same results as their TV campaign," explains Mary Crosse, the Executive Producer of Content at digital studio Click 3X. "Brands forget that their 30-second commercials that they're paying a lot of money to get viewers to watch are not going to attract the same views when consumers have the choice of which content they're going to spend time with online."

Another mistake Mary reminds her clients to avoid is devoting all their time and effort to the video and not leaving enough time in the digital strategy and seeding to promote the video launch. Some brands do this: They spend a lot of effort and money producing a video that gets 400 views but looks like it could have easily garnered 40,000 with the proper strategy in place. The distribution strategy should be a part of the conversation and budget from the beginning.

Mary thinks it's important for brands to stay true to their brand DNA when creating content online but to step away from their traditional advertising formulas and create content that gives more value to their audience. As for how you define value, that's entirely up to you. It can be informative, entertaining, or inspiring.

Although the vast majority of branded "viral videos" use humor, compelling informative videos are quickly catching up.

When you're developing video content, bear in mind that your goal is not to go viral. This is a very dated term and is not something you should ever try to force. In fact, one of the easiest ways to ensure you don't go viral is to have that goal in mind. Instead, develop a compelling video with the goal of reaching the right people, not everyone. Also, don't put too much pressure on your initial efforts. It's a good idea to start with something easy, such as interviewing your customers and employees. You can do this on an ongoing basis and build it into your editorial calendar. Plus, you can keep on repeating the format, provided you don't run out of employees or customers. And let's face it: If you're running out of customers, you have much bigger problems than a lack of video content.

If you're looking to do something truly stellar with video content, rest assured that online video has far from reached its potential yet. Right now, "video is a high-functioning blunt object in the greater structure of the web," says Michael Mendelsohn, a veteran creative director and videographer. "Video still feels like it's an end point in interactivity. I've seen video used in interesting interactive campaigns where it becomes invaluable in disseminating information, but video on the web is still too passive an experience."

While innovative and truly interactive video is far from a mature phase right now, there are plenty of examples of brands pushing the envelope to elicit more engagement. To celebrate the launch of their McBites snack, McDonald's crowdsourced ten miniature movies, 30 seconds apiece, from its audience, with creators of the top ideas winning cash prizes. Experimental fashion designer Norma Kamali launched Norma Kamali 3D, featuring a 3D fashion show. Norma found multiple ways to make the video more engaging. Because it was a 3D movie, she offered 3D glasses she had designed to her audience as a mail order item; expecting 500 requests, she received instead nearly 38,000 when the offer was shared and reshared on Facebook. Not only that, Norma built a game into the movie, hiding six items in the film that did not belong; viewers of the video who found all six could email Norma for a chance to win a special prize.

Building Engagement Using Social Gaming

Social gaming is increasingly becoming an important driver for developing relationships with your audience through play, and it is a fairly powerful way for brands to promote engagement. Tablet owners are particularly big on games, with 66 percent of them playing games daily. The social gaming audience is somewhat evenly divided, with women aged 35–44 comprising the largest group.[6] One of the best things about branded social games is that companies are offered the opportunity to drive purchases and increased loyalty through something other than discounts and freebies.

In Nike's Winter's Angry perseverance campaign, players help famous athletes, such as women's soccer player Alex Morgan and Olympic gold medalist sprinter Allyson Felix, "beat the cold" by completing a few trials. Members of Nike's social audience who achieved the highest scores could win a trip for two to meet a world-class athlete.

MAC Cosmetics launched Cute Pinball to celebrate its new Quite Cute Collection, inspired by the Japanese culture of passion for all things cute. The game, housed on MAC's Facebook page, allowed players to easily challenge friends and post badges signifying achievements. The stickiness of the game resulted in MAC's achieving 56 percent higher like growth over the previous month.[7]

Whereas MAC created their own game, it is becoming increasingly popular to tie your brand into a hit game with a built-in audience. That's exactly what Best Buy did with CityVille, Zynga's hit game that has over 40 million Facebook users playing monthly. The whole point of CityVille is that players create their own city; the more successful they are, the more game features they can unlock, including purchasing businesses. While most businesses people can buy have generic names, Best Buy is the first real-life retail chain to branch out into the game, allowing players to show their affinity for the electronics retailer.

. . . . **GUEST POST** . . . .

Should Social Gaming Be Part of Your Strategy?

Erica May works on Social Games Strategy at Facebook, where she manages the advertising and community relationships with game developers Zynga, Playdom, and Kabam.

I'd advise companies looking to advertise in social games to talk to developers and make sure the audience of a particular game is the demographic they're trying to reach. Social games are becoming hot in the advertising world, and it's kind of like when iPhone applications first launched: Everybody felt as though they needed to have one. However, not all brands need to use gaming as part of their strategy.

Brand sponsorships within social games are not about being intrusive; they are about taking interest in what a customer cares about instead of trying to tell them what to do. For instance, in a game like CityVille, if you are going to sponsor a building . . . that's a premium good valued by a customer, and going to potentially remain in their city for a while. You're adding value to their gaming, not giving direction or trying to control the conversation. The way we are moving, if brands don't have good content, they're not going to get surfaced, whether they are paying for it or not. We want to provide a really engaging, organic experience for our users, and we don't just want to throw ads in front of them that they won't be interested in.

CASE IN POINT: Whistler Blackcomb's Evergreen Content

Whistler Blackcomb is a ski resort located in Whistler, British Columbia. Each January, the resort hosts the Deep Winter Photo Challenge, a competition held in which six pro ski and snowboard photographers are personally selected by Whistler Blackcomb to team up with athletes of their choice to capture the "epic powder days, stormy conditions and deep tree skiing" of a typical January. Each photographer's collection of photos is then edited into slideshows and presented in front of an audience of about 1,000 winter sports enthusiasts.

Whistler Blackcomb's Deep Winter Photo Challenge predates the social marketing age, so the initial competition didn't include social media. The challenge was originally created as an experience to bring people to the resort during the quieter time period of mid-January, but the competition has other advantages. For one, the photos often find themselves in industry publications, creating one more way to engage with potential customers. The competition also keeps Whistler Blackcomb top-of-mind with key influencers in the ski and snowboarding industry, making such individuals more likely to engage with the resort on an ongoing basis.

As the competition has grown over the last seven years, social media's role has grown: Both competitors and audience members are live-tweeting; postevent slideshows are uploaded on Vimeo and YouTube, embedded on websites, and posted on Facebook. Social media are actually helping to increase Whistler's original goal: resonating within the ski and snowboard world by getting engaging imagery out into social channels.

The Challenge has yielded a lot of evergreen content, as Whistler can leverage content created over the past few Challenges to drum up interest ahead of this year's competition. In the Challenge, Whistler has a campaign that is deeply rooted in the brand's love for the outdoors, adventure, and winter sports. Having an ongoing event to plan the calendar around is also helpful for Whistler Blackcomb's social marketing team because it knows, going into each season, that there's a pretty robust campaign from which to draw audience engagement.

Likes Versus Engagement and Quantity Versus Quality

To get to work every morning, most of us drive past billboards. We may or may not process these billboards or mentally file away the brands we encounter. However, in the digital age, the targeted equivalent of a billboard is a company's page on Facebook. When customers decide to like a page, they are essentially saving a marketing billboard to market to them later. A like, by itself, doesn't really mean much. Sure, if you're in charge of growing your brand's social audience, getting more likes for your page will make you look good; however, it's more important to get people to engage after they like your product's page. The sad reality is that many people never visit that Facebook page—or engage with that brand—again. According to best-selling social media author Pam Moore, founder & CEO of FruitZoom, "A Facebook 'Like' is the beginning, not the end, of a relationship." In the age in which anything with indeterminate ROI is immediately cut from the budget, you can't afford not to engage with your audience post-like.

As in the example of the company in Chapter 2 that used provocative but irrelevant Facebook posts to promote their product, creating an online media presence is not about quantity: It's about quality. It's better to have a few hundred engaged fans who encourage their social circles to try out your product than to have thousands who liked your page and have been MIA ever since.

Too many brands send out e-mails encouraging their customers to "Fan Us" on Facebook. Getting that like from a prospect who's on the fence about your brand is a good first step. I don't want to denigrate a Facebook like as a step in the sales funnel. But it's just that—a single step, only part of a longer sales process.

Although curating the content of others can gain you a following, it's simply not the same thing as creating your own brand content. Curation tends to take less time than creating your own content, but it tends to be lower risk, lower reward.

Although raising awareness among nonbuyers shouldn't be your top priority, it can still have long-term benefits. Long before I had a car, I saw plenty of Geico commercials touting their car insurance. In no way was I in the market for their services at the time, but years later when I purchased a car, I turned to Geico immediately for my car insurance. Because of this principal, I advise brands to widen their audiences whenever possible. That's why throughout this book I tend to say "customers and prospects"—because, even if you are in a B2B or B2C line of business, there is absolute value in creating relationships with people who are not yet ready to buy.

· · · · · · · **GUEST POST** · · · · · · ·

Maya Grinberg, Social Media Manager at Wildfire, on:
The Evolution from Likes to Engagement

The focus *used* to be on getting as many people as you could to commit to being consumers of your content. This commitment used to be called being a fan, but now the verb is to *like*. The focus was on growing this community of fans for your brand as fast as possible. Now, the extension of that thought—and a really important question—is: "Once users have committed to being your fan, *then* what do you do with them?"

The next wave of Facebook marketing will be all about, "How do we keep those fans and future fans engaged from day one? How do we continue that relationship throughout the lifetime of their being a fan of our page?" The challenge for marketers will be to craft a strategy around making sure that fans don't get bored with the branded content, making sure they don't unsubscribe from the brand in the feed, and making sure that the brand is actively putting together marketing and promotional campaigns that give fans a reason to come back to the fan page. Increasingly, the content that gets put out can't be static; it needs to be consistently compelling. Marketers will find themselves studying fans to try to determine what they actually like from the branded page and what they don't like, then constantly adjusting the social media plan to serve their users better catered content.

What's a Facebook Like Worth?

Facebook fans provide value for a brand in a few ways, including loyalizing fans by increasing their engagement, increasing fans' incremental purchasing behavior, and influencing friends of fans.

If you're a fan of your local florist, your friends might be interested in the business as well. A Facebook study of the top 100 Facebook brand pages found that, for every like a brand amasses, the brand is capable of reaching 34 friends of the liker. There is no reason why this does not hold true for smaller businesses: Getting fans gives you the ability to start an interesting conversation with others.

The report found that Facebook fans of Starbucks were 418 percent more likely to visit starbucks.com, with friends of those fans 230 percent more likely.

Bear in mind that, even if you're posting, you might not be reaching all your fans; far from that, in fact. For brands that post content every weekday, 16 percent of fans are reached, on average. It's a catch-22 for many brands: If you post too infrequently, fans might miss their content; post too often, and fans may get irritated, tune you out, and unsubscribe. "There isn't one way to do this," reinforces Maria, Head of Community at Yammer. "You really need to listen and understand what people are saying, what they need, and where they are, and address their needs."

To be successful in engaging with customers after the like, it is important to develop a strategy beforehand. The best way to see a return on your social media investment is to develop pragmatic, realistic goals and objectives, and a step-by-step plan for getting from point A to point B.

Although content is king when it comes to engagement, it's the king of a pretty small kingdom unless you marry it with caring about your customers and making their happiness your focal point.

In the next chapter, we'll discuss how social platforms have made becoming customer-centric a more manageable proposition for many brands.

going further · · · · · · · · · · · · · · ·

For bonus materials and updates pertaining to this chapter's topics, please visit: *http://goingsocial.jeremygoldman.com/ch4.*

become truly
customer-centric—
and reap the advantages

IT'S NOT ENOUGH to say that you're customer-centric. A decade ago, if your brand posted ongoing advertisements about how customer-centric you were, the only way for the consumer to verify whether this was true was to ask friends and acquaintances. Now the consumer can just run a quick search online or post a question to social connections to find out whether the brand in question is truly focused on the customer or merely spouting marketing speak.

Many companies are getting into social marketing simply because they've realized that people are talking about their brand's customer service on Facebook, Twitter, and blogs often powered with commenting systems such as Disqus and Intense Debate. This new paradigm means that it's impossible to provide any type of product or service without having to deal with the social ramifications, and therefore it's impossible *not* to participate in discussions on social media. These days, a company with a great product but poor customer service becomes known as a bad brand. Customer service is a Jabba the Hutt–sized tiebreaker; most customers are not going to bother with a brand that doesn't provide good service, even if they like the product. Addressing customer concerns and resolving complaints quickly makes it more likely that customers will give you positive word of mouth that will spread across your social marketing channels.

This being said, I trust you not to drive yourself out of business for offering free shipping on a product that costs $120 to ship or if you offer a 50 percent–off coupon more often than you can afford to, all in the name of being customer-centric. You have to strike the right balance between being customer friendly and being an intelligent businessperson. Pleasing the customer is important, but running a viable business is equally vital. If you give away everything for free, you won't be around very long. The goal should be to figure out what will surprise and delight your customers, at the same time ensuring you have a long-term plan for profitability.

The Dawn of Social Customer Service

Traditional customer service has changed significantly in the past five years, due to platforms such as Facebook, Twitter, Yelp, and more. Customers have a voice as never before. As a result, they are speaking up and sharing their experiences with your brand and others, and their fellow customers are listening, commenting, and sharing these stories of both great and horrible customer service experiences far spam to a minimum. Direct messages are a platform for communication and feedback, as opposed to sales pitches.

One caution: With the increased customers and brands on Facebook, keeping up with questions and comments through yet another channel in a timely manner can be a challenge for companies. It's not just publishing content; it's managing a two-way communication, which is a lot of work for brands. That being said, isn't providing stellar service the kind of work that's well worth it?

. . . . GUEST POST . . . .

Christi McNeil, Emerging Media Specialist and Spokesperson at Southwest Airlines, on:
Expanding Customer Service to Online Channels

While our dedication to customer service hasn't changed as a result of social media—we've always had a business built on serving our customers—it has definitely evolved. We've expanded our Customer Relations team to the online channels, which has increased the ways that customers can reach out to us. Social media has required our business to become fast responders and problem solvers.

We treat all of our customers equally, whether we are dealing with an issue via phone, letter, email, or Twitter. When we are handling an issue, we are moving so quickly to get the details and research the issue that we don't have time to pay much attention to Klout scores or how many friends someone has. We try to understand the issue or concern and presumably assist them the best that we can. Although contacting us through Twitter does not mean we can grant an exception to policy or overturn a decision that's been made at the airport, we can still use Twitter to help improve our communications with the customer.

and wide. As an organization, you may have gotten used to thinking of your customer service as being squarely focused in your call center, but that is quickly changing. You have to start thinking of communications on Twitter and other platforms as being part of the overall customer service experience. You're not just selling your product; you're selling the combined perceived value of your product and your service.

As a result of the new paradigm in social marketing, customer service has gone from a reactive department to a proactive part of your business. Even though at times you have to react to a crisis, your customer service group should be a strategic, forward-thinking team organized around providing the best customer experience possible and creating fantastic word of mouth. If your company ignores product or service issues, then your customers are going to use forums and social networks to sully your good name. Customer service has also become a hot topic for journalists; they love writing exposés on companies that provide either stellar or horrific customer service. There is a direct correlation between the ease with which unhappy customers can now gripe publicly and the increased importance of good customer service as a marketing strategy.

Although a public complaint isn't the type of thing you look forward to, the shifting paradigm has plenty of advantages. For one, you'll get feedback in real time from your current customers, as well as from prospects. One of the best sources of inexpensive research is listening to those who aren't yet buying your product but are mentioning you on social platforms. If prospects are giving lots of feedback that your price point is too high, you know there might be a market for a simplified version of your product at a lower price point.

Many companies that have become good at this social customer service are finding significant cost savings over traditional customer service. Faster resolution times mean fewer manpower hours to take care of the same number of customers. As a result of moving customer service to social platforms, many companies have found that their customers are ultimately happier and more likely to purchase more and/or have good things to say about the brand.

Finally and probably most importantly: moving customer service online also lets you respond to customers in real time, allowing your customer service team to engage in multiple conversations at once rather than making a customer leave a message. Typically, you and your customers are going to notice that a customer support issue dealt with online can be resolved faster than via phone or e-mail. The end result typically is happier customers who are more likely to become repeat customers. If that isn't a good enough reason to go social, what is?

If you are planning to develop a social marketing program revolving around customer support, you're going to need a qualified team to make it work. The best pick for an assignment like this is a customer support representative who has a good understanding of social media, rather than a social media expert without customer service experience or the empathy needed to succeed as a service-oriented problem solver.

While I advocate speedy customer service across all channels, that advice is easier to follow across your company's social channels. All customer issues should be solved or redirected in a timely manner, not just to the satisfaction of the customer who is directly affected, but for anyone else in the social audience who has been paying attention. To speed up the process, it's a good idea to have a well-documented internal customer service policy for managers of social media accounts. This way, all those on your team engaging directly with the brand's social audience know exactly what they can and cannot say; this liberates them and allows them to respond speedily.

When faced with a public social customer service probl ommend publicly making your intentions of fixing the crystal clear, so that everyone paying attention can see you uinely trying to solve the problem. Scott Monty, head o Media at Ford Motor Company, echoes the importance o transparent: "Because social media touches so many elements business (or at least has the potential to do so), we try to ensur our very public efforts online are visible to all."

"Facebook and Twitter have completely replaced traditi Customer Service for a lot of consumers," agrees digital marke strategist Abby Lane Whitmer. However, because of the limitati and public nature of these channels, Abby and other digital mark ing professionals often end up sending people from Facebook Twitter to their brands' more traditional customer service channe to get a more in-depth response. Often, there's a proper point i time to take the conversation offline. In cases like these, it's a good idea to contact disgruntled customers privately to resolve any service issues. Once you're out of the public eye, however, make sure to have the same level of professionalism in your communications: Don't say or do anything in private interactions that you wouldn't want to see the customer make public.

Although Twitter has had DMs (direct messages) since its early days, direct messaging is a relatively new addition to Facebook. It's a way for companies to communicate and interact with their customers and fans on Facebook, especially when situations call for a more personalized approach than a quick, public reply. From a customer's point of view, getting individualized attention from a favorite brand—or a direct response to a complaint—can be a nice customer service touch and make them feel special. The dialogue has to be initiated on the customer's end because Facebook does not allow companies to send unsolicited messages, which helps keep

> Our online engagement is hard work, but it results in people wanting to fly and interact with a brand they trust and love. We have a legion of fans online who want to interact and "talk" with us, and that loyalty is increased with each tweet or message we send to them.

The Immediacy of Social Customer Service

Because of the immediacy of the social web, customers have more of a voice than ever. What each customer is thinking and saying matters greatly. A few years ago, it was relatively unheard of for a customer to be involved in the inner workings of your business, but now customers are demanding the ability to contribute new development ideas, potential new features for your product, branding suggestions, and so on.

Karen Yung, Manager of Social and Mobile at Coach, agrees that "the upside to customer service via social media is the immediacy and intimacy of the experience." She notes that "customers are engaging with brands and companies in environments that are comfortable to them—places they would be in already—without having to step out of those boundaries to seek help or attention."

Increasingly, customers are more likely to try to resolve customer service issues over social platforms because they expect to receive a faster, more empathetic response from the company through this medium—or another customer to chime in with help. Customers are more likely to expect an immediate answer when something goes wrong. Nobody looked forward to a 40-minute wait time on the customer service line in the old days, but now, given the immediacy of the social web, most people find it completely unacceptable—myself included.

For years, I have been experiencing a customer service issue with Papa John's pizza. For some reason, when it came to online ordering, my building was outside the delivery radius of the two stores closest to me. It turned out that this was due to just a programming error on the website; in reality, I was within the delivery radius of both stores. However, each and every time I placed my order online, I had to call the store and switch it from carryout to delivery because the website seemed to constantly think I was outside the delivery radius. Needless to say, this was very frustrating and defeated the entire purpose of ordering online. I called Papa John's customer service line as a customer trying to give positive feedback so that they could fix this issue. Each time I called, there was approximately a 30-minute wait and I gave up, deciding to simply order from Papa John's considerably less than I would have otherwise. Finally, after a particularly bad service experience with Papa John's, I tweeted about the poor service, and Papa John's responded back to me within 10 minutes. Lesson: Once customers get this type of immediacy, the odds of their going back to the old paradigm are next to zero.

Companies that are moving more of their customer service functions to social platforms are overwhelmingly feeling the benefits of the move more than the drawbacks. Responsiveness is often cited as one of the major benefits. "I can't tell you how many times we've been able to turn an unhappy customer into a brand advocate just by listening to a potential issue, responding honestly, and doing our best to fix it," says Jason Keith of Vistaprint, a leading provider of professional marketing products and services to small businesses. "Just those simple actions go further than you could possibly imagine."

Getting Good at Listening

Under the new paradigm, companies need to be good at active listening. This means not just engaging in a dialogue with customers but actually listening to what they have to say and taking that feedback to heart.

Engaging in a two-way conversation doesn't just lead to refinement of an existing product; in some cases, it can even be responsible for the product's existence in the first place. That's the case with John Siuntres and *Word Balloon*. In 2004, the veteran radio host began a video documentary about crime comic books. Unfortunately, John's videographer had to depart mid-project, and John was left with four interviews with such prominent comic book creators as Brian Azzarello, cocreator of *100 Bullets* and one of the most popular comics writers of the last two decades, and Max Allan Collins, who had created the *Road to Perdition* comic on which the Tom Hanks film was based. To salvage what he could from the project, John edited down the audio from the interviews and uploaded them as MP3 files onto his website. A frequent message board participant, John shared links to his interviews on such boards as top creator Brian Michael Bendis's *Jinxworld*. Users on the message board told John that he was, in essence, a podcaster and that iTunes would be a great place to begin placing his content to attract more listeners. John used the feedback to convert his audio files into a podcast, leading to the creation of *Word Balloon*, the "comic book conversation show" considered to be the top comics podcast, with an average rating of five out of five on iTunes. Think about it: If John weren't a good listener, all of this might not have happened.

Although you don't necessarily need to always follow their directions, if you ignore what they're asking for, make sure you have a good reason for doing so. One brand I'm familiar with was repeatedly asked for a new product innovation from its audience. The company's executives, however, believed its future lay in a different direction. Rather than changing directions, the company continually ignored the feedback it was getting from its audience. A competitor wound up offering an innovation similar to what the audience had requested, and a large number of customers left for that competitor. The company didn't have a compelling reason to ignore its audience, and it paid the consequences.

Listening is one of the most important things a brand can do online. If your brand is just broadcasting its own agenda, it isn't truly engaging in a conversation. Listening comes in two forms: passive listening and active listening. Passive listening involves allowing your customers to speak without interruption. Active listening, on the other hand, involves listening followed by giving your audience cues that you're listening and working on the main points that they raise. For the purposes of social marketing, active listening helps you begin a conversation and create connections with customers.

Giantnerd is a perfect example of a company that listens: The outdoor equipment company uses its site's social features to make adjustments to their products. Giantnerd receives actionable data by seeing how many audience members Love, Dislike, or Want a product and then uses the data to improve its manufacturing processes and decisions. When Giantnerd sees a large percentage of Dislikes or lackluster reviewers on a particular bike it manufactures, the company makes changes. Feedback on the smallest of details, such as the location of the toecap on the pedal, has led to changes in a bike's manufacturing; these changes have led to demonstrably increased sales on the reconfigured models.

Giantnerd has found that it can tell what sales work and what sales don't, just from Loves, Dislikes, comments, shares, and general feedback. In this way, the company's social marketing efforts are not just a way for it to message customers; they're a way for the company to drive its future development. "The community is really driving the ship," offers up Brad Fredricks, the company's Vice President of Ecommerce. "They're core to our decisions."

Does Giantnerd's approach sound similar to yours? If yes, you're on the right track. If not, ask yourself whether you talk more than you listen. If you're wondering about this, there is a good chance you're talking too much. Marketers are typically trained to talk more than listen. If you think you're a poor listener, work on becoming a good listener as soon as possible. If you think you're already a good listener, then work on becoming a great listener. There is no limit to the improvement you can make in listening to your customers.

Without a culture of listening, you run the risk of a social media misstep, as McDonald's experienced with a recent Twitter promotion. The campaign started with the hashtag #MeetTheFarmers, which was used to tell the story of McDonald's fresh produce guarantee. Later in the day, however, the company switched to using the vague hashtag #McDstories. This vagueness backfired bigtime, as customers began sharing their least favorite McDonald's experiences. McDonald's was paying to promote this hashtag, and dissatisfied customers were "brandjacking" the hashtag. McDonald's was actually paying for its brand to be denigrated! Although McDonald's does a lot right when it comes to going social, in that instance it didn't fully realize that a successful social marketing campaign has to be rooted in people's perceptions of the brand. McDonald's chose to ignore what their customers had to say and wasn't listening, leading to a public relations fiasco. It's impossible for a brand to be in charge unless it truly cares about what their audience has to say.

Listen? Always. Participate? Sometimes.

Let customers talk among themselves, and inject your brand into a conversation only when it is appropriate. Goozex, the video game and movie trading community mentioned earlier, handles social marketing with a mandate to interject only when doing so will add value. "Any comment directly made to Goozex on Facebook or Twitter will get a response from us, unless it's overtly negative or inflammatory," explains Mark Nebesky of Goozex. "Oftentimes on Twitter there is a @Goozex mention that is not intended for our response, but rather for our attention. My rule of thumb is: if I respond to someone, does it fit in within a conversation frame, or will it stick out as some kind of intrusive experience? Customer service issues get a helpful response with some kind of actionable step."

Vistaprint USA, a leading provider of professional marketing products and services to small businesses, has been recognized for its stellar social engagement, with multiple New England Direct Marketing Association (NEDMA) Awards to its credit. The company attributes its overall social marketing success, in part, to striking the right balance between being intrusive and being helpful. As an organization, Vistaprint tries to not let any comment about the company go unanswered, be it positive or negative. "If someone had a positive experience and gives us a shout-out because of that, we want to thank them," explains Jason Keith, Vistaprint's Senior Manager of Public Relations and Social Media. Negative experiences, while infrequent, are treated as equally valid as positive ones by Jason and his team. "If a customer has had a negative experience, we want to see how we can potentially rectify that through social media."

Indeed, there are no set rules about when to let your customers talk among themselves and when to intrude in the conversation. All things being equal, the best situation is if you can get your customers to articulate the brand's vision for you because that comes across as a much more genuine peer-to-peer recommendation. There aren't many things more satisfying than seeing one of my customers ask for a specific product recommendation and, before I can chime in, having another of my customers answer the question by recommending the same product I was about to recommend.

"You should participate when appropriate—generally, when something is asked of you that a fan won't necessarily provide," says Maria Ogneva, Head of Community at Yammer. "For example, when someone tweets for support, it's directed toward the company—and even if the brand doesn't have an answer right then, it's important to let people know that they are heard and cared for."

When it comes to participating on message boards, the slope is considerably more slippery. "In a forum, it's a balancing act between allowing users to talk to each other about best practices versus jumping in with a fix or maybe jump-starting a conversation," Maria explains. If you can build a network of influential fans on these message boards, however, they can act as effective ambassadors on your behalf. "Your primary task should be to create advocates via positive brand experiences (product, service, everything); those advocates can come to your rescue when you need it. That's much better than defending yourself when someone tries to bash you in a forum," says Maria.

CASE IN POINT: Fresh Brothers Wins Loyalty Through Listening

Fresh Brothers, a Los Angeles–based pizza chain, was launched in 2008 by Debbie Goldberg and her husband Adam; they now operate six stores. In addition to their fantastic pizza, the company has developed a powerful reputation by being extremely responsive on social channels. Fresh Brothers averages four stars out of five on most major review sites, including Yelp. Debbie wasn't always active on Yelp, but when the daily Google Alerts delivered to her e-mail inbox kept showing mentions of Fresh Brothers on Yelp, Debbie decided to spend more time on Yelp and other review sites.

Fresh Brothers does a few things that stand out with its reviewers. For one, Debbie thanks reviewers who share strong reviews and rewards those users by mailing them gift certificates. When reviewers post negative reviews, Debbie will typically offer them a gift certificate and entice the reviewers to visit the restaurant again soon. One of the ways Fresh Brothers succeeds is in its responses to negative reviews: Many business owners might argue and get into a fight with a negative reviewer. Fresh Brothers takes the opposite approach, acknowledging the reviewer's points and softening the reviewer's stance about Fresh Brothers at the same time. It's not uncommon that an initially unhappy reviewer will visit Fresh Brothers and amend their opinion about the chain. Fresh Brothers encourages its audience to update any reviews after the fact.

Not everyone thinks of Yelp as a social platform, but that's exactly what it is. After all, users can tag other user reviews as Useful, Funny, or Cool, befriend other reviewers, and participate in message board forums. Debbie succeeds on Yelp because she understands the nature of the channel. Yelp is a social platform in which complaints, often employing creative language, are the norm. To engage on Yelp, Debbie learned to develop a thick skin. After all, it's incredibly easy to take what someone says on Yelp personally. "The brand, the business that you build, is very personal but what these people are saying is not. It's not a slam against me if they say something negative, but it is something worthy of taking note of and researching and learning from what everybody has to say, whether it's positive or negative."

It was shocking to some customers—in a good way—that the owner of the business actually responds. People love that a founder of the company is identifying herself as a real person and following up. In that sense, even when someone posts about a subpar experience, Fresh Brothers scores points for responsiveness.

When it comes to the good experiences of customers, Debbie quickly discovered that positive Yelp reviews were better than paid advertising. "People who do like what you're doing are advertising for you, so you would be crazy not to recognize what they are doing and jump on the bandwagon and encourage them to keep doing it."

Debbie can't remember that anyone has reacted negatively to receiving a response from the owner. Even if someone gives Fresh Brothers a poor review, getting a note from the owner saying, "Hey, I'm really sorry you had this experience" is a very positive experience.

The end result isn't just a profitable, rewarding business, but a fanatical fan base as well. Fresh Brothers has customers who come in fresh off the plane and stopping in

> to get a pizza even before going back home. One cus-
> tomer in particular stopped by to get his Fresh Brothers
> fix after spending a week in Italy, which goes to show how
> loyalized the restaurant chain's customers have become.

Moderating Your Audience

Often, the best way to ensure you don't have to continually lead your community is by empowering members of your audience with the knowledge and tools to lead on your behalf. "The best online communities don't actually work on a one-to-many principal; they work on a one-to-one-to-many," says Heather A. Taylor, the Editorial Director of Econsultancy, who has served as a social strategist on brands such as the BBC and Paypal. "When you have a community of people who are really involved and care for that community, they become moderators themselves; they become super users."

Unfortunately, though, something inappropriate is occasionally said on your social channel, and you have to decide what to do about it. This is a relatively divisive topic among social strategists; some don't believe in deleting comments or moderating in any way, under any circumstances. I'm a bit less liberal on this topic: On pages that I manage, an audience member's content needs to be particularly irrelevant or offensive to be removed. Under most circumstances, a valid complaint about a company's product or services shouldn't be grounds for removal.

When it comes to managing their community, Vistaprint tries to avoid censorship. As Jason Keith explains:

> Truthfully, we never delete posts from customers or non-customers because we don't feel that's how the social space works. Everyone is entitled to their opinion, and if they've

had a bad experience we welcome them telling us about it. We want the chance to make things right, to get the correct information out there, and to better educate our customers on who we are and what we're doing. The only time we'll delete a post is on our Facebook page when someone uses profanity.

Of course there are times when we have to "disengage" with a social conversation because it's unproductive, but those times are few and far between. For the most part people are respectful and even if there's a dispute it's always handled in the most respectful way.

For what it's worth, I'm an advocate for avoiding censorship whenever possible. If your brand receives a negative comment reaction on your Facebook fan page, I believe it looks far better to address it there in the best way possible than to delete it. After all, there's a good chance others have seen it already. There are, however, times when you do need to delete and even ban fans.

Customer Service: Everyone's Responsibility

Customer Service isn't a niche part of your business; it's what keeps the lights on! Whether a customer or prospect connects with your Twitter controlled by your Customer Service Department, contacts your Facebook page run by Marketing, or even calls headquarters and gets the Accounting Department, all of these functions need to be in the business of being customer-centric.

Customers expect to have a seamless conversation and to be treated consistently across all parts of your organization. This becomes a greater challenge as your organization grows, and your phone-based customer service representatives are a separate function—maybe even in a separate physical location—from your online community manager. Regardless of your size, consumers see your brand as one entity. That entity should provide a consistent experience, regardless of department.

As an organization grows, seamless conversation between departments becomes more difficult. Just as you might build up a set of super users external to your company, you can do the same within your company. "Your brand managers, product developers, and customer service teams are the ones who will have the answers to your community's questions and you'll need to coordinate a workflow system for getting those answers responded to quickly," says Heather of Econsultancy, who has helped set up similar systems in the past. "You may be met with resistance, especially if your coworkers are busy and unengaged with social media, so incentivize them, explain how their involvement will benefit them, help them get feedback and ideas for product development; you need their buy-in."

It's hard to ensure that customers have a seamless conversation with your brand across all your engagement channels, but Caty Kobe, who manages community at the customer service hub software provider Get Satisfaction, has a relatively simple solution. In the social marketing age, everyone in your organization must operate in a customer-centric fashion. Doing so ensures seamless conversations as the organization grows. Caty feels that frontline customer service reps and community managers must feel empowered to do what's right for the customer, regardless of the situation. She attributes part of her success to leveraging the right tools to ensure that all of her communications stay in the same place. She uses Nimble, for instance, which imports all of Exchange, Twitter, and LinkedIn information into a unified inbox, so that every customer conversation is visible.

CASE IN POINT: eFlirt Expert's Customer Service Becomes Its Marketing

Laurie Davis started eFlirt Expert with just $50 and a Twitter account. Now it's largely considered one of the leading online dating coaching services around, inspiring countless others. The company works with men and women, regardless of age and sexual orientation, and helps them create "unique and powerful dating opportunities" via connections made online.

Above all else, eFlirt Expert tries to be approachable; the service's tone is always conversational to encourage discussion. The company wants @eFlirtExpert or @eFlirt JillofAll to be the first place singles turn to when they (or friends) are having a digital dating challenge. On Twitter, eFlirt Expert follows back everyone who follows them, with the exception of spammers, in case they need to send eFlirt Expert a DM (direct message) regarding a private matter. Of course, if you have an advice-based business such as Laurie's, you have to walk a fine line between not giving away enough free advice for prospecting purposes and giving up so much that prospects never become paying customers. Rather than taking a hard-line stance toward billing, eFlirt Expert has a standing policy of giving complimentary advice if it can be achieved within three DMs. In this way, the company is able to demonstrate value to prospects without engaging in hard selling.

eFlirt Expert believes in a when-in-doubt-respond policy. Whether it's a comment about the company's work or a suggestion regarding how its services could be improved, eFlirt Expert tries to always respond. No tweet, wall post, or even Foursquare comment goes unanswered. The company has adopted a policy of being equally responsive to customers before, during, and after their dating consultations.

For Laurie and her team, the successful use of social marketing channels has centered on finding and engaging consumers in real time. Social channels, particularly Twitter, have allowed Laurie and her team to weigh in on digital dating challenges discussed by users. The company has been able to focus its content around offering dating advice. In addition, the success stories of eFlirt Expert's customers have made for compelling content, which in turn reinforces the company's value proposition and helps educate prospects on the eFlirt Expert's services.

One such service is eFlirt Expert's Lip Service Live, an ongoing feature on Facebook in which singles can ask questions, and eFlirt Expert answers them in real time. The success of this program has led to semiregular eFlirt Expert Twitter chats using the #eFlirtLive hashtag.

In addition to using hashtags, eFlirt Expert uses Twitter to retweet its audience liberally. eFlirt Expert saves the best testimonials to their Twitter favorites, so testimonials are easily accessible to new followers. Some of the favorites are:

> @Jennimafer: Met a great guy on an online dating site. 4 dates in 6 days and going strong. Thanks for the advice @eFlirtExpert!

@adamjgmiller: Love is a beautiful thing. @eFlirt
Engine and @eFlirtExpert are helping me find it!

In its quest to be customer-centric, eFlirt Expert has created
ongoing engagement mechanisms such as the Sexy Techie
series, where Laurie and her team profile clients who are
also tech entrepreneurs, asking them questions ranging
from professional experiences to dating preferences.

On Facebook, eFlirt Expert has turned success stories
into a point of engagement. For example, when one of
their clients made his relationship official by adding it to
his Facebook profile, the company celebrated by mentioning it via its own status update and then polling its
audience: "Do you notice when your Facebook friends
change their relationship status?"

Like many brands successful at online engagement,
eFlirt Expert rewards fans and followers who interact
with the brand. Laurie and her team have found that giving members of their audience recognition works quite
well. For example, on Twitter, every Friday, eFlirt Expert
uses the #FF (Follow Friday) hashtag to feature five men
and five women who it considers to be Twitter's Most
Eligible. Each week has a different focus; one week, the
list might be Twitter's Most Eligible Entrepreneurs,
with Twitter's Most Eligible Musicians the theme the
next week. eFlirt Expert prides itself in finding fun ways
to highlight members of the audience beyond simply
interacting with them and retweeting them.

All of this customer-centricity sounds great, but it isn't
really worth the effort if it doesn't yield paying clientele.

Thankfully, that's not a problem for eFlirt Expert, which has quantified 40 percent of its new clients signing up as a result of its customer-centric social marketing.

Let Them Eat Pie!

A lot of companies think about what their brand is and where they want to go with it—and *then* think about what their customers want as an afterthought. This has always been a bad idea—like sleeping with a coworker. But now that we have direct access to consumers, it's an even poorer decision—like sleeping with a coworker whose desk is right next to yours. Your customers' concerns and needs must be the first and foremost thing on your corporate agenda. Marketers need to think about what kinds of information they need to learn about their customers in order to serve them better. Sales teams need to be selling the right products and services to the customers, lest they go elsewhere.

So if you're a bakery specializing in cakes and your customers repeatedly ask you on your social channels to start making pie, by all means, listen to them! That's what being customer-centric is all about. Let them eat pie!

Incorporating Customer Feedback into Product Development

Sometimes the best thing a brand can do to reward its customers is to include them in the product development lifecycle. In Aliza Sherman's *The Complete Idiot's Guide to Crowdsourcing*, the Wine Sisterhood is featured as an example of tapping into the crowd, via their Facebook following, to get input from their target market about their current and upcoming wine brands. They've made specific changes to wine labels based on crowd input and have used brand names for new wines that were voted on by their fan base. The Wine Sisterhood is in a continuous dialogue with the women who follow them on Facebook and Twitter to learn what women want out of their wine experiences and to form stronger relationships with their customers.

"We've received lots of helpful feedback via social channels," says Brandie Feuer, a longtime hotel marketer. "Everything from customer insights into advertising, new products and promotions that might be effective, to customer service experiences that could be improved. We've used that feedback to make both our marketing efforts as well as guest experiences exceptional." Brandie has taken fan feedback and used it to develop features that fans have requested, including the ability to book two hotel rooms in a single online transaction.

Steve Huffman knows a thing or two about using customer feedback to improve his products: He founded the early social news site Reddit in 2005 and cofounded Hipmunk in 2010 with the stated mission of taking the pain out of travel planning. Steve recommends involving users in your product development process, but with a caveat: Users' opinions are often useful, but not obviously so because users typically aren't very good at designing products. "When users give us feedback, we have to run it through some filters," Steve explains. "The first is whether that user is representative of the user base as a whole; the second is whether the user is complaining about something we actually have control over; and the third filter is whether the user is complaining about a symptom or a cause. Generally, we use feedback from users to help adjust our priorities, but not to steer the actual product." While the vast majority of feedback Hipmunk receives is positive, Steve recommends not overlooking feedback that is somewhat negative because "that's the stuff that helps steer the product."

CASE IN POINT: *Kodak Modernizes Itself by Listening*

When you think of companies that are forward-thinking, Eastman Kodak probably doesn't come to mind. After all, the company has been on the decline for years, falling so far as to declare Chapter 11 bankruptcy in 2012. That said, the iconic company, founded in 1889, has used social media to help stave off its losses of the last decade.

Traditional new product development consists of market research, trend analysis, and focus groups. Kodak realized that its social platforms could be of major assistance in its product development efforts, helping the camera maker deliver better products with a greater insight into demand.

Kodak launched its first pocket camera, the Zi6, at the same time the company began engaging on Twitter. Kodak began with Twitter slowly, primarily taking notes about what people liked and didn't like about the Zi6. Although feedback was generally positive, Kodak's social audience had a few criticisms. For one thing, it was difficult to get quality sound when in a crowd. Another concern was that the USB arm was situated too close to other plugs on the camera, making it hard to use. Kodak created a list of these and other desired features that consumers discussed on social platforms and used that data as a product road map for its Zi8. The social media team then shared these concerns with their internal product development teams. The next pocket camera, the Zi8, included an external mic jack for better sound and a flexible USB arm to make it easier to plug in. Although the improvements were welcome, Kodak's social audience didn't understand the reason the company's cameras had names like Zi6 and Zi8. Kodak responded, asking its social audience to help them name their next pocket camera. Kodak developed a social contest in which fans could submit name ideas for the company's next camera via Twitter and the Kodak blog, and Kodak would select the most appropriate name. Winners would be invited to attend the Consumer Electronics Show in Las Vegas as guests of Kodak and be featured as part of the product launch. One fan suggested Play, and another suggested Sport. Kodak decided that the names were perfect together, and the PlaySport was born. The end result? Kodak's new pocket camera has sold over 1 million units and has been a major success for Kodak, consistently ranking highly in sales charts. Not bad for a stodgy old company.

Letting Customers Lead

One of the most important things that any company must do in the social space is listen to its customers and, when appropriate, engage in an honest way. To some extent, being responsive to what your audience wants to hear means letting your audience dictate your strategy—again, to some extent. This can be nerve-racking for you if you're in a corporate leadership position and used to determining by yourself what your brand's message ought to be. Under the new paradigm, you are essentially making those decisions in collaboration with your audience. This is a pretty big step, but it's an incredibly important one: If you discuss only what you want to and nobody's really listening, you're not only wasting your time, you could also be encouraging your audience to tune out your marketing.

CASE IN POINT: giffgaff's Customers Take the Reins
UK-based giffgaff is a mobile phone service that functions as a mobile virtual network operator. Unlike traditional mobile phone operators, giffgaff allows the service's users to participate in aspects of the company's operations, such as sales, customer service, and marketing. In fact, the company's slogan is "The mobile network run by you." "All we did was take feedback from the customer," says Heather A. Taylor, who served as giffgaff's Social Media and PR manager. "In fact, our whole model was based on that. Products were created with our users in mind and often came from their suggestions." At last count, giffgaff had received 4,800 product suggestions from its customers. On a routine basis, giffgaff will test new product ideas in giffgaff labs and make these features available to all members for a brief period. Some features fail and never make it into the main product, but others that prove popular are often beta-tested, then incorporated into the company's main product.

It's not just product development that giffgaff crowdsources: Its customer service is managed by users, with its top ten users spending over 12 hours per day answering audience questions. To date, 75,000 questions have been asked, and more than 880,000 answers have been provided.

Of course, customers won't literally run your business for you for free, nor should they. In return for participation in giffgaff's business, a customer is paid through a system called Payback. The greater contribution a user makes, the greater the Payback. For instance, when a user recruits a new customer, he or she receives 500 points for each new activation. Users can also earn points by assisting other users in the giffgaff forum.

The result of this innovative approach? giffgaff is growing at an incredible rate, with its community grown roughly 600 percent in 2011. The start-up has also won multiple industry awards, including the Most Innovative Community Award at the Social CRM Customer Excellence Awards and the Forrester Groundswell Award, and it has been rated the number one global online community by Lithium, a leading provider of social community solutions.

going further · · · · · · · · · · · · ·

For bonus materials and updates pertaining to this chapter's topics, please visit: *http://goingsocial.jeremygoldman.com/ch5.*

6

how to avoid pitfalls, deal with crises, and keep your brand's reputation intact

OBVIOUSLY, WHEN going social, your company is going to do whatever it can to avoid missteps. Despite your best intentions, however, there's always the possibility you'll have to deal with a major or minor faux pas or two at some point. Your company has to be able to respond—and respond quickly—if a crisis arises. When something really goes wrong, you need to have a good plan for dealing with it. Is there a good chance you won't have to use it? Absolutely. But if you don't develop a strategy to address crises before they occur, is there a possibility that you'll really, really regret it later? Definitely.

Doing Your Homework Before Engaging

While social channels tend to be filled with over-the-top communications, tread carefully when you're talking about sensitive issues. Kenneth Cole saw an outpouring of negative feedback about the brand's insensitivity in February 2011 when it tweeted, "Millions are in uproar in #Cairo. Rumor is they heard our new spring collection is now available online." Although Kenneth Cole impressions and awareness skyrocketed briefly, the company was forced into crisis management mode, with the designer having to apologize on the brand's Facebook page. Authenticity is great, but coupling it with sensitivity is even better.

Sometimes, a social marketer can say something insensitive completely by accident. One of the costs of engagement in a real-time society is that you must be well informed if you want to engage on current events. When Ashton Kutcher heard that legendary Penn State football coach Joe Paterno was fired, he tweeted the following:

> How do you fire Jo Pa? as a hawkeye fan I find it in poor taste #insult #noclass.[1]

Of course, Kutcher had no idea he was seemingly voicing support of a football program that had allegedly covered up the sexual molestation of young children. Kutcher meant well, but he was behind the news cycle and hadn't Googled to see exactly what Paterno was accused of. If your brand is going to engage in a discussion about current events, stay abreast of the latest developments on the subject.

Dealing with Negative Feedback

If you have a friend who perpetually offers criticism, however constructive, it's not uncommon to get upset and even a little bit defensive—especially if you weren't asking for any feedback in the first place. However, if you see a customer complaining on Twitter about your product or service, you can turn the criticism to your advantage. Think about it: If somebody cares enough about your brand to take the time to comment to the world about an aspect that's unsatisfying, you must use the opportunity to win that person back with amazing customer service. People who complain publicly and are treated well often post a glowing comment afterward.

Through social marketing, you can put a human face on your company. Before the advent of social networks, it was much easier for corporations to remain faceless and thus less responsible—and responsive—to their customers. However, with the rise of social technologies, it's more difficult for a consumer to bear ill will toward a company that makes him or her feel like a real person is there to help solve problems. Putting a caring face in the customer's mind goes a long way. One example of a company that did this to great effect is Comcast, with Frank Eliason managing their @comcastcares Twitter account. Although Frank has since moved on to become Senior Vice President of Social Media at Citi, his experience building @comcastcares is featured in seemingly two out of every three social media books of the last few years. Frank became one of the most recognizable online customer service experts around by improving Comcast's brand and reputation, largely by humanizing the monolithic (and oft berated) cable provider.

It's important that negative feedback be handled diplomatically. Even with the most diligent managing of social networks, it's almost certain that at some point your brand will inadvertently post something that is incorrect. In that event, you can easily post a polite retraction, and customers will forgive you. Likewise, if something untrue is said about your organization and you have developed a strong following, another customer may speak up to defend your reputation. (It's always nice to not have to defend yourself.) If the customer gives you honest constructive criticism regarding some component of your product or service that doesn't work the way it should, acknowledge the feedback, apologize if it's appropriate to do so, and show that you're thankful for the feedback. Customers may be annoyed momentarily when you make a mistake as a brand, but a hasty retraction and some damage control will turn this negative feedback into a positive for your brand.

· · · · · · · **GUEST POST** · · · · · · ·

Abby Lane Whitmer, Director of Ecommerce and Social Media at Ahava North America, on:

The Gap Between Marketing and Customer Service

I'd love to see an online marketing manager who hasn't ever had to deal with an irate customer on social media. I think it's now the first choice of venue for unhappy customers to lash out on because it's easier than a phone call, they usually get a quicker response, and they feel some sense of satisfaction in publicly denouncing a company.

Here's my general response process to irate customers on social media:

1. Notice the angry post and grimace.

2. Send the customer a private message, expressing deep concern for their situation, and direct them to customer service's e-mail address. Now with Facebook's new brand pages, sometimes I will post a public comment asking them to Message the brand.

3. On occasion, I might delete the original post depending on its content. I know this can get some

backlash, but it *is* our brand's Facebook page. We don't have to leave a degrading comment up for all those new potential customers to see, so I delete such comments within minutes (after messaging).

Sending customers to customer service representatives is always my first choice because they have some fantastic leeway as to what they can do to calm an unhappy customer, and it's then out of the public eye. If you have a good customer service team, they should also be simply better at handling people in that capacity. This frees up the social media space to be used for all of the exciting, positive messages and leaves the complaints to the professionals.

Making Things Right

Not admitting an error can cause even more problems down the line. When musician Dave Carroll had his $3,500 guitar broken by United Airlines in 2008, he tried to resolve the situation through traditional customer channels, to no avail. Frustrated, he responded by posting three videos detailing what the airline had done to him. The first of those videos has 12 million views as of this writing. In the five months after the first video was posted, United's stock dropped 10 percent, eroding $180 million of shareholder value. Although it's hard to peg the videos as the sole culprit for the stock drop, the negative publicity associated with the YouTube videos pushed the company in the wrong direction. United Airlines didn't rectify their error, and they paid the consequences.

Many executives, upon encountering service challenges, try to whitewash the problem, demanding that their community managers delete customer problems from their Facebook pages. In the preceding Guest Post, for example, Abby Lane Whitmer argues in favor of deleting a customer complaint from what she considers a marketing channel. I feel you should try to avoid deleting posts outright, if your brand does make a mistake and says something it shouldn't have, because it comes across as heavy-handed. It's certainly a divisive issue, and, although I agree there might occasionally be appropriate times to consider deletion, removing customer concerns can give the impression that you're hiding something. Responding publicly, on the other hand, lets customers know a few things about your brand. For one, you're not hiding anything. Also, you're clearly quick to respond when there is a problem, which instills confidence in prospective customers who may be on the fence about your product.

It's generally better to acknowledge and learn from mistakes you make on your social channels rather than pretend they haven't happened. Naturally, you should try not to make any "unforced errors" on your social channels, but it's inevitable some will occur. When this happens, you need to apologize, explain what went wrong, and move on.

If you screw up, don't feel too bad. There's an upside to being imperfect! If your brand admits a mistake, it will earn social credibility, but that's just the start. If you really want to win over your customers' hearts and minds, further action is needed. For example, suppose your company doesn't do overnight shipping on the weekends, and somebody points out that this isn't mentioned on your website. Don't just acknowledge that feedback; let that customer (as well as all other customers) know when the situation has been resolved. Make superstars out of the people who give your brand constructive criticism. This way, you create major brand advocates who will stay loyal to your company even when future issues arise.

To really transform your business, you should have a strong process for prioritizing and processing customer feedback. Toyota is one company that not only tweeted about their own car's defects but also placed a prominent banner on its Twitter page, letting customers know where to go to find more information about the recall. In response, many customers tweeted that they appreciated the company's transparency.

All in all, it's actually a good thing when customers complain to you! Research suggests that only between 3 and 5 percent of your customers complain when they're experiencing a problem.[2] What this means is that, for every one person who posts a complaint on your Facebook page, there are some 20 to 35 people could also be experiencing the very same issue. Let's imagine what those people are likely to be doing if they're not posting about your product: A few of them might be suffering in silence, but the bulk of these people would quietly give up on your product, putting it in storage. Out of those people, what percentage do you think are ever going to turn into major brand advocates who lead the way to new customer acquisition? Maybe . . . no one? Exactly.

Regardless of your approach, you simply cannot make everybody happy all the time; face the fact that you will have negative customer feedback directed at your brand at some point or another. This is the cost of doing business in a world where social media is becoming ever more prevalent. To deal with negative customer feedback, you need a policy for making people happy when they are unhappy and for moving the conversation to a less public channel. But, you might ask, "Isn't this book about transparency and public engagement?" To a large extent, yes, but the art of going social involves understanding that different types of communication are appropriate for different channels. The same principle applies in your personal life: Would you break up with your boyfriend over the phone? In a text message? A conversation of that significance would be better held in person. Likewise, if a customer requires a lengthy back-and-forth with the brand, it makes sense to settle the issue over the phone, in-person, or via a private message on the customer's social platform of choice.

CASE IN POINT: Digg's Censorship Dilemma

In May 2007 (I know, practically the Stone Age when it comes to social media), social news site Digg received a cease-and-desist letter from the Advanced Access Content System (AACS), a consortium owning rights to an HD DVD encryption key that had been cracked. This cracked key would allow users to essentially break the DRM (digital rights management) restrictions on HD DVD discs, and Digg had news stories on its site about the cracked key. The translation in non-nerd terms: Digg was essentially publishing content informing its audience how to pull content off HD DVD discs.

The team behind Digg doesn't actually publish news. It allows its users to post news, and the community votes on the overall value of individual stories. Stories are placed on the site as determined by the level of importance they've been given through these votes.

The AACS argued that, by allowing stories about the HD DVD crack to remain on the site, Digg was breaking the law. In response, Digg CEO Jay Adelson wrote that the site would be pulling news stories relating to the cracked encryption key. The Digg community members, notoriously opinionated and opposed to any and all forms of censorship, revolted. "The Digg community is one that loves to have their voice heard, and this has been something that struck a chord with them," said Digg founder Kevin Rose. The outpouring was such that all of the top-voted technology stories on Digg pertained to the cracked key and Digg's censorship of the original story. In trying to make the cracked key issue go away, the AACS's letter (and Digg's response) succeeded only in making the story bigger.

Digg's customers were not happy about the company's capitulation to the AACS, and Rose took their opinions to heart. That night, he began a post. "After seeing hundreds of stories and reading thousands of comments, you've made it clear . . . you'd rather see Digg go down fighting than bow down to a bigger company," read Rose's post. "Effective immediately, we won't delete stories or comments containing the code, and will deal with whatever the consequences might be."

Under the old business model, Kevin Rose and Digg could have looked at this direct interaction with their audience as a negative. After all, they were dealing with angry feedback from their readership. However, Rose wisely took a different stance, listening to the audience and responding in a way that let customers know they had been heard. Threats of legal action soon subsided, and Rose has gone on to success as a senior product manager at Google. The way Digg handled its DRM situation is a terrific example of active listening and strategic response to an emerging crisis.

Avoiding Heavy-Handedness

I've seen brands, both fledgling and old-school, determine that the risk of getting negative comments from customers and prospects is so high that they would rather not create a social media presence. Or, if they have a social media presence, they treat it as a broadcast medium rather than as a channel for conversation. The problem with this thinking is that the conversation is occurring online whether you participate or not. If your brand is part of the conversation, you can direct it in a specific direction. If you're not part of the conversation, you maximize the risk that a detrimental discussion about your company or your products will take place—and you don't want that to happen.

In March 2010, Greenpeace activists took action to tell Nestlé, the world's largest food company, to end its sourcing of palm oil from companies that destroy rainforests. The action took place after the debut of a report, "Caught Red Handed: How Nestlé's Use of Palm Oil Is Having a Devastating Impact on Rainforest, the Climate and Orangutans." The report exposed how Nestlé's palm oil usage was directly related to the destruction of the environment in Southeast Asia.

Nestlé, a monolithic company not yet well versed in social marketing tactics, petitioned YouTube to remove Greenpeace UK's new campaign video, "Have a Break?" Nestlé argued that it violated copyright laws. Unfortunately for Nestlé, the legal wrangling backfired. The company's attempts at stifling the conversation actually just amplified the palm oil controversy, with coverage in mainstream media, such as *Forbes*. Although the video in question was deleted from YouTube, Greenpeace simply posted the video on Vimeo, where it has over 530,000 views.

Apologizing When You Screw Up

If you slight a friend in some way, the smartest thing to do is to apologize, right? That's the easiest way to keep a friend. The same principle is at work when it comes to keeping your customers as friends. A beauty brand I'm familiar with posted a touched-up picture of a model using its product. When the picture was posted to Facebook, people noticed the touch-up and began commenting on it almost immediately. It turns out that the pictures were supposed to be used for a press junket, not specifically for social media. Perhaps the creative team didn't think about the customers' ability to deliver snarky comments directly to the brand's Facebook page in real time, but that's exactly what happened. The brand deleted the offensive comments. However, they probably should have addressed the error, commented on the page to show people how to get stellar results using the product, and had an internal discussion about how it's better to display actual product results than faking ones.

If you're an entrepreneur building your brand online, you may possibly find yourself in a social marketing crisis of your own making. That's what happened mid-2011 to Robert Scoble, the noted author and technology evangelist. After a few articles written by him critical of Twitter were published with mistakes, his professional reputation took a hit. Scoble did what few others do: He fully owned up to his mistakes. Posting his phone number publicly on Google+ for all to see, he wrote:

> I'd be happy to sit down with anyone from the company and any investor too to give their side of the story . . . I'm sorry. I should have done fact checking as to the particulars of the story . . . that was lame and poor journalism . . . am I responsible?

Absolutely. My reputation lives and dies on the accuracy of what I write. I was inaccurate today so my reputation has taken a huge hit. I'm sorry that I screwed up so badly.[3]

Scoble's detailed Google+ post led to hundreds of responses. Although not all were positive, the response was overwhelmingly supportive of how Scoble handled the situation. When a brand screws up and takes full ownership of that mistake, the typical response of a customer is to show appreciation for the apology and transparency. If your brand is stuck in a situation like the one Scoble got into, be open with your customers, and own it.

On the Facebook pages I have personally managed, my team and I do not delete posts that contain minor errors. I assume that somebody, somewhere has already seen them; instead, we issue a follow-up correction message. I also double-check my links and content to make sure they are accurate, but mistakes do happen. Undesirable grammatical errors happen when you're trying to do 12 things at once. When it comes to factual inaccuracies, however, take extra special care to get things right the first time!

CASE IN POINT: Bonobos Turns Crisis into Opportunity

Expectations were high when it came to Bonobos, the fast growing men's clothing retailer, on Cyber Monday 2011. The company was expecting a record-breaking sales day, and customers were expecting a major sale. Bonobos geared up to make sure it had the right website infrastructure to support its sales volume that day, but, given the company's rapid growth, it had been hard to figure out exactly how much traffic to expect. As it turns out, the traffic bonobos.com saw was unlike anything it had experienced previously. High demand for the sale, a LivingSocial partnership that drove considerably more volume than expected, and an unexpected piece of PR hitting that morning all added to the chaos. Not much time passed before bonobos.com crashed due to the unexpected volume.

Bonobos had all hands on deck to talk to its audience, keeping everyone in the loop as much as possible. "Even though we knew we were getting dozens and dozens and dozens of people letting us know that we were down, we didn't want to do a blanket response," says John Rote, Senior Director of Operations and Customer Experience at Bonobos. "We didn't want to just put a message out that said 'Hey guys, thanks for letting us know; we know we're down.' We wanted to actually respond to everybody on a case-by-case basis, letting each person know we heard you, we will get back to you, and we will let you know when we are back up—that type of thing." Rather than treating each customer as a statistic and limiting engagement, Bonobos took the Cyber Monday challenge as an opportunity to engage more. Instead of deflecting blame and point out that site crashes have happened to much larger companies like Target and Walmart in the past, Bonobos took responsibility, saying it should have foreseen the issues. Bonobos took the authentic angle of giving an explanation while being crystal clear that it wasn't giving an excuse.

After bonobos.com was back up and operational and taking orders, Bonobos noticed a bug that impacted many of its orders, requiring a manual fix on all affected orders.

The company was concerned orders would take longer to ship. "Frankly, we could have left the site up and taken a lot of orders, but it was creating a high enough number of cases where customers were getting a suboptimal experience," explains John. "We decided it was better to shut down and be very open and ultra communicative about what we were doing and when we would be back up, than it would be to leave up a site that we know is leaky and cause people issues."

Bonobos' leadership team made the usually difficult decision to shut down the site until further notice. That's a hard decision to make on a normal day; on a Cyber Monday it's an even harder conclusion to reach. However, Bonobos is ultimately trying to build a much larger company than its current size, so executives would rather take a short-term hit than risk alienating customers with a bad customer experience. Most companies might not even consider this option, but at customer-centric Bonobos, the decision to shut down was the right call to make.

The company enlisted all departments to team up to address the fallout of the site's temporary close. Bonobos' customer service Ninjas—as the company affectionately calls its service team—and other team members went into overdrive, reorganizing their schedules for the rest of the week to work through all issues as quickly as possible. A cross-departmental team from marketing, merchandising, IT, operations, and service was constantly taking the pulse of customers, analyzing how the site was recovering from its crash, and looking for the right time to remessage its sale. While the site was down, John and his team continued actively engaging with people, being transparent about what had occurred, and letting customers know that Bonobos "had their back" and would extend the sale once the technical issues were worked out.

After a few days, Bonobos relaunched the site. Once it was confident the site could withstand a spike in volume, the company sent its audience an e-mail announcing the return of the sale. To make sure everyone could participate, Bonobos left the sale running longer than its originally planned 24 hours. For any customers who missed the remessaged sale, Bonobos made exceptions to ensure no customer would be left out.

Despite the week's stress, Bonobos found ways to inject its traditional sense of humor into the situation. When customers visited the bonobos.com homepage, they saw a photograph of a man's feet and ankles in Bonobos pants and socks, with his pants dropped. Even in a crisis situation, Bonobos communications were clearly in line with the brand.

As a result, for several days after the Cyber Monday fiasco, Bonobos received tremendous positive word of mouth for their handling of the crash. "There were a lot of people whose very first Bonobos brand experience was actually ending up on our fail page; many of them said it was a deal breaker for them and I totally understand that," says John. "But a lot of new customers seemed to say 'Okay, it's a bummer that the site is down, but this seems like a company I might be interested in doing business with or having a conversation with.'"

: Take a lesson from Bonobos: Use every touch point to
: build a little bit of trust, demonstrate that you're human,
: and make people a little bit more likely to tell other peo-
: ple about you.

going further · · · · · · · · · · · · · · ·

For bonus materials and updates pertaining to this chapter's topics, please visit: *http://goingsocial.jeremygoldman.com/ch6.*

7

how to staff your social team and organize for more effective engagement

IN MOST CASES, engaging in a daily social marketing conversation with your customers should not be the marketing director's job. After all, the director's job hasn't become any less important, so don't take them away from what they're doing currently. Likewise, a PR professional who is experienced in pitching traditional media outlets (and even bloggers) might not be the best brand community manager. For many organizations, this probably should be a brand new hire, not someone already on staff being given added duties. And it definitely should be a full-time position. When you seriously invest in building meaningful relationships directly with your customers, you'll enhance brand equity and likely increase demand for your products and services. This begs the question: Who manages your social media presence every day? Many brands still operate as though updating one's Facebook presence is a job that requires little to no experience, perfect for a recent college grad or an intern. Make no mistake: This is an important job, not an afterthought. Would you let an intern write (and approve) the ad copy for a national magazine campaign? Probably not, if you're looking to stay in business. Yet many brands think that a nonessential team member can be put in charge of outbound communications to their best customers.

Sure, a younger, inexperienced team member may have strong Facebook acumen, but you must have someone capable of developing a sophisticated promotional calendar that will engage your fans. Your social marketing campaign should have the same amount of forethought and planning as your campaign for marketing in traditional channels. Arguably, it has to be even more planned out, given the need to be marketing 24/7 on the social web.

Depending on the size of your organization, you might be looking for a community manager (responsible for day-to-day interactions with your fans and followers), a social media manager/director (responsible for developing the company's content and strategy for social media), or a combination of the two.

The Perfect Community Manager

Finding the perfect community manager isn't easy, but it's important to find someone who is empathic with the audience and especially mindful of building relationships. Ideally, you are looking for someone who has an impeccable memory when it comes to previous interactions. Obviously, friendliness and affability are key to making the right hire. On top of everything, the candidate should be professional but not too "professional" to the point of appearing aloof or stuffy. Good community managers will be enthusiastic and completely immersed in their job. They need to be a part of their community at all times, which can get exhausting. So make sure they have downtime to avoid burnout.

Although they should be enthusiastic about contributing, good community managers do their best to avoid overinvolvement once the community gets going. It's important to allow members to engage and ask questions; to encourage this, the community manager has to try to avoid jumping in and providing immediate answers. Community managers need to let the community build a true sense of unity, communicate among themselves, and help one another. If peer-to-peer engagement is slower than expected, good community managers know how to bring out the best in their members, such as by sending a private message to the more engaged community members asking them if they could respond to online questions or comments from other members.

Garick Chan, who is in charge of community management at Nimble, a social CRM (customer relationship management) company, has studied what works and what doesn't for a community manager role. Based on his experiences, a community manager must be, above all else, a passionate individual dedicated to helping others. Think of the friend who goes above and beyond the call of duty to wow you; that's the kind of person you want as your community manager. At the same time, a good community manager ought to maintain a balance between friendly social engagement and business needs. At the end of the day, sales and profits must remain aligned with business goals. Someone who understands the social aspects of business and creates new business contacts seamlessly is the type of individual who can succeed not just as a community manager, but as a community builder as well. While a community manager must be a strong listener, the word *manager* indicates the ability to lead the audience toward a conversation about the company's product.

When hiring a community manager, Garick feels you ought to avoid somebody with a big ego. There are plenty of self-described social media gurus, which he feels is a ridiculous label given the constant growth and evolution in the social marketing industry.

I asked Caty Kobe, who manages community at Focus, a leading Q&A community focused on making business expertise available to everyone, what makes a strong community manager. She had plenty of suggestions. According to Caty, a strong community manager must have a vibrant personality to handle the marketing, PR, customer service, and sales elements of the role. In addition, the manager has to be comfortable attending industry events and speaking with thought leaders, but humble enough to be able to reply to everyday customer concerns with solid answers and thoughtfulness. Your ideal community manager, according to Caty, must be resourceful, able to work with a variety of personalities, and passionate about the brand. In some ways, Caty argues, your community manager serves as the face of the company and, as such, should be someone you are comfortable having as a key brand representative.

While this may be pretty obvious, I'm going to advise against hiring individuals who are somewhat abrasive or difficult to work with. Have you heard the story of the stellar community manager who was dismissive of her audience? Me neither—because that's an oxymoron. In some jobs you can afford to have a talented employee who's a little grumpy at times, but community manager is not a role where you should take that risk. There's a fine line between being too passionate about the brand and just passionate enough to be able to compromise. The ideal community manager should, of course, be closer to the latter.

When you're hiring someone to be in command of your social media presence, make sure you're looking for the right qualities in candidates. *Passion* is arguably the most important quality to look for in a people-facing role such as customer service or community management. If someone isn't passionate in the role, most people the manager speaks to on behalf of your brand will realize that passion is missing. Moreover, enthusiasm is contagious: If you have passionate, excited people managing your social marketing, that passion will spread to your followers. In turn, they will feel energized by the product and the vision behind it, rather than just feeling that they're being sold to. This passion can extend to your other employees as well, turning them into better brand emissaries.

Passion is also important in a role like this because it leads to *dedication*. For an "always-on" job like community management, where a crisis can occur during off hours and someone might be asked to tweet at 10 p.m. on a moment's notice, dedication is vital. This person has to have a service mindset—enough that they get jazzed to jump in and help out when you're in crisis management mode.

As important as passion can be, credibility is also critical. When I hire community managers and advise others on their hires, I can't overemphasize how crucial it is to get someone who knows the business or industry, or at least has a fair degree of familiarity with it. For the better part of the last decade, I've worked for beauty and lifestyle companies in customer-facing roles. Knowing a significant amount about my company's products and those of our competitors, combined with general industry knowledge, allows me to speak to customers competently and credibly.

If your company wants someone with *credibility*, first look within your industry (as well as at bloggers who cover the industry) for people to interview and for recommendations on whom to contact. Keep in mind that, in an official or unofficial capacity, this person will wind up being a spokesperson for your company; you must be sure it's someone you're proud to say represents you. If your company sells environmentally friendly clothing, it's important to have a community manager who also lives life in an ecofriendly way.

Although you certainly don't want a community manager to be dismissive or to check out, be aware that an overly dedicated community manager can be a liability too. "Most community managers are checking their smartphones from the moment they wake up until the second they go to sleep," shares Heather A. Taylor. "I'm guilty of this, too. Though it's admirable, it's also a surefire route to exhaustion. You need balance and downtime to actually be a better community manager, plus it will give you perspective, which you won't have if you are in the community 24/7." Find a community manager who treats managing their community as a true privilege, yet who also takes the time to recharge, and your brand will have a major advantage when it comes to going social.

. . . . **GUEST POST** . . . .

The Relationship Between Community Management and Customer Service

Kelly Kim is the cofounder of Twylah, a company that helps celebrities and brands create customizable, personalized Twitter landing pages.

Before cofounding Twylah, I was a nonprofit executive for almost 20 years. I worked at large institutions and small agencies alike, but they both held the same values and were similar in many key respects.

Most importantly, in the nonprofit world, we put our constituents first; we "serve" them. Service is deeply embedded in the culture and in the conversation. Indeed, customer service is not a department; it's truly an activity and an attitude.

If anything, this is my approach as a community manager now: a strong focus on customer service. I can't solve all customer service problems, but I can respond to each and every inquiry in a timely manner and with a helpful demeanor. And I can and do respond to each e-mail, each tweet, and each comment on any forum as quickly and as courteously as possible.

What nonprofits understand (and corporations are still learning) is that customer service activities are not primarily about answering customers' concerns; they are mainly a way of establishing significant connections and positive associations between your brand and your constituents. In other words, customer service is about building relationships. The truth is, it is almost synonymous with relationship building depending on the attitude you bring to it.

It's been my experience that a strong focus on customer service is critical for community managers as long as they are using these opportunities to build relationships and not just to answer questions.

Thankfully, the experience I gained and the values I learned in the nonprofit world are still in my heart and in my habits, and they've been an important part of any success I may have had as a community manager.

Engagement Versus Analysis: Two Different Jobs

Depending on your objectives, your social marketing program may be managed by one of many departments: marketing, public relations, customer service, or another department entirely. More likely, the program will be shared by more than one department because social media is a tool for communication in the same way a fax machine is. It would be silly to say that the finance team is the only group in your organization allowed to use the fax machine. Each department within your company has its own objectives and targets, and you can leverage social marketing techniques to help all of them achieve their goals.

It is not necessarily in your best interest to have your day-to-day community manager also focused on KPI (key performance indicator) measurement. Your community manager probably has her hands full continually engaging customers and creating content to support the brand's objectives. Not everybody who's engaging in the social marketing space has a business background and might not have the analytical mindset necessary. Rather than try to turn a creative, socially minded individual into a data analysis person, look within your organization to see who are strong data analysis team members and put them in charge of measurement. (For more on measurement, check out Chapter 12.)

Predictions for the Future

A few years from now, it might be commonplace for all organizations to have a director or vice president of social media engagement (or something along those lines) to lead cross-functional social strategy. That being said, I don't think most organizations will have a position titled Social Media Manager for a number of reasons. First, that title will soon be considered too generic. Second, you can't have just one function focusing on such a high growth area for your company. In fact, there will be a social marketing component to many management positions in PR, communications, marketing, and customer service. There won't really be as many jobs where you can say 0 percent of that job relates to social engagement. Sure, you might have a specialist or two on staff, but, for the most part, social media will be an embedded part of everybody's job at a certain point.

"I don't think a social media manager position is a sustainable position in any organization," agrees Amber Turnau of Whistler Blackcomb. "Eventually, it will be like learning how to type. Forty years ago typing was a special skill that only certain people had and now everybody can type, thanks to computers. In the next couple of years, social media will be something everyone needs to have to be in marketing."

Your Audience Doesn't Turn Off at 5 p.m.

Not long ago, marketers had the pleasure of actually leaving work and "turning off" until the next work day, but this has changed, with many companies giving their staffers smartphones so that they can be reached at all hours. Our customers, too, are online and engaging all the time. If you want credibility as a brand, you have to be ready to respond as soon as humanly possible. Once your business grows to a certain level, it might even make sense to have somebody watching this around the clock. Like most busy social marketing professionals, I don't have 24 hours a day in which to engage in social monitoring, but I do check for any relevant posts about my brand just before I go to sleep and as soon as I wake up to make sure that no new crises have to be managed that instant.

Your organization has to make sure you have the resources to manage a community. If you need more than one person to manage the community, ask yourself whether you have more than one person who can take the reins. When Heather A. Taylor worked for PayPal, three people took shifts managing the @AskPaypal Twitter community, which ensured continuous coverage and dedication.

Another thing that customers expect is ongoing communication. I have seen all too many brands spend hundreds of thousands of dollars on the media by associating with a particular campaign designed to get thousands of fans and followers, only to do nothing to engage that audience after the initial media blitz. If you want ongoing loyalty, you have to engage frequently and with valid messages.

Under the new paradigm, real-time responses are needed. It doesn't matter if most of your online product reviews are great; if the most recent one is poor, that has a better chance of showing up when potential buyers are looking for your product. If you get a scathing review late on a Friday night and you sit on the problem until Monday morning, the bad experience will be communicated to many potential customers without any social output from your brand to ameliorate the situation.

Given the immediacy of this environment, you can't waste time preparing the perfect response for each minicrisis. It's best if your organization develops its own terms of engagement for when something like this happens, so that your community manager knows how best and most immediately to deal with any crisis.

Brandie Feuer, Director of Marketing for Las Vegas's Tropicana Hotel, makes a terrific point: If customers tweet at your brand, they are expecting a response from the moment they send it to you. This is a large contrast to the older paradigm: When customers wrote to your brand via postal mail, they didn't reasonably expect an answer for a few weeks. Customers calling and e-mailing brands still wouldn't expect to have an answer for at least 24 hours. The cycle is speeding up. I just had a bad experience while writing at Starbucks.

A barista had the chutzpah (and inexcusably poor taste) to play Rebecca Black's "Friday" out loud on her iPhone while she was on shift. I tweeted @Starbucks expressing my annoyance and was mildly annoyed that the brand hadn't responded five minutes later. Irrational? Probably. But that's how I felt at the time, and it's increasingly the way your customers will feel when they don't get an immediate response.

If it's really impossible or impractical for your business to be responsive 24/7, consider listing your company's hours of operation prominently on your social presences.

Marketing Automation

Considering the 24/7 nature of social marketing, many companies are finding ways in which automation can help them operate more efficiently. While automation can make a huge contribution to your social marketing, there's good automation and then there's bad automation. Good automation will allow you to spend less time on what amounts to manual labor and frees you up to focus on more value-added work. Bad automation, on the other hand, decreases the odds of social interaction with your fans. It might save you from working, but it's also going to kill your ROI. When Temptu debuted on QVC, we used the tweet scheduling features in CoTweet and HootSuite to schedule reminders to our audience that we would soon be on television for the first time. This wasn't so that we wouldn't have to do any work at the time of the show; it was so that we could focus our energies on watching the broadcast and tweeting in real time with our followers who were also watching our television appearance.

Plenty of tools will simplify or automate posting your long-form (i.e., blog) content to Facebook, Twitter, and other social platforms. One of my favorite tools is called ifttt, which stands for "if {this} then {that}." Ifttt simply lets users stitch together all their digital properties so that *if this* particular event occurs, *then* do *that* (something else) in response. For example, if your brand's Facebook profile picture has changed, then automatically update Twitter with that same profile picture. Or if it's supposed to rain tomorrow, send out a specific tweet with a reminder to your fans to take an umbrella with them in the morning. Best of all, ifttt integrates with over 40 different services, so the number of if {this} then {that} combinations that you can run is pretty close to infinite.

One of the best uses I have found for ifttt is to connect it to Buffer, a tool that lets you optimize all your brand's sharing across its social platforms. Buffer gives you an easy interface to schedule when you'll be sharing the great content that you find on the web, as well as any of your own content that you wish to share. Simply set up a posting schedule in Buffer, then fill up your Buffer queue with engaging content, and the application will "automagically" set up your posts over the course of the day. At present, Buffer works across Twitter, Facebook, and LinkedIn, with the option to add up to six unique social accounts, making it a great tool to help grow your brand presence across a number of platforms.

Buffer and ifttt are such a terrific pairing because you can set up an ifttt task that will watch your company's RSS feeds. If any new updates are published, they get updated to your Buffer. Of course, I'd still recommend going into your Buffer queue and optimizing your copy, especially at the beginning. Either way, ifttt and Buffer can be amazing time-savers and especially useful for marketing automation during off hours. You can use ifttt to watch other RSS feeds, such as Google News, and then Buffer up news, photos, and other content that may be interesting to your audience.

We've all gotten diet advice at one point or another saying that everything is okay in moderation—eggs, meat, deep-fried Twinkies, and so on. (Well, maybe not the Twinkies.) The same principle applies to marketing automation. Tools that let you automate some of your engagement can certainly save you time, but posting a link to a blog post yourself and formulating the ideal lead-in and lead-out copy for the link typically bring your brand more likes, comments, and retweets. There's a trade-off when it comes to marketing automation, which changes considerably from business to business, so I recommend wading into the automation waters before fully diving in. Use automation wisely, and I guarantee you'll want to thank me with a deep-fried Twinkie or two.

Setting a Social Marketing Schedule

If I had to do a shot of tequila every time I heard someone say that social media is free, I'd be comatose. Personally, the statement drives me a bit crazy. People don't factor in the time drain associated with determining what your strategy should be, what types of content your audience is interested in consuming, and everything else that goes into your social marketing plan.

Talking to your audience is time-consuming. The actual day-to-day engagement can take a significant amount of time, but the time you'll have to spend thinking about what to talk about, what topics you will blog on, and what pictures and videos to add to your social presence is often underestimated.

Set aside the time to create a social media schedule. This can be over a weekly conference call, in a biweekly sit-down meeting, or in any format that works for you and your team. The important thing is that you set the schedule and keep to it. Schedule time to brainstorm ideas for new content, determine what content gets posted when, and divvy up responsibilities if you're involving multiple people. This process can be as complex or as simple as it needs to be, depending on your brand needs. If you're engaging with 10,000 fans online, you'll probably want to put more thought into the plan than if your community consists of 14 fans. The important thing is getting organized and knowing what you will be talking about. Having a calendar that jibes with your goals and objectives will help set you up for success.

When it comes to content ideation, it's a good idea to have a good group brainstorming session to determine the types of content. Try to bring a diverse group of people together: Your community manager, head of product development, event coordinator, head of marketing, and PR team are all good people to include. After all, if one of your goals of social marketing was to understand what your customers want from your company, all of these functions would clearly benefit from such information. In addition, try to vary the group of individuals from time to time so you get a diverse set of ideas.

One of the key inputs into how to develop your editorial calendar is your audience: What are they looking for? Knowing the identity of your audience and what they'll be interested in knowing about or discussing is going to make or break your social marketing efforts. At every brand I've managed, one of my most significant time expenditures has been tracking the clickthrough rate (CTR) from social networks to our blog (basically, the percentage of unique visitors that have gone from viewing our social network content to clicking over to our blog content). I have filtered and analyzed the types of topics that are most likely to get clicked on and most likely to be shared; from that, I get a sense of what my audience is interested in and what isn't so important to them.

To help its clients, social media agency Conversify has created a conversation guide. "Typically, an agency asks the client, 'What are the three messages that you want to get out?'" explains Monique Elwell of Conversify. "Our conversation guide is, 'What are the conversations we should be having with our customers?' From that, we create a social media editorial calendar, which is half reactive and half proactive. As a social marketer, about half of what we talk about is reactive—in other words, talking about what the customers want us to talk about, and letting them lead the conversation."

If your community manager works only during regular business hours, it's a good idea to engage and respond to overnight inquiries upon arrival at the office in the morning. Of course, if your company is able to support someone engaging on off hours as needed, that would be ideal.

If you're working on social marketing engagement, like anything else in a workplace, you have to set deadlines for yourself. If you categorize all the blog posts you're generating into Tier A posts (more important) and Tier B (less important) and allow yourself three hours to develop a Tier A post and one hour for a Tier B, then block out time in your Outlook or Google Calendar, and allow yourself three hours for that Tier A so you can move on to that Tier B at the right time. Having a strict schedule within your line of sight will keep you on point.

Optimizing Your Engagement Schedule

After you set aside time to develop your content, you need to decide the best time to publish that content to your audience.

Buddy Media, one of the leading providers of social marketing products, conducted a study of 200 clients' brand pages on Facebook to assess factors impacting engagement. One of the key findings was that the time of a brand's Facebook post is a critical factor in determining the post's success. Office hours are often the *worst* time to blast content. Blasts outside of business hours had 20 percent higher engagement rates.

Generally, Facebook activity peaks at three times: early morning (7 a.m. EST), after work (5 p.m. EST), and late night (11 p.m. EST).[1] Of course, you should take these times as general guidelines rather than rules because you know more about your audience than a generic study does. The timings of your posts ought to be tailored to when people are thinking about your brand. If you run an adult-themed brand, for example, you might consider scheduling engagement for the wee hours of the morning. Use tools such as Crowdbooster or Tweriod to better pinpoint the times your audience is most likely to be paying attention to your content.

When determining a posting schedule, bear in mind that the day of the week matters as well. On average, Thursdays and Fridays have 18 percent more engagement than other days, but each industry is different. For example, engagement with entertainment brands peaks on Fridays, Saturdays, and Sundays; automotive and retail brand engagement rises on Sundays; and travel and hospitality brands do well on Thursdays and Fridays.[2] There's a certain intuition behind when different industries do well: For instance, people tend to be thinking about entertainment plans most often Friday to Sunday, so it makes sense that engagement would be up during that part of the week. Try to think intuitively about when your prospects and customers will be interested in your content.

Twitter's Chief Revenue Officer Adam Bain also recently stated that Twitter users are more engaged with tweets on Fridays. This can be for a number of reasons: One theory is that workers are mentally exhausted from the work week and are more likely to check out going into the weekend. Another reason is that there tend to be fewer brand posts on Fridays, meaning higher overall clickthrough. Most brands don't seem to have realized this phenomenon, however. In addition, most brands don't realize that posts published after work hours are capable of getting significantly more engagement. Mondays tend to be the noisiest time to post.

If you have the budget to spare and want to take your engagement to the next level, you can commission a social analytics firm like PeopleBrowsr to do a specific study of when your audience is looking to engage. For example, one consumer products company asked PeopleBrowsr to investigate the so-called need state of coffee, tobacco, and alcohol users, so that the client could discover the times when its audience would most likely talk about these on social media. Apparently, the need for coffee spiked at 9:00 a.m., alcohol at 5:00 p.m., and cigarettes at 9:00 p.m. The client used this data to optimize its media placement and ensure that its ads were visible at the times when prospects were most likely to be thinking about their vices. Even if your company isn't engaging in paid placements, you can use this type of information to figure out the best time to get your brand's content in front of your audience.

The Importance of Consistent Engagement

If you do a good job with respect to your engagement and content creation, your audience will start to count on you. Do you think it's okay for your social channels to go into hibernation when your community manager goes on her honeymoon? Sorry. Consistency and reliability are important to maintaining your reputation. What if CBS forgets to air *Big Bang Theory* one week? You'd think they don't have their act together. The same can happen to your brand.

John Siuntres of *Word Balloon* realized from his background in radio that continuity was key. "Especially early on, I thought it was really important to be there every week and have a consistent product people could depend on," says John. Rather than just one podcast episode, *Word Balloon* would post multiple podcast episodes at once, so that if its audience members enjoyed the first podcast, they would have something available for immediate consumption afterward. Rather than release one piece of content and then disappear for a few months, *Word Balloon* has a relatively consistent posting schedule, to which John credits its ongoing success. Since his early days, John has also branched out, starting a second podcast series with Art Baltazar and Franco Aureliani, creators of the award-winning *Tiny Titans* comic book series. *Word Balloon*'s consistent approach to content creation and engagement has built the brand's authenticity.

Getting Organized—But Not Too Organized!

Now that I've helped you get organized, I'm going to tell you something that might sound contrary. Although it's important to plan ahead, it's also imperative that you stay flexible and don't overlook real-time opportunities as they pop up. "It's good to have a content calendar, but by definition, the more rigorous the calendar, the less nimble you are as an organization," warns noted social media advisor Jay Baer. Staying nimble is key, especially when you encounter some unexpected good fortune in the form of late-breaking news that you can use to power your social marketing strategy. Whenever possible, you should take advantage of serendipity, particularly when the opportunity is too good to pass up.

If your company makes the jumpsuits Kim Jong-il has worn for nearly three decades and he passes away, feel free to break into your "regularly scheduled programming" to acknowledge his passing. If your creative team has to be involved or if your organization requires multiple approvals, all that could slow down your response time. So consider making your messaging as minimalist as possible. "When you're trying to incorporate serendipitous events into your social marketing plan, the sooner, the better," advises Lara

Eurdolian, founder of social strategy firm Pretty Social NYC. When Lara managed day-to-day social marketing at Kiehl's, a coworker noticed Regis Philbin unexpectedly announcing on LIVE! with Regis & Kelly that he uses Kiehl's Close-Shavers Shaving Formula. Lara worked quickly, putting up this quick Facebook post:

> This just in! This morning on "LIVE! with Regis & Kelly," Regis announced that he uses Kiehl's pre-shave to help him with razor burn! [http://bit.ly/f5D8og]

The status update, with a link to the product mentioned, netted hundreds of clicks the day it was posted. Lara could have waited to post official footage from the episode by having her PR department liaise with the *LIVE! with Regis & Kelly* production team, but the footage could have been two days old by that point.

Brevity is the Soul of Wit

When it comes to the length of posts, it's important to be concise. Reading on a computer screen tires the eyes more, and people read approximately 25 percent slower when they're reading on a computer screen as opposed to paper. So the more concise you are in your posts, the more likely people are to actually read the entire post, as opposed to just scanning it. The aforementioned Buddy Media study found that posts with 80 characters or fewer had 27 percent more engagement than 80-plus character posts. Ironically, only 19 percent of posts in the study were under 80 characters.[3]

Though your posts should be short, it's a good idea when including a link to let customers know where they'll be taken. Posts with a full-length URL had three times as much engagement as posts with URLs shortened by generic URL shorteners such as bit.ly and ow.ly. If your brand is able to invest in a brand-specific

URL shortener, such as bddy.me for Buddy Media or on.mash for Mashable, it's a nice compromise between brevity and letting your audience know where a link will take them.

Knowing How to Ask a Question

It's important to know what you want to ask your audience, but, for optimal engagement, it's crucial to ask a question in the right way. To get a like on a post, just ask in a simple, outright manner, such as "Like us if. . . ." To get comments, ask outright, such as "Care to comment. . . ?" or "Tell us if you. . . ." And so on. To get responses to questions, position *where* or *when* or *would* at the end of the post because that gets you 15 percent more engagement than those same words buried in the middle of the post. Interestingly enough, *why* questions don't work that well; they are perceived as more intrusive and require more effort to answer than *what* questions.[4]

Of course, bear in mind that the data set in this study was limited to large brands. For small businesses, balance this data with known specifics about your own brand. Furthermore, social marketing is always evolving, and these statistics may change. Still, it's nice to have somewhere to start.

Posting Just the Right Amount

Recently, social media agency Ignite analyzed the top 50 Facebook brand pages over a three-month period (May 1–July 31, 2011). The group included 15 fashion apparel retailers, 13 packaged food/drinks companies, 10 tech companies, six brands in entertainment/recreation, and five food establishments/chains.

The study found that the average number of posts was 38 per month, with entertainment brands posting nearly twice as frequently (70 posts a month). What's interesting is how many more impressions the top-posting brands generated: The top five posting pages generate over 32 times more impressions than the bottom five.[5] Although this doesn't mean you should give up on quality, in the social world, quantity is pretty important as well.

There are two ways to increase your brand's overall number of impressions: posting more and generating more fan engagement. To succeed, your brand ought to do both and find a happy medium between quantity and quality.

> ### CASE IN POINT: Whistler Blackcomb Organizes for Success
>
> Whistler Blackcomb is a ski resort 75 miles north of Vancouver in British Columbia, Canada, and is widely considered to be the largest in North America, typically entertaining over 2 million guests a year.
>
> Amber Turnau has been working on the PR team of Whistler Blackcomb since 2007. She was originally hired to work "completely unrelated to social media," as she puts it. Although Whistler has a brand marketing team, interactive team, and PR team, engagement across all channels has always lived in the public relations department. This is different from many companies, which manage engagement from the marketing side or the interactive/e-commerce side of the business (though the structure definitely varies from company to company). Amber's role has evolved over time so that it is now connected to brand and interactive marketing, even though it is still a PR functionality.
>
> Amber is the lead for Whistler Blackcomb's social marketing efforts. She heads a team of people from different areas of marketing and sales. Although the other team

members are not admins or regular contributors to any particular social channel, they assist with respect to specific campaigns and cover for one another as needed. The PR team does more administration on the channels than any other team, but Amber is definitely the point person engaging daily on the social front lines.

Within Whistler's brand team, some individuals specialize in doing marketing for the ski school team, while others help retail outlets. Whistler also has a team managing the food and beverage arm. Amber makes sure that each of those areas is on her cross-functional team responsible for social engagement. In this way, they can learn how to plug social media into the marketing initiatives for all the different ancillary business units. Amber has seen them grow over the last year and a half since she has been working with them. Now they're asking questions like, "How can we use QR codes to help drive people to the showcase snowboard shop Facebook fan page?" They've come around to the understanding that social can be a major boon to the company.

going further · · · · · · · · · · · · · ·

For bonus materials and updates pertaining to this chapter's topics, please visit: *http://goingsocial.jeremygoldman.com/ch7*.

8

tools for producing more relevant, targeted engagement

TARGETING AND subtlety are part of the allure of social marketing. Holly Alexander, founder of social media firm Topspin Communications, puts it this way: "If a traditional advertisement was a blind broadcast to the world about your product, then think of social media as a tap on your customer's shoulder."[1] The sad thing is that, as businesses begin getting approval to spend more and more of their traditional media budget on social marketing, they run the risk of forgetting this truism. Make sure your business doesn't make that mistake! Don't throw away one of the key benefits of marketing on social channels.

Have you ever had a birthday party where people from different parts of your life are present? Some are from high school; some are from college; some are family members; some are neighbors; and some are colleagues from your previous job, as well as from your current company. In a situation like this, your social contexts for knowing all these people are quite different, and you must subtly adjust your conversation to each group. For instance, if you talk about how your last employer was probably the best job you've ever had, you're likely going to have that conversation with people who worked with you at that same employer. There's a good chance you're not going to have a discussion like that in front of the team you're working with currently. Likewise, you might not talk about office politics with friends from high school; with them, you're probably asking them about their wives and kids or about what they've heard about former classmates.

When it comes to connecting with your customers, the same principle applies. The more you understand individual customers, the more you can tailor relevant discussions to each one of them. Targeting and segmenting are incredibly useful tools because they help you ensure you're delivering a relevant message to each and every customer.

A lot of web evangelists talk about targeting as if it didn't exist before the Internet. Of course, it's been here all along. A perfect example is Geico's print advertisements in *Fortune* magazine. In *Fortune* magazine's Fortune 500 issue, where the top 500 U.S. corporations are ranked and analyzed, Geico runs ads tailored to *Fortune*'s more affluent and financially savvy readers, discussing the company's ownership (Berkshire-Hathaway, Warren Buffet's conglomerate). This is the kind of ad that would be particularly powerful to *Fortune*'s readership but would probably be ignored if the same advertisement ran in, say, *Lucky* magazine.

What the Internet has done is democratize targeting, making it relatively simple to target on a small budget. Even a small company such as Temptu has the opportunity to target, using tools like Facebook's advertising platform.

E-mail and CRM, aka Bread and Butter

You're probably aware that there's little correlation between the "hottest" tool in your marketing toolbox and the most useful one. In many cases, flashier and newer tools aren't going to deliver the same tried-and-true value of some battle-tested tools like customer relationship management (CRM) and e-mail marketing.

"Though e-mail isn't the sexiest tool in the digital marketing toolbox, it continues to be an excellent way to target specific messages to specific customers, especially when paired with a strong CRM database," says Tamar Koifman, a digital strategist who has worked on beauty brands such as Kerastase, Chanel, Clinique, and Kiehl's.

E-mail is certainly one of the older tools in the digital marketer's toolbox, yet it can still be quite effective. Some experts, such as Web pioneer and author Aliza Sherman, think that tried-and-true older technologies can pay huge dividends when used properly.

"I think going old-school and using your website and an e-newsletter in smart, fresh ways can get you back to more intimate— and less noisy—ways of reaching your customer," shares Aliza.

If you use social media, you must socialize, but you don't always have to socialize with your customer to make a strong impact. An uncluttered, action-oriented website with an archive of useful resources will never go out of style. Of course, don't forget to prominently let visitors know where they can interact with you in the social mediasphere. And a short, concise e-newsletter chock full of really useful, right-now information can't be beat. Short is the operative word, along with some links to quality information that add value without overloading the reader.

· · · · · · · **GUEST POST** · · · · · · ·

Integrating E-Mail and CRM

Christopher S. Penn is the cofounder of the PodCamp Unconference movement and is cohost of the popular Marketing Over Coffee podcast. Named one of the top 50 most influential people in social media by Forbes, *Christopher currently serves as the Director of Inbound Marketing for enterprise e-mail company WhatCounts.*

Imagine for a moment a field of wheat. Amber waves of grain bowing softly in the wind. This field means life, health, and sustenance for people. Each head of wheat contains the kernels that can be milled and refined to flours for breads, noodles, cakes, and a variety of other foods.

Now imagine that same field of wheat with only the most primitive tools to harvest it. You can definitely cut down enough wheat with a scythe to feed a family. You can take that wheat and pound it on a stone with a crude hammer or a rock, soak it in water, and grind it to a mealy gruel. Nutritious, yes, but not necessarily tasty and certainly not scalable.

This is the state that most marketers find themselves in when it comes to e-mail marketing and a CRM.

Marketers by and large have no trouble acquiring e-mail addresses one way or another, from retail point of sale to mobile to social to plain but effective calls to action on your website. Like the fields of wheat, e-mail addresses are relatively abundant, but their value isn't in the possession of them. Their value must be unlocked and transformed.

Most marketers are like the field owners who are harvesting with a sickle and milling with a crude wheel. You can sustain a small company with primitive e-mail practices, just as you can sustain a small community on a field of wheat and primitive tools, but to scale—to grow—you need much more.

That's where a CRM comes into play. Careful integration of your e-mail marketing with your CRM lets you reap the full potential of your e-mail database, tracking your most valuable prospects and customers, monitoring behavior, and targeting your campaigns to individual segments of your audience. From your CRM, you can microsegment (almost to the point of truly unique personalization) and track behaviors in aggregate and longitudinally over the life cycle of your customers, giving you a very big picture of what works and what doesn't for your most valuable customers.

The integration of the two isn't easy or for the technologically faint of heart, but the value you derive from tight integration will multiply your e-mail marketing ROI by orders of magnitudes.

Improve Targeting with Social Login and Registration

When it comes to social platforms, the sooner you can cut through the clutter and start engaging, the better. This is one reason why social login systems can benefit your brand.

"Registering to JibJab using Facebook involves far less friction than filling out a bunch of web form fields, so we see a much better conversion rate for this approach," says JibJab Media's cofounder and CEO, Gregg Spiridellis.

> More important than the conversion rate is the data that comes from the users who register using their Facebook account. When a user registers with our direct form, we get their email and first name. When a user registers using Facebook, we get access to the profile information they authorize, a list of their friends, and easy access to their photos so we can make it easier to create Starring You® videos. We can build products that create much better user experiences for people who register via Facebook compared to those that register direct.

One of the leaders in achieving what JibJab does is Gigya, a company that offers social media tools to brands that want to integrate their sites with social platforms such as Facebook, Twitter, Google+, LinkedIn, and others. According to the company, Gigya's service now reaches over 1 billion users a month. Moreover, their 500+ clients include more than four out of every ten of the top 100 sites ranked by Comscore. "Our mission is to make every site social," says Ryan Salyer, Gigya's CEO. "We're not going to stop until people think about us with those large social players."[2]

For targeting and segmentation purposes, the heart of Gigya's offering is its Identity Management Platform, which lets brands have permission-based access to their users' data across a number of areas, including social interactions, profile information, and behavioral data. Also, a tool like this makes it possible for your brand to target e-mail campaigns and onsite content better. In fact, it's not that hard to have two completely different campaigns going on at the same time on your website, with one geared toward one set of users and one optimized for another completely different group. For example, you can easily run a campaign on your site geared only toward college graduates who enjoy sports and have an above-average number of social interactions.

Gigya offers a number of different social plug-ins as well, such as allowing users to add comments on a brand website and an activity feed that allows users to see what their Facebook friends are purchasing or interacting with on the website. Gigya also has a gamification suite, which lets your brand add things like leader boards and badges to your site in order to encourage users to interact more with it.

When websites add a social login, they can create more personalized content aimed at specific sets of users. Brands can learn a lot about individual users based on their interests, particularly when using a data-rich platform like Facebook or Google+. This can make your marketing much more customized and targeted, encouraging more engagement.

Targeting Using Facebook

When Temptu was on QVC, testing out its first few shows, it wasn't that difficult for me to place targeted Facebook ads or teach my community manager to do this herself. What's more impressive is that she did this almost absentmindedly while on a conference call that had been going on far too long. It's that easy!

First, I found people on Facebook ages 25–49 who had listed both Beauty and QVC as interests. I then ran a targeted Facebook ad featuring Temptu's upcoming appearance on QVC. The ad was connected to a like button, so Facebook users could easily like the ad and then start receiving Temptu updates in the news feed.

At the same time this ad was running, of course, other Temptu ads were running on Facebook. These ads, however, were focusing on different aspects of the brand; most focused on the company's groundbreaking AIRbrush Makeup System, the first airbrush system made for at-home use. These ads made no mention of QVC because they were not focused on QVC users: They were targeted to people who had indicated they were interested in Beauty and Technology. In this sense, the brand was putting their best—or most appropriate—face forward for their first interaction with any specific fan. The more relevant the message is to any given fan, the more likely you are as a marketer to have that fan begin a conversation with you.

If you want to analyze the sizes of different market segments on Facebook, it's not that difficult to do some testing. You can go to https://www.facebook.com/ads/create/ and fill in the mandatory fields to get past step 1. When you get to step 2, aka targeting, you select criteria that best describe your target audience. As you tweak what you are looking for, Facebook will automatically show you how many of its members fit that profile.

Let's say I'm starting a wedding-planning business based out of New York City. I can target my ad by city, selecting New York City, of course, and adding Jersey City, New Jersey, and Brooklyn, New York, for good measure. A box asks whether I would like to include cities within 50 miles, and I leave that checked. I think my target audience is somewhere between 22 and 35 years old, so I select those as the minimum and maximum ages I'd like to have see my ads. Under advanced demographics, when I get up to relationship status, I select Engaged because I'm pretty much only looking to market to these women. Finally, given that I'm looking for more sophisticated clientele, for education, I indicate that I would like to display only to college grads. My query results in approximately 40,000 people who live within 50 miles of New York, Jersey City, or Brooklyn, between the ages of 22 and 35 inclusive, who are female, who have graduated from college, and who are engaged. Of course, this is not an exact science, but it does give me a sense of how large my market is in relation to other potential business opportunities. Let's say I wanted to start exactly the same business, but aimed at women 36 to 55: My potential Facebook ad target has dropped to about 12,000 people, indicating that the previous opportunity targeted to women 22 to 35 is somewhat larger—at least on Facebook.

On Facebook, brands can engage with their customers using advertisements that are targeted to specific geographic locations, demographics, interests, and more.

Targeting After the Like

The Facebook like isn't the end of targeting and segmenting; it's just the beginning. When companies post links, status updates, and photos, Facebook allows the company to segment, focusing on specific countries, cities, and languages. This allows the company to tailor its message to particular demographics. Kiehl's used this to great effect when Facebook first launched targeting on Fan Pages. Although Kiehl's is a global brand, the vast majority of the brand's fans are in the United States. A significant minority, however, are based in the United Kingdom. When the UK launched its own e-commerce website for the first time in 2009 (I worked on the launch with the local market), it featured a variety of promotions to celebrate the launch. Though we live in a particularly promotional economic environment, especially post-2008, Kiehl's has fought that trend more than many other brands. Thus, it was a relatively big deal that Kiehl's was offering any type of price concession.

A great way to let Facebook fans in the UK know that this promotion was happening would be to simply post a graphic or text message to the global Kiehl's Facebook page to let UK-based customers know that a great deal awaited them. However, that would have significantly irked the rest of the Facebook page's fans, who weren't going to get any promo of that nature.

The solution was relatively simple: Target a message to fans in the UK by posting to the wall and displaying this message only to fans in the United Kingdom. However, they actually could have gotten even more specific because Facebook at that time allowed targeting by city or state/province, not just by country. (As of this writing, you're now limited to targeting only by country and language, but look for more options to be added back over time.) At the time, Kiehl's had just a few stores in the UK, all located in or around London. In that situation, Kiehl's could have gone further by posting two different messages:

1. One ad focused on London and its vicinity, telling patrons of the stores that they now had the option of shopping online when they couldn't get to the store.

2. Another focused on cities and towns farther from London, such as Cardiff and Wolverhampton, telling people who had heard of Kiehl's but who didn't have the opportunity to visit any of its shops directly that they now could shop the skincare brand online without having to make a trip into London.

Minor differences in messaging, such as this example, can lead to a significant change in conversion rates. If you walk into a Starbucks and say, "I'll have a Venti coffee" to no one in particular, there is a good chance you won't get a response. But if you walk up to the counter, look a barista in the eye, notice that his name is Robert, and say, "Hi, Robert, can I get a Venti coffee?" there is a much better chance you'll get an answer—and, if the line isn't too long, a coffee. It's the same thing with messages to your customers: The more customers felt as though someone is specifically talking to them, the more likely they are to respond.

Targeting with Twitter

While Twitter is currently an all-or-nothing communications tool in that you can send a public tweet to everyone simultaneously or a DM to just one person, there are plenty of ways to target specific demographics. Targeted Twitter searches can also help you figure out exactly whom to have a conversation with. Use a site such as Followerwonk.com to search Twitter bios and to find people who work for specific companies you're looking to sell to. Also, if you're a B2B organization focused much more on the quality of followers versus the quantity, perhaps you can set up every member of your business development team with a Twitter account. Then teach them how to use Hootsuite or Tweetdeck to segment their feeds and find the content and users most relevant to their specific functions.

Twitter's Lists feature is a great way to segment your audience. Twitter Lists allow you to sort your most ardent followers, top brands that you want to build a relationship with, people you're following but who aren't following you back, and so on, into different groups. Lists can also be used for competitive analysis: For one, you actually don't have to follow someone to place them on a list, so you can follow the competition without technically following them. On top of that, you can make a list completely private, hidden to everyone but you. These two conditions allow you to create a list, name it, say, "competitors I want to steal market share from," and place all of your competitors' Twitter IDs on that list— all without actually following those accounts, which would give them a heads-up that you're following what they're doing.

Another cost-effective way of segmenting your audience is simply to create multiple social accounts for different facets of your business. On some of Whistler Blackcomb's social platforms, the ski resort maintains multiple accounts, so that its audience receives only the types of messages they're most interested in. Whole Foods does most of its tweeting from @WholeFoods but also has accounts that cater to specific stores, cities, and even foods, including one focused on cheese. I'm not kidding about that last one; Global Cheese Buyer Cathy Strange runs @WFMCheese. As a cheese lover, she finds it a pleasure to be able to tune in and hear about the latest in Gouda and Manchego. However, by sharing these tweets from an account appealing to a niche segment, @WholeFoods doesn't need to turn off its roughly 3 million followers who are less fanatical about cheese.

Targeting Specific Niches

Another good method of targeting is to find outside communities and join a social marketing conversation. A brand doesn't have to start a conversation to wind up becoming part of it. One example is Meetup, the popular platform for helping like-minded individuals meet up in real life. A new feature, Meetup Perks, allows businesses to market offers to members of specific groups. Brands can visit the Meetup Perks page and search groups by topic, location, and more. They can then offer, for $5 per month per group, a deal tailored to that group's specific interests.

> ### CASE IN POINT: JamaicansMusic.com Makes Sweet Music by Focusing on Targeting
>
> After being unable to find a website focused on the reggae and dance hall music he was passionate about, Alex Morrissey founded JamaicansMusic.com while he was still in college. Initially, "the site was for me," Alex admits, but when he noticed how many visitors his site was getting, he started going social and asking them questions about what they wanted on the site. Rather than simply trying to broaden his social audience and expand to focusing on all types of music, however, Alex specifically targeted individuals interested in the same music as he was.
>
> As traffic to JamaicansMusic.com increased, Alex improved the content and began promoting the site heavily through Facebook. Alex attributes the site's momentum largely to the growing Facebook traffic; he used Facebook from early on to grow both its fan base and its revenue. The company's Facebook page now has more than 2 million fans from around the world, having grown from 470,000 fans in September 2011 and with nearly 1,000 joining every day, making it one of the largest Facebook pages in the Caribbean. Alex uses Facebook to engage with existing fans and attract new ones, with the key to his success being his targeted approach in developing targeted content, hosting targeted giveaways, and geographic targeting of promotions.

Alex credits his success in attracting advertisers and sponsors in large part to the page's ability to provide specific demographic data. By using tools such as Facebook Insights and Google Analytics, he is able to view the breakdown of fans by country, gender, and age—information he then shares with potential sponsors and advertisers. "Since we have such a large fan base in each country, we feel we can get a lot more awareness [for sponsors]," Alex says. "It's better than traditional media or even advertising. We can target countries, so advertisers get better results."[3] He has learned, for instance, that JamaicansMusic.com fans come from over 230 different countries, with the greatest number of Facebook fans hailing from Indonesia. By using geospecific targeting, JamaicansMusic.com can be relevant to a specific geographic segment of fans without alienating others: posts and promotions can be directed only to certain segments of the Facebook audience. For instance, when Bob Marley's son Damian released an album last year, JamaicansMusic.com partnered with him and used Facebook geographic targeting to reach fans in South America in particular.

JamaicansMusic.com draws people to the Facebook page with engaging and fresh content. For example, the team posts several new items on the wall each day, usually music videos, which typically generate hundreds of likes and many comments. Beyond the main wall, the site offers engaging content; multiple tabs lead to such features as a top ten chart, new videos, and access to the company's Internet radio station, JADIO. Fans can also play Song Writa, a popular game created by the company, where they can mix their own music. Jamaicans Music.com launched the Song Writa game with an event that took place on its Facebook page. To increase attendance, the company offered BlackBerry Curve smartphones and a $5,000 (Jamaican) credit from mobile phone company Digicel. The launch helped drive Facebook traffic up by 7,000 fans over the course of four weeks, and, at its peak, about 15,000 users were playing the game. All of this content has one thing in common: It is focused on a very specific target Alex is trying to reach.

JamaicansMusic.com is now a multimedia company that hosts live events. A launch party in Indonesia drew 1,000 people when only 200 had been invited and even started its own Internet radio station and magazine. The company has found that a strong Facebook presence and a robust website can go hand in hand; the actual JamaicansMusic.com website now receives 300,000 views per month. As a result of Alex's efforts to reach a specific target rather than trying to be a jack of all trades, JamaicansMusic.com continues to thrive. The business now has five employees and is profitable.

going further · · · · · · · · · · · · · · ·

For bonus materials and updates pertaining to this chapter's topics, please visit: *http://goingsocial.jeremygoldman.com/ch8*.

9

how to identify influencers, work with vips, and grow word of mouth substantially

SOME PEOPLE are more influential than others. There is an unwritten rule when it comes to social marketing: About 1 percent of your fans and followers online will comprise most of the social sharing pertaining to your organization. They're more likely to comment, post on your wall, share statuses, and retweet. When you develop an offer, these are the people most likely to share it. When you post a recap of your brand's participation in NY Fashion Week or a special in-store event, these fans are the ones most likely to comment.

Just as not all customers are created alike, so too not all influencers are created alike. Some of your influencers might be superinfluencers, who can make or break a campaign based on what they think about it. A superinfluencer might manage an influential blog, speak at prominent conferences, and have a substantial professional presence online. Many of your influencers fall under a lesser but still important umbrella, accounting for the majority of social interaction on any of your campaigns.[1] These influencers are still valuable because they are most likely to be active online as sharers of information; however, they are not generally considered to be experts in any one area.

One of the best things about being different and unique is that you have a much better chance of your customers socializing your content for you. This doesn't just apply to brands that live on social media; if you have an offline brand that has unique content, social technologies can allow your content to spread like wildfire. A perfect example: The NBC show *Parks and Recreation* featured an annual tradition called Treat Yo' Self on an October 2011 episode. In early November, a Foursquare user named Alisha M. created a Foursquare list indicating her favorite New York City pampering spots, in line with Aziz Ansari's *Parks and Recreation* character's original concept. The Treat Yo' Self list went viral on sites such as Buzzfeed and Popsugar, among others. "I have no affiliation with the show, it's simply my own homage to the show and of course the city I love," explained Alisha.[2]

From Peas to People: The Pareto Principle

The Pareto Principle was named for Italian economist Vilfredo Pareto, who in 1906 observed that 80 percent of Italy was owned by only 20 percent of its population. On a microeconomic level, he also noticed that 80 percent of the peas in his garden could be found within just 20 percent of the pea pods. This 80/20 rule has since been found to be oddly relevant to most businesses. In the social marketing world, this translates to approximately 80 percent of your brand's online feedback and interaction originating from just 20 percent of your audience.[3]

There are all sorts of 80/20 rules based on the Pareto Principle. One of my favorites asserts that 80 percent of your marketing dollars and efforts go to customer acquisition, with the remaining 20 percent to customer retention. In my personal experience I've found this to be more or less accurate. When you flip the Pareto Principle around, you'll find somewhat of a problem: You're getting most of your revenues (about 80 percent, give or take) from your ongoing customers, the very same ones you're giving only about 20 percent of your attention to. Be careful!

Influencers in your social community can make or break your brand; if you keep them happy, they can continually spread goodwill to potential prospects. Given how likely superinfluencers are to help grow your brand, it makes sense to develop special content and promotions exclusively for them. Identifying these fans is as easy as simply watching the community over time. However, there are also tools out on the marketplace that will help you identify your top fans. Tools such as Booshaka analyze your Facebook page and help you identify your page's top contributors. These fans are then incentivized to participate even more by earning points based on the quality of their participation.

Nearly every user exerts some influence online, but only a handful of them are true influencers, and here we can see a slight variation of the 80/20 rule working in the online world. A study by Josh Bernoff and Augie Ray, authors of *Groundswell*, found that only 6.2 percent of adults using the Internet generated 80 percent of all influence impressions on social networks, with 13.4 percent of adults online generating 80 percent of influence on blogs and forums.

Influencers don't necessarily resemble each other across industries or sectors. Bernoff and Ray's study of mass influencers within the consumer electronics market, for example, found that those influencers are more affluent than the average, more likely to be male, and somewhat geographically concentrated. Understanding what your mass influencers probably look like will help identify the best methods to market to and communicate with them.[4]

Identifying Your Brand Promoters

What we're trying to learn right now is whether the same person who purchases a lot from us is also one of our best influencers, or is there a different path to the influencers. They may not be the best purchasers in terms of quantity or dollars, but they might be influencing 1,000 people in their network who then become the buyers.

—Tracy Benson, Senior Director of Interactive
Marketing & Emerging Media at Best Buy[5]

I'm including Tracy's quote to make you feel better. Identifying the influencers within your audience is hardly a perfect science, even if you're a company with the resources of Best Buy. After all, it can be very difficult to analyze all your customer comments from multiple social media sites on a very large scale. To complicate matters, some comments are video- or image-based, and not even Google has cracked the code on how to best parse that type of messaging. In other words, finding the influencers within your audience and developing deeper relationships with them is far from a perfect science. To that I say, so what? If your brand makes an effort to identify and build strong connections with influencers, you will have a major advantage over brands that don't.

How do you identify your influencers? Now, more than ever, it is relatively easy to compile a list of who has e-mailed you the most, who has purchased the most from your website, and who has retweeted your messages most often. It starts to become difficult when you want to collect information from multiple sources into one cohesive database.

Once you've identified your influencers, it's important that you treat them as though they're really special. Make it about them, not you; your social marketing relationships should be more about your customers' needs than about your own. This holds even truer when it comes to your influencers. If you spend the majority of your time talking about yourself in an overly promotional tone, your customers will tune you out as an old-school marketer, not a social marketer. This is even more critical to remember when it comes to your best customers. Make it about them and their needs because your business needs them to continue its growth.

Find out what your best customers are interested in. In some cases, it's as easy as giving them an exclusive shopping opportunity. Some sites, like Shoebuy.com, offer private sales for their best customers. When customers purchase enough and/or visit the site often enough, they are invited to these private sales; these invitations go to only a small percentage of the entire mailing list. While the perception of exclusivity is exciting, the actual reality of exclusivity makes it clear to customers that they are being rewarded for supporting your business.

You can also communicate your appreciation to influencers by allowing them access to some of your products *before* they've been released to the rest of the world. This type of access makes customers feel special and important to your brand. This is a great example of meeting customer needs in a way that is perfectly aligned with what your organization is trying to accomplish: Identifying how to serve your customers better. By giving customers prerelease access to products, you can solicit feedback from your key customers and then use those findings to better inform your marketing to the rest of your customers.

Augie Ray and Josh Bernoff of Forrester Research recently conducted a study about online peer influence. They found that consumers generated over 500 billion online impressions about products and services. However, over 80 percent of these impressions (both favorable and unfavorable opinions) were generated by only about 16 percent of the U.S. population.[6] (There's that 80/20 rule again.)

Ray and Bernoff identified these people as mass influencers. This subset of the population, about 30 million people in total, will most likely be the source of your success or failure when it comes to social marketing. These are the people you need to keep engaged and happy.

If you're trying to reach the mass influencers on your marketing lists and social networks but have absolutely no idea where to start, you can look at a few traits.

Age, for instance, is an easy one. Mass influencers tend to be between 32 and 38, whereas the average American digital citizen is 44. Finding customers roughly in that 32-to-38 range will let you find people who are young enough to be proficient with digital communication techniques but old enough to have generated meaningful relationships with their peers.

Income is another important factor. Mass influencers tend to have average incomes of $89,000–98,000, a significant step above the U.S. online average of $79,000. If you think about it, it makes sense that you're more likely to trust the opinion of someone who has the disposable income to try multiple products in the same category rather than just settle for one thing that meets their needs.[7]

Another way of identifying influencers within your audience is to look at rating and reviews websites. About 32 percent of influential impressions take place on these sites. Another 29 percent take place on discussion boards and forums. This means that disgruntled customers who might be giving you grief on Yelp shouldn't be viewed as unimportant outliers. They actually matter—big-time!

When you're trying to identify your more influential customers, keep in mind that early adopters of the latest technology tend to be more influential. Approximately 25 percent of the U.S. population visits the Internet from a mobile device; among mass influencers, however, the percentage is almost twice that number.[8] A few years ago, your customers who first purchased smartphones were likely to be influencers. Now, the influencers in your audience are more likely to be the ones using QR codes, purchasing tablet devices, and using augmented reality apps.

If you're in customer acquisition mode, don't just focus on your existing influencers—you can recruit new ones, too. Twitter's API (application programming interface, which is just a nerd term for code that lets software communicate with other software) has allowed developers to create plenty of helpful apps to identify your brand's existing and potential influencers. We Follow, one way to find influential Twitter users, is organized into topics, or interests, that you can delve into to identify the most influential people in each category. You can also add yourself or your brand to the most appropriate lists to expand your odds of being found and recognized as an influencer. Topsy tracks Twitter conversations in real time and identifies the most popular tweets based on how often they've been retweeted. Whatever industry you're in, you can use Topsy to figure out the top conversations going on now and who is leading them. Once you've determined that, you can start a relationship with these influencers.

Don't feel bad about treating certain people differently. When I was single, I had many female friends, and my relationship with each of them was about the same. However, eventually I noticed that one of them, Victoria, had an especially positive effect on my happiness. Once I realized that Victoria was truly special and my future happiness depended on her, I would have been an idiot to treat her exactly like the others. It's the same thing in the digital world; not everyone is created equal. I'm not saying to treat some customers poorly and some well; I'm telling you to treat some customers well and some even better.

Finding, Then Nurturing

Finding influencers is important, but it isn't enough for your brand to grow. Rather, after finding them, you must nurture those relationships and motivate these influencers to share your content and offerings. As your brand grows, one of your marketing goals should be to increase the number of influencers who are engaged with your brand. By engaging directly in conversations with super influencers, you will have a much better idea of what these individuals are looking for. Once you have this knowledge, you can find other people out there who are similar to your super influencers.

Most Valuable Customers (MVCs)

If some customers are of marginal value, the opposite is also true: Some are incredibly valuable. Your MVCs can be important in different ways:

- *Loyalists:* These customers come back time after time, and they probably have a long history with your brand. If your average customer has come into your store three times, loyalists have visited more than 20 times.

- *Heavy Hitters:* These customers may not visit as frequently, but they spend more than the average when they do purchase.

If the average basket on your e-commerce site is $60, the heavy hitter's average is closer to $200.

- *MVCs:* Finally, MVCs are more influencers than they are purchasers; they might spend only $60, but they're enamored enough with the product to get six friends to try your brand for the very first time. If each friend spends $60 with you, and three of the six become repeat customers, imagine how much that initial referral is worth to you.

Deepening Your Relationship with MVCs

If your business is concerned with how to treat these influencers, fearing their potential wrath, you're not alone. Cosmetics company Sephora didn't want to let customers comment on sephora.com, lest bad reviews stop people from buying their makeup and fragrance offerings. That was in 2009. Eventually, the company realized that Facebook and Twitter conversations were leading people to sephora.com to make purchases. Why not take control of that conversation by encouraging it to happen on the company's own website? Sephora turned to Lithium Technologies, a leading provider of social community solutions, to find a way for Sephora's superusers to be able answer other customers' questions.

"We had such a robust natural conversation on Facebook," said Bridget Dolan, Sephora's Vice President of Interactive Media. "We saw that women were asking each other questions—they'd say, 'What's a great waterproof mascara?' And within an hour, they'd have about 17 really well-thought-out answers."[9]

Lithium is at the forefront of Social CRM, a fast growing arena that includes Jive Software and others. According to Gartner, spending on social software that is used to promote sales will top $1 billion in 2012. Lithium alone has more than doubled its revenue from 2009 to 2010. Companies such as Lithium and Jive help clients monitor social media conversations on their Facebook pages. This close monitoring allows companies to address customer issues more expediently, and it also covers other functions that were previously managed by four or five separate agencies. More and more, the one-stop-shop model is gaining in popularity.[10]

Sephora isn't alone in engaging Lithium; other clients include HP and Best Buy, which now receives over 2.5 million visits per year from its online community. Approximately three out of every 10 questions posted by users are answered by 25 superusers.

"Is it material to Best Buy's overall sales volume? No," says Lisa Smith, Vice President of Enterprise Customer Care. "Is it extremely helpful and a loyalty builder? Yes."[11]

Building loyalty in this day and age shouldn't be taken for granted, as customer loyalty just doesn't exist the way it used to. It used to be you had to have a product that was slightly better than somebody else's to get people to start buying from you. Then there was a decent chance that people would continue to buy from you for a long time. Now, however, loyalty has to be earned. Just like your company's sales representatives have to be concerned more with the long view, building a profitable relationship with the customer over time, your community manager has to think the same way. Not every brand can inspire the kind of passion Best Buy does. There are many social-enabled websites without much in the way of actual interaction.

"In terms of building communities on your own website— there's been mixed results," says Gartner analyst Gene Alvarez. "Some organizations have not been able to lure people away from Facebook." Christopher Morace, Jive Software's Senior VP of Products, seconds that notion: "Any company who thinks that 'If you build it, they will come,' is probably wrong."[12] If you think about it, that shouldn't be a surprise. When customers are completely comfortable hanging out on Facebook for a large percentage of their week, they might want to simply stay there rather than visit your meager social presence—unless you can offer something different and worthwhile. Jive built Nike a community hub that lets users schedule meet-ups and track running statistics, which are exactly the kind of things that Nike's social audience will stop by for. "If you can figure out what it is your customers and prospects are really looking for, then they'll absolutely come," Morace said. For Nike, that certainly seems to be the case, with its Jive community now topping 1 million registered users.[13]

Engage with your fans and followers online, and you're more likely to build loyal followers who have your back. At Temptu, we have one particularly active fan, Jess, who engages in our posts about once a week, acting as a great brand ambassador. Let's look at the one-angry-customer example and how she was able to diffuse the situation without corporate intervention.

Social media doesn't keep regular business hours, and one night a frustrated customer publicly complained about her inability to use one of our products. While the Temptu social media team does regularly monitor brand mentions, Jess stepped in before the team had a chance to respond. She offered the unhappy customer some courteous and helpful advice, letting her know what she was doing wrong. As important as it is for the customer to get attention from the brand, it's more effective when that communication comes in the form of peer-to-peer interaction because Jess is not an incentivized brand representative. This is something Clara Shih outlined to great effect in *The Facebook Era*. If I know a woman named Natalie, and Natalie knows Leslie, then I am more likely to have a positive opinion about Leslie when I'm introduced to her for the first time because some of the trust that I have put in Natalie is transferred to Leslie. Therefore, Leslie has an in if she is trying to sell me something; our mutual connection helps her get her foot in the door. Jess's relationship with Temptu gives the brand an in with Jess's connections. Finding an outside brand loyalist willing to fight on your behalf is an invaluable resource, and it is something you won't be able to earn without building strong relationships with your customers via social channels.

> ### CASE IN POINT: popchips' Approach to Finding and Loyalizing MVCs
>
> Snack maker popchips is a brand that clearly goes the extra mile with respect to treating its audience well. popchips' philosophy is "one snacker at a time," meaning that dedication is associated with getting each and every snacker onboard as a customer. To that end, popchips has focused on developing influencers and taste makers in its key markets. Of course, snackers are hardly one easily defined niche audience, so popchips has identified a few subniches of categories they need to market to. These range from nutritionists and fitness trainers to PTA moms, marketing professionals, college ambassadors, and, on occasion, celebrities. popchips' goal is to find everyday snackers, convert them into passionate fans of the brand, and eventually turn them into brand evangelists.
>
> popchips employs a variety of sampling programs to help it build its relationships with influencers. The company will occasionally select fans to host a snack break at their company, turning them into the office snack heroes. Another one of popchips' approaches is to send a personalized care package to a brand evangelist. These packages

come with a handwritten note and even include instructions for how the influencer can "pop it forward" and have the company send samples to three of the influencer's friends. As someone who has been the recipient of one of these boxes, I can say they make a big impression—enough so that many recipients of these boxes tell multiple friends via social channels, as well as offline, about their swag. I purchase from luxury retailers relatively frequently, partly for work and partly due to a shopping addiction that I should probably discuss with my therapist at some point. Quite a few of them don't put as much love into their packaging as this snack company puts into a care package that wasn't even paid for. Don't take my word for it, though. "I sent out a tweet one day about how I was obsessed with popchips' Salt & Pepper chips," shares Shannon Downey of agency Pivotal Chicago. "popchips thanked me on Twitter and then three hours later, there was a knock at my office door; they had delivered a basket full of popchips and a thank-you note! popchips now has a brand advocate for life."

popchips knows that if it can get its product into influencers' hands early to get honest feedback about the product's pros and cons, there are obvious advantages. In fact, another motto at popchips is the proclamation that "if it doesn't taste good, it isn't a snack." With that in mind, getting feedback from its snackers is essential to popchips' product development. To ensure that the brand is getting candid feedback, popchips has created a tasting panel among its evangelists that gives the brand the kind of candid feedback it needs to succeed. Rather than shying away from constructive feedback, the brand deliberately goes out of its way to find fans who are committed to letting popchips know how it's doing. Once a product is finalized, popchips will send samples out to its evangelists and other influencers to help generate buzz and excitement, as well as retailer interest.

The combination of a compelling product, personal outreach by the brand's employees, and smart use of marketing tools has helped turn popchips' fans into passionate ambassadors and evangelists for the brand. Says Brian Pope, popchips' Vice President of Marketing: "No ad is more powerful than an excited fan sharing a new passion."

Klout and Other Influence Analysis Platforms

Can you imagine someday in the near future when you might be graded or treated differently based on your influence level? For better or for worse, we're already at that point in time. Services such as Klout, Peerindex, and Kred are algorithmically ranking individuals (and brands) based on their influence levels. They accomplish this by analyzing users' influence across a number of social channels, including Facebook, Twitter, Google+, and more. These services are creating millions of social scores based on users' aggregate influence levels. To a lot of people, this is a good thing: No longer do you have to be a movie star, television pundit, or another media celebrity to be defined as truly influential. At the same time, services like Klout do have some detractors, who claim that their algorithm is imperfect. The company receives e-mails and messages constantly debating one person's influence over another, asserting that the algorithms are not correct. My take? Platforms like Klout and Kred are trying to do something incredibly difficult, and even if they're not perfect, you should not discount the value they can add when you're going social.

Whether you like it or not, social media participants are assigned a number in a public manner that correlates to their overall influence, accessible to people whom you might work with, be friends with, and so on. Klout's argument for measuring people based on their influence levels is that traditional broadcast media such as television and radio are measured, and due to sites such as Facebook, Twitter, and YouTube, we have all become broadcasters. Therefore, all those broadcasters should be measured.

While knowing your customers' scores can help you understand their importance to your business, it can be a double-edged sword. Klout can empower your business in some ways, but it can empower your customers as well. A high Klout score quantifiably lets your customers know that they have a voice. As a result, it becomes even more important to keep your customers happy—regardless of their scores.

What's great about companies such as Klout and Peerindex—for marketers, at least—is that they are incentivized to do a great job at finding out who is and who isn't influential. This means that they go beyond the numbers of fans and followers to determine who truly creates engagement and motivates followers to take action. Klout has created upward of 100 million scores to date and is integrated into a number of social apps, such as Hootsuite, making it the dominant player in this space. So, for the most part we'll be focusing on Klout.

Influence scores on Klout range from 1 to 100, with most users falling in the high teens. To give you an example of some real-life Klout scores: Justin Bieber has a 100. Ashton Kutcher is an 82. Me? As of this writing, I'm a 59. I used to be in the 70s, but Klout recently updated their algorithm, knocking me down a few pegs. Boo.

Today, over 3,500 companies are using Klout's data to reward users with better customer service, recruit new customers, and for other purposes.[14] Of course, Klout has been working hard to monetize itself by officially partnering with some of these companies. Klout launched its Perks program in early 2010, geared toward putting sponsored products into the hands of influencers. Perks have been launched across a number of different categories, such as technology, entertainment, and consumer packaged goods. To date, hundreds of such deals have been made, with the frequency of deals gaining in velocity in recent months. According to CEO Joe Fernandez, four out of every five companies who have done a Klout Perk reengage with Klout to create a new Perk.[15]

In June 2011, carmaker Audi began to offer promotions to Facebook users based on their Klout scores; Klout partnered with Facebook fan page provider Involver to allow brands to offer customers personalized experiences based on their Klout scores. In Audi's case, influencers with high enough scores were invited to test-drive the new 2011 A8 in San Francisco. Audi isn't the only company jumping on this trend. Some airlines, such as Virgin America, have used Klout scores to offer free round-trip flights to highly rated influencers; in Las Vegas, shows have offered tickets to highly rated guests.

If you're a brand looking to work with the Perks program, Klout is getting pretty good at allowing you to reach out to exactly the customers you want, based on their influence, geography, and demographics. So, if you're looking to find women in the Midwest who are influential in technology and cooking, Klout can help you reach out to this segment.

There's a bit of a legal gray area when it comes to Klout Perks: Brands might be breaching FTC guidelines if influencers don't disclose that they've received a freebie.[16] Klout includes a card with all Perks letting influencers know that they should disclose that they've received a free item, should they wish to write about the item. In theory, this puts the onus on the influencer. So, when I was one of 500 chosen to receive a Klout Perk of a Windows Phone running the new Mango software update in November 2011, I was responsible for disclosing that I received a freebie should I ever write about it—which, now that I think about it, is what I'm doing right now.

If you're a brand, chances are you'll want to know how to improve your Klout score. To maximize your own Klout ranking, it's important to focus on a few specific areas of interest when it comes to your social content. This way, you can develop an area of expertise rather than being a generalist. In other words, it's better to be a knowledgeable, trustworthy specialist in a specific area than a jack-of-all-trades and a master of none.

Right now, these services obviously are not perfect; in fact, they are far from it. Influence in the physical world, for one, has not factored into these counts whatsoever.

A number of custom Facebook brand page providers can integrate with services like Klout. One such provider, Involver, has an app that can be used to integrate with Klout so that brands can reward their high influencers with extra perks.

CASE IN POINT: Secret Leverages Klout to Identify Word-of-Mouth Influencers

Procter & Gamble, the multibillion-dollar consumer products company, is always testing out new platforms by way of its Futureworks division, which is charged with driving new, breakthrough innovations. Futureworks' Associate Marketing Director, Sonny Jandial, wanted to test-drive Klout for a social influence campaign and identified Secret as the perfect P&G brand to test it with. The deodorant brand was looking to launch its Clinical Strength Waterproof deodorant with strong word of mouth—something Klout could potentially help them with.

Secret wanted to find key influencers with preidentified interest areas and utilize those influencers to amplify the message that the new product offers waterproof wetness protection and delivers through heat, humidity, and water. As part of the campaign, Secret supported 61-year-old distance swimmer Diana Nyad in her attempt to swim 103 miles from Cuba to Florida—without a shark cage. Diana was the perfect influencer to reinforce Secret's message: a product promising waterproof protection geared toward self-confident, fearless women. "The general consumer isn't going to talk about a new ingredient in deodorant," Sonny reasons, "but they will talk about what Diana is doing, how it is cool, how she is being fearless." Generating this type of conversation is especially fruitful when it ties back to the product.

Although the concept for the campaign was developed completely by the brand, Secret used Klout to identify women who possessed the qualities it sought to embody: confidence, entrepreneurship, and an active interest in fitness. The 2,500 selected influencers received a year's supply of deodorant and were told about the story behind the new product and the Diana Nyad sponsorship.

To gauge the success of the promotion, Secret looked at the number of impressions generated, the impression quality, the number of tweets from the 2,500 influencers, and the number of retweets of those influencers' messages. With Klout's help, Secret was able to quantify the messages that went out: 6,000 tweets from 2,500 different influencers, resulting in 15–16 million impressions. The results of the campaign were also quantifiable: During this time, Clinical Strength Waterproof deodorant was number one in sales in its category. In addition, a consumer survey revealed that over 75 percent of users said they would recommend the new product to a friend. With results like this after only an initial foray, it's evident why influencer outreach programs like Secret's are on the rise.

Treating the Treatworthy

Treating your MVCs better than the rest of your customers isn't a new idea, and it's certainly not confined to the online world. If you're a frequent flier, for instance, you're going to accumulate more miles than your great aunt who hasn't flown since Uncle Milton left her for that no-good hussy. It's the same concept with your local coffee shop's loyalty card that rewards you with a free coffee for every nine purchased. Social media takes it one step further: Those who fly most often and drink your coffee most frequently now have a voice, and they demand to be heard, both by you and by their fellow customers.

Many smaller organizations might get uncomfortable with the idea of adding more to their workload. If you already have a full-time community manager fostering relationships on social media, you might not want to pile even more work on his or her plate. However, it's crucial to create special promotions, content, and so on. It's not like influencers are waiting around to be thanked; it's up to you to be proactive and tell them how much you appreciate their service as brand ambassadors.

When it is time to reward your customers, pay close attention to the perceived value of what you are going to offer them. Perceptions are incredibly important. If people perceive something is scarce, it tends to get them more excited when they receive it. A perfect example is the launch of a new product. There might be 100,000 units waiting in the warehouse somewhere, but if you're giving five away to lucky customers before the product is released, the fact that no one can buy it anywhere spikes its perceived value significantly.

Don't assume that all your users want discounts in exchange for their loyalty. Wealthy social media users aren't following brands to get discounts and coupons. A recent survey from The Affluence Collaborative found those who pull in serious salaries follow a brand on social media because they like it.[17] According to *eMarketer*, the survey results showed that those earning $200,000-plus a year are more likely to follow a brand on social media out of sheer loyalty. Only 29 percent of respondents making $500,000 or more a year followed a brand for discounts and special offers; instead, the majority (52 percent) cited "I love the brand and want to follow it" as their primary motivator. While many making $200,000 or more a year follow for deals and discounts (39 percent), that figure is lower than the general population of 44 percent.

Developing influencer-only content is a great reward. Beauty brands such as MAC Cosmetics and Bumble and Bumble create newsletters for their professional users, sharing tips of the trade with them, loyalizing these influencers and increasing the odds that they'll recommend the brand's products to end consumers. Exclu - sive offers, such as private sales, are also good ways to let influencers know that they're special, but there's a caveat. While the "private" sale has been a nice promotional lever to pull and can definitely promote engagement, it has become relatively commonplace in a short period of time. As a result, audiences have figured out that private sales aren't all that private and thus don't make influencers feel as special. "We see this offline too with the proliferation of 'Friends and Family' sales that no longer have anything to do with being a friend or family member," explains Tamar Koifman, a digital strategist who's worked with beauty brands Kerastase, Chanel, Clinique, and Kiehl's. Tamar's right: Your audience is smart and going a step past the expected will be more likely to get your influencers excited. If you develop a campaign catering to influencers unlike anything you've seen in your market before, you're on the right path toward strong word of mouth.

If your business sells a physical product, make sure you have that product in inventory a few months before it goes on sale so that you can get it into your influencers' hands prior to launch. If you do this, you'll be in a great win-win situation: you'll be able to show your influencers how much you appreciate them by giving something that they have empirical proof isn't available anywhere else in the marketplace. Moreover, you'll be able to get early, honest feedback about the product's pros and cons, so you can mitigate any negatives and develop marketing campaigns around what your influencers consider to be the key selling points. There's a good chance these points will differ somewhat from what your marketing team was going to launch with.

When you're trying to identify your influencers, keep in mind they're not always going to be obvious just by looking at your Facebook and Twitter fans and followers. It's not uncommon to find that one of your Twitter followers who has only 1,000 followers is actually a major contributor to a prominent blog with 90,000 unique visits per month. It could just be that they've built their social audience independent of Twitter. Likewise, even those who have middling Klout scores can be incredibly influential offline.

Influence scoring platform Kred saw this as a possible differentiator from Klout, creating an Offline Kred feature that integrates offline achievements with a user's online identity to create a more representative picture of that user's influence.

You can reward the influencers in your audience in many ways. Giving them individual attention is a good idea. If it's their birthday or if there's something interesting going on in their life, why not put a Facebook gift on their wall if you have a personal connection with them or send them a targeted message?

The Old Spice deodorant company signed up former NFL wide receiver Isaiah Mustafa to make a series of hilarious television commercials revolving around the core message that if men would wear Old Spice, they could be as manly as he is. If you watch television even infrequently, chances are you've seen the campaign. However, the campaign reached new heights when Mustafa began responding to bloggers and Internet celebrities with personalized video messages on YouTube. What made these videos so successful is how targeted they were, laser-focused on responding to very specific niche groups and individuals.

> **CASE IN POINT: Tripping Trains an Advisory Board to Be Its Best Advocates**
>
> Tripping International is a San Francisco–based Internet start-up that caters to world travelers by connecting them with local hosts to offer sightseeing tips, conversation, and free places to stay. When 200 people applied for an internship, the cofounders were surprised by the number of young people who wanted to work with the company. They decided to establish a ten-person social media board consisting of 20-somethings to advise on marketing strategies and encourage the best internship applicants to

apply for a spot on this board. A novel idea, sure, but the rationale for the decision was strong. For one, Tripping's primary users were college students, so marketing techniques had to be tailored accordingly. Furthermore, college students and 20-somethings grew up with technology and more experienced/older candidates did not.

To establish the board, Tripping's cofounders challenged the top 40 candidates to vie for spots on the advisory committee. Each candidate had three weeks to generate as much online buzz as possible around Tripping and its services. The goal was to determine which candidates had the most creativity, enthusiasm, and ability to spread the word about Tripping.

As part of the competition, participants pushed the limits of creativity, including streaming online video of people lined up at a popular college doughnut shop hangout at 1 a.m., contacting popular travel bloggers and raving about the site, and posting information on Twitter regarding Tripping's service.

Once Tripping's leadership selected ten board members, the board began helping the company almost immediately. One of the improvements the board initiated was a Video validation feature, in which Tripping remotely interviews potential hosts via Skype and retains passports and proof of address as an extra layer of verification/safety for young travelers. The board also helped Tripping understand its audience better, which helped the start-up select more relevant marketing activities. For example, the Board helped Tripping nix the idea of hosting evening events on Barcelona college campuses because young Europeans are "relaxing at wine bars and local cafes" at night, not hanging out on campus. Board members also helped Tripping sign up six new promotional partners, including AmeriCorps, the student volunteer organization with 600,000-plus alumni.

Although board members don't have daily responsibilities, they act as brand ambassadors and offer opinions, advice, and ideas. Although these positions are unpaid, the full-time Tripping team makes sure board members benefit from the relationship. As such, board members received training on how to program and create Facebook ads, assistance with their postcollege job hunts, introductions to other entrepreneurs in Silicon Valley, and exposure to the process of developing promotional partnerships.

The potential value, perspective, and insight added by college students or 20-somethings—who may have little in the way of formal work experience—can be quite helpful in the realm of social media marketing.

The creation of the advisory board helped Tripping engage with its social audience. Perceiving that social media engagement was key to the company's success, Tripping looked to the board to give feedback about how to increase Tripping's engagement rates. Given that Tripping actively recruited board members within its own target demographic and pool of active travelers, they had a number of great ideas on how to encourage activity among fans, followers, and members. Because the majority of Tripping's board members came of age after Facebook's launch, they possessed a natural aptitude for social media. In addition to supporting Tripping's current efforts, they contribute ideas and create content for Tripping's upcoming blog and social channels. For instance, Tripping recently ran a photo contest largely designed and promoted by the board across Facebook, Twitter, and other social channels. As a result of this groundswell, Tripping received hundreds of submissions and grew its following across all social channels by over 10 percent in just one campaign.

In addition to the expected benefits, the creation of the board had a few unintended positive consequences. CEO Jen O'Neal and her team were aware that board members were interested in marketing and social media, but they were not expecting them to be equally excited by other areas of the business. For example, one of the company's first board members, Katy Birnbaum, expressed an interest in technology right away. The Tripping team invited Katy to work directly with Tripping's CTO, and Katy quickly proved herself to be a fast learner and talented developer. This led to Katy becoming a full-time engineer at Tripping and a well-respected member of the team. Other exceptional board members were presented with opportunities for full-time employment: To date, four board members have been hired as full-time Tripping employees.

going further · · · · · · · · · · · · ·

For bonus materials and updates pertaining to this chapter's topics, please visit: *http://goingsocial.jeremygoldman.com/ch9.*

how to build strong relationships with bloggers and work with online personalities

IN THE PAST few years, the media industry has changed drastically. Although plenty of "old media" magazines and newspapers are still around, and many traditional-style journalists make a living exclusively off digital content, the rise of bloggers has been a major sea change. When I'm talking about bloggers, I'm not referring to everyone who has a blog. I blog on and off at jeremygoldman.com, but I wouldn't call myself a blogger. In fact, the term *blogger* doesn't really do justice to most of the highly trusted experts who have risen over the past few years as online royalty. Today many individuals, who might have previously built their personal brand while working at a magazine or on a brand, have been creating their own personal brands. Even better, they can make a living from it!

Let's face it: Brands are often used to putting up advertisements as opposed to having authentic conversations with their customers. One way for brands to market in a more conversational manner to potential customers is to develop relationships with influential bloggers. Brands that are building strong relationships with bloggers have a good understanding of the value of the word-of-mouth buzz bloggers can generate. Unlike old media journalists, bloggers generally let their guard down and allow their audiences to peer into their world. Blog readers—and viewers, since many are becoming video based—get to see details of a blogger's everyday life.

"If you're a brand that builds a marketing partnership with a blogger, or any other noncelebrity endorser, you can win points for authenticity," says Gabrielle Archambault, a social media manager who specializes in blogger relations and buzz-building campaigns. "You're working with someone that your customers look up to and relate to. Your customers feel like they have a personal connection to the bloggers that they follow. If you build a strong relationship with a blogger, that gives your customers more of a personal connection to your brand." Because they ring of authenticity and accessibility, bloggers can help brands they work with reap the benefits of targeted customer acquisition, as well as loyalizing their existing customers.

Brands such as MAC Cosmetics, Gap, and Coach are increasingly collaborating with bloggers to develop new social marketing campaigns. For instance, a brand might invite a blogger to serve as a guest blogger or post a video of the blogger talking about the brand or using one of its products. These sponsored campaigns can stretch over weeks or months. One of the more popular ways for brands to collaborate with bloggers has been to create limited-edition products.

MAC, for example, has worked with beauty bloggers such as Christine Mielke of Temptalia and Patrice Grell Yursik of Afrobella to custom-create their own makeup collections to be made exclusively online. Often, bloggers are compensated in free merchandise, but that's quickly changing; some top bloggers can command thousands of dollars for large sponsorships.

Although these collaborations are popular, their rise has been met with a bit of controversy. After all, these campaigns often blur the line between what's editorial content and what would typically be considered advertising. Generally, publications such as *Better Homes and Gardens* and *Sports Illustrated* are careful to delineate between editorial and advertising. Some bloggers, who didn't work in old media or journalistic backgrounds, tend to observe that divide less strictly. That being said, the controversy about brands going social with bloggers is likely to die down over time. The FTC recently added to their guidelines the requirement that bloggers disclose when they receive free products or are being monetarily compensated by a brand. Increasingly, customers are used to seeing brand–blogger collaborations. If there's an advertising relationship between a blogger and a brand, provided the nature of the relationship is disclosed, blog audiences don't generally have a problem with it.

Given the rising importance of bloggers, your relationships with them should not be treated as a tacked-on part of your PR strategy to get some last-second buzz in case all your national print pitches fall through: They should be a meaningful part of your strategy. After all, your social marketing channels provide a great opportunity to further engage with and promote members of the press.

Just as I've been trying not to generalize what's in a marketer's head over the course of this book, so too I try to stay away from generalizations about bloggers. Instead, I've spoken to my colleagues in the blogging world to get their thoughts, and then asked my blogger friends to reach out to their own circles of bloggers, and subsequently to their circles' circles, to get a more diverse set of opinions.

Strategically Selecting Your Key Blogger Relationships

With a finite number of hours in the day and with the average worker stretched thin, there's obviously a limit to the number of influencer relationships you can manage. Given that limit, you must choose whom to work with carefully. There are literally thousands of new blogs launched every day by thousands of diverse authors, not to mention all the traditionally accredited publications out in the world. Engaging them all is impossible, so why try?

It's best to identify key influencers that fit your brand and create lists so that you can better manage those relationships. Talk to everyone you can, especially if they are reaching out to you; however, make sure it's a good investment of your time, and make the decisions in advance on how you'd like to engage your community. Suppose you have the opportunity to engage with three different bloggers: The first has 7,000 followers but a website full of typos and banners and questionable content. The second has 214 followers and a well-designed site with content that would resonate with your demographic. The third has 10,000 followers, a great site, and perfect alignment with your brand's demographics. Which should you choose to engage with? Possibly all three, although on different levels. You may want to host a giveaway with the first blogger. The second blogger may be suited for an offline relationship; add it to your media list to send out company updates in hopes they'll post about you. With regard to the third blogger, you might want to engage with them on all levels and develop a strong relationship to gain their support. If you're a small brand and have limited resources, you may want to go after only the Blogger 3's of this world—and that would be a logical decision.

In a perfect world, all three would love the opportunity to work with you, right? After all, you're offering them products, giveaways, content for their websites, exclusive events, and promoting them through your social marketing channels. However, you may find they are not that responsive or that they are taking up a lot of your time for little reward: you've sent several products and have no posts to show for it. Why is this happening? Sometimes when you're pitching a blogger hard, so is every other brand in your field. If you're pitching bloggers who work in organizations of one to three individuals and hundreds of PR professionals are trying to get in with them, there's clearly a bandwidth issue. So for you to be chosen, first and foremost, be sure that you have your act together from a social marketing channel standpoint, urges Yvonne Kai of HeyDOYou. "A vacant Facebook page or abandoned Twitter account never sends the right message," says Yvonne.

Also, be careful not to be too self-absorbed, warns Simon Mainwaring at Fast Company. "When a brand continues to talk about itself using traditional media, or makes the fatal mistake of using social media to talk about itself rather than listen to its customer community, then I'm no longer interested in that brand and would not promote it to somebody else."

It is also extremely important to be creative and know the individuals you're dealing with. What's their background? Are they industry professionals, or are they teenage bloggers with too much time on their hands? What type of content do they write about? Show them you know who they are and that you read their blog. If they write about luxury goods and are being offered Prada bags as freebies, but you're developing a new line for Walmart, don't be surprised if you don't get a response. On the flip side, if the blogger is responding to you and is enthusiastic about working with you, encourage that relationship.

Think of it as an experimental game of talking to different sources and figuring out the strategy best suited to you. Depending on your product and resources, it may be more worthwhile to talk to a few highly influential blogger/members of the press. Or you could reach out to twice as many medium-sized bloggers who could offer you a higher return or response.

Successfully Pitching to Bloggers

Traditional media pitches can be very formal; social media communications often lean toward the more casual side. To professionals used to communicating under the old paradigm, this new approach can take some getting used to.

Many bloggers feel that an informal tweet can be the start of a relationship, one that will later develop via another communications channel such as e-mail or phone. To many bloggers, the source of the pitch doesn't matter nearly as much as the respect that the brand conveys in that pitch. Bloggers are often pitched on Facebook, Twitter, LinkedIn, and blog comments, but most seem to appreciate e-mail pitches, citing that they often feel more personal and professional.

Striking the right tone in your pitch is important. Keep in mind that while bloggers want to be treated with a modicum of respect, pitching them too formally can be a faux pas. "I prefer to be treated as a 'close friend' as opposed to very formal and too 'business,'" says Koren Zander of beauty site Enkore Makeup.

Casual and personal do not, however, mean sloppy; although many bloggers don't consistently use proper grammar and might be prone to typos, your pitch needs to be beyond reproach. Just because you're writing to somebody from a smartphone doesn't make it okay to butcher the English language.

Let me say something here that should be obvious but isn't always: Sometimes the best way to pitch is to not really pitch at all. Often, the best way to develop a positive relationship with online personalities is simply to treat them as if they were any other customer being given terrific customer service. "I love when I make a comment or talk about a brand experience I have had and the brand responds unprompted," says Shannon Downey, a blogger at digital production agency Pivotal Chicago. She shares: "I complained in my blog about an experience I had at Bank of America. They then asked if they could call me to discuss, and they promptly did. The brands that go far above and beyond the bare minimum are the most memorable and powerful."

If you send an untargeted pitch to bloggers without an understanding of what they do and what they cover, that's a good way to show that you're not really interested in working with them. Not doing research before reaching out can backfire. Says Elessa Jade of *Pursebuzz*, the popular beauty reviews site: "There have been times where I get an email about a household cleaning product, telling me how I'd be very interested in the product, when I clearly talk about beauty products." When pitching, make sure not to force-feed stories that don't apply to a blogger's subject of expertise and interest. "Being treated like a number" was voiced as a major grievance by a number of bloggers. Showing that you've taken the time to read and understand their voice and content will help you build authentic relationships.

Many bloggers prefer the efficiency of online communications, and express annoyance at receiving cold calls. "Don't call me to pitch to me. I don't have the time," says Shannon Downey.

"I do not like the word 'blogger,' so emails that start out that way are a turn-off," says Alison Blackman, a relationship expert and cocreator of the Advice Sisters blog. "Try to use my name. If you don't know my name, I know that by starting an email with 'Hi,' or 'Friends,' you are mass mailing something. That's usually a turn-off." Glen Hellman agrees: "I hate the Dear Blogger thing. Call me Glen or just start off with your pitch."

Indeed, when communicating with online influencers, be aware that they are likely to be more technically savvy than you. If you do something clever like try to pass off a mass mailing as a targeted e-mail, there is a good chance they will see through it.

Personal subject lines are a good idea, and send a message right off the bat that the blogger is getting a pitch that is truly meant for them, not a mass mailing. "If [the brand] can reference anything that shows that I was worth taking a moment to learn some simple fact about me, or my work, or acquaintances," says Downey, "I will open that email."

"I don't mind being mass emailed, as long as the email is not cheesy and off topic," voices Elessa Jade of *Pursebuzz*. "I do not like emails when they try to tie in current events and it has nothing to do with their product. And while I don't mind being addressed as 'blogger,' I have never considered myself as a blogger." Some bloggers definitely require a bit more of a personal touch. "Always address pitches to my name," says Koren Zander. "If not—I consider it a chain mail. I'm sure they would love the same courtesy. I mean, wouldn't it be odd if I emailed them and addressed them 'Dear Brand Person'?"

There is no one magic way to guarantee a response from a blogger, just as there is no guaranteed way to start up a friendship. That being said, being courteous and engaging will help point you in the right direction. If you are human and relatable when approaching a blogger for the first time, you have a much better chance of striking up a positive relationship. "With any pitch, I think the most critical determinant is the humanity that a brand builds into their marketing message or sales proposition," says Simon Mainwaring, branding consultant, speaker, author, and *FastCompany* blogger. "The more it resonates with me as a human being, the more I find I have an emotional connection and want to share that product or service with others. The most compelling presentation a brand can make is when it really does the hard work to find and distill the human element in what they're bringing to the marketplace."

A pitch that is to the point and has a good sense of humor has a solid chance at getting a blogger's attention. Bloggers will typically respond favorably to well-thought-out messages that immediately explain what the e-mail is about. "Clear and concise will let me know right away if it's something I want to pursue," explains Alison Blackman of Advice Sisters. She echoes the sentiment of many bloggers: The subject line is a good precursor, but the rest of the pitch has to build on that and impress. "You have to wow me after I open the email."

Dean Takahashi, lead writer for GamesBeat at VentureBeat, covers video games and technology extensively. A former writer at the *Wall Street Journal* and *LA Times*, among others, Dean is also the author of the books *Opening the Xbox* and *The Xbox 360 Uncloaked.* He is approached on a daily basis to cover new products and has his pick of what to cover and what to quickly discard to his Gmail's trash. Takahashi admits he is more likely to cover a brand when it has a human approach. He genuinely cares about his readers' needs, so he gives extra weight to those who take the time to make a tailored pitch with direct relevance to his readers and are pitching quality stories that will generally interest his readers. If you're pitching Dean and you're not being self-serving, even better: A story of significance above and beyond the self-interest of the company makes a compelling case that the pitch is relevant and interesting to a larger industry or community. That has a much better chance of intriguing him.

Creative and funny subject lines can sometimes grab somebody's attention. "Most pitches are boring, and quite standard," laments Alison of Advice Sisters. "Every now and then someone will send me a pitch that is truly funny, or amusing; if nothing else, that will make it stand out, and make my day." For many bloggers, who are used to being approached pretty frequently, creative pitches hold a significant amount of sway. "I appreciate out-of-the-box thinking," says Charu Suri of Butterfly Diary. "Pitches like 'Tips to make your skin sun-savvy' have been done to death. Give me a different spin or scientific hook."

When it comes to out-of-the-box thinking, the PR team I worked with at Kiehl's was terrific. Rather than deliver a deluxe sample of our fan favorite, Creamy Eye Treatment with Avocado, to bloggers and journalists, the team worked with our creative department to put together a one-of-a-kind, unofficial limited edition gift set containing a small amount of the product, some background information, and a box illustration you couldn't find anywhere else. Best of all, Kiehl's didn't promote this limited edition whatsoever, showing that all the PR team wanted to do was deliver something great to the media and not receive any ancillary attention.

When pitching bloggers, it is crucial to send them the basic information they require out of the gate rather than making them work too hard. It might sound obvious to send bloggers all the information they need if you'd like them to cover your product or initiative, but many bloggers interviewed for this book had the same complaint: disorganized pitches without all the key information needed. Bloggers typically don't have the time to track you down and get information and assets you should have sent in the first place.

In addition, don't send large attachments unless the blogger has asked for them; clogging someone's inbox without permission isn't the best way to start a relationship. Instead, include a link to any large files, such as high-resolution images, so bloggers can download them as needed. Be sure to include a press release. Says Koren Zander of EnkoreMakeup: "I prefer a press release attached, with a photo of the product, and the press release should include key elements and the reason why the product is different from what is already out in the market. Then, offer up a direct contact in case I have further inquiries; that's important. That makes me feel that I can really call them if I need more info. And if I do call for more info, I expect the brand to know what info has already been shared with me." Also, whenever possible, a product sample should be part of the pitch: Many reputable bloggers write only about products they have personally sampled. To increase the odds of engaging successfully with bloggers, have samples to send. This might mean engaging with your operations team and explaining the importance of having a product launching in October in the warehouse by August so that it can be ready to send to your blogger contacts.

Keeping a Relationship Positive

While trying to get on a blogger's good side, it's critical that you don't accidentally incur their wrath. One of the most common complaints bloggers have about brands is that they can be rude and aggressive in their pursuit of getting covered. "If I tell you [being covered might take] 4–6 weeks, please wait until after that point before following up," says Elessa Jade of *Pursebuzz*. Alison of Advice Sisters agrees: "I don't like getting six copies of the same email. Send it once—then follow up if you really want me to read it." Generally, one well-thought-out e-mail and follow-up are sufficient. The blogger who is interested will respond. For time-sensitive events, reminders are generally appreciated.

Another faux pas is to add bloggers to your standard consumer database without their permission. Media lists, which are reserved for journalists and bloggers, are typically lists that bloggers are happy to be on, but to be opted in to all of your brand's promotional communications? That's another matter entirely. Why would you be pushy with the people you can least afford to annoy? Says Shannon Downey: "If you add me to your Facebook group or email list without my permission I will unsubscribe and you will never have another chance to pitch to me again. Consider yourself blocked!"

"A mistargeted pitch annoys me," shares Dean Takahashi, the lead writer for GamesBeat at VentureBeat. "Also, a pitch that assumes I can be bought also annoys me. We're independent thinkers."

To Koren Zander, the biggest sin a brand can commit is having an uninformed PR person. "Don't pitch if you're unable to answer my follow-up questions! One phrase I hate hearing is 'I will have to get back to you on that question'—I get many of those—and I don't always get a follow-up. And some of my questions are pretty easy, like asking what their product's target market is. How do you not know the answer to that?"

All bloggers are not created equal. Everyone has a voice; that's both a good and a bad thing. In many cases, you're dealing with an individual personality, as opposed to a brand. Don't expect the same level of professionalism. Some bloggers may understand your budget restrictions or that you have to prioritize a major publication over their small blog, whereas others may offer criticism or act like spoiled children if they don't get everything they want. It's important not to lose your cool, to stay diplomatic, and to be as professional as possible. Being the bigger person does not mean giving in to their demands. If the relationship is important to you, take the conversation offline and find another way to work with the blogger in order to satisfy him or her and salvage the relationship. Do not publicly humiliate bloggers or try to "put them in their place." Getting into an ongoing feud with bloggers simply causes unnecessary drama. And remember, any written communication could possibly cast your brand in a negative light. Moreover, private communications sometimes find their way into the public eye and could come back and haunt you. Treat bloggers with kindness even when you have to decline a request of theirs. They'll typically understand, and you'll leave the door open for a relationship in the future.

· · · · · · · **GUEST POST** · · · · · · ·

Charlotte Adjchavanich, Vice President of Digital and Communications at Maybelline, on:

Building a Successful Brand–Blogger Collaboration

There are several keys to generating buzz with a brand–blogger collaboration. First, identifying someone who is brand appropriate and who has the type of following your company wants to attract is critical. Investigate Klout scores and research blogs where your brand is being truly endorsed or mentioned in a positive light. There has to be authenticity in the partnership because your brand can be perceived negatively if it looks as though it is jumping on the social media bandwagon. Good bloggers know that, to stay credible and build a sustainable practice, they should work commercially in only a mutually beneficial way.

As with any successful campaign, there need to be an objective, vision, and strategy. Why does your brand want to associate with a blogger? How long do you want to work with the blogger? What are the creative parameters for the partnership? Do you give carte blanche to create content, or does your brand have strict guidelines? All these questions should be used as filters before embarking on securing your digital influencer. Be sure to negotiate, upfront contractually with the blogger, your wish list of requirements for the partnership.

Buzz can be generated in a multitude of ways:

- Partner with a blogger and "discover" her before any other company.

- Leveraging a blogger's fan base and his circle of online peers helps tremendously to spread messages virally.

- Set timing of the launch and duration of the campaign; choose an appropriate season and date.

- Placing exclusives with high-traffic and industry-trade online sites can start your campaign buzz.

- Create teaser campaigns; cleverly branded content via video, photos, or blog posts; or "reality-style" content of before-and-after or theme-based content

You should have KPIs planned to measure the success of your campaign. KPIs include video views, online media impressions, twitter reach, retweets, trending topics, likes on Facebook, and reblogs on Tumblr. If you're going to do all the work to develop a strong relationship, make sure it's worth it!

Bloggers and Brand Discovery

For most bloggers, the recipe for deciding what to cover and what to pass on is quite simple: Find brands that will be of interest to their audience. "I cover a brand when I find it interesting or my readers find it interesting," says Elessa Jade of *Pursebuzz*. Also keep in mind that most bloggers aren't sitting at home passively waiting for pitches; most are actively looking for new topics to cover. "I have discovered products through Twitter and Facebook, and also in person. I don't only write about things pitched to me; I often seek out unique brands and products and post about it," explains Kai. "I'll then look for the PR contact so they know we wrote about it—assuming, of course, their Google Alerts haven't already informed them."

Don't assume a blogger has to be familiar with your product prior to the pitch. Alison Blackman is one of many who said she has covered many brands that she wouldn't have otherwise known about simply because they were pitched to her. Bloggers cover brands that they weren't previously familiar with all the time, simply by virtue of a promising product and a great pitch.

Simon Mainwaring, the *FastCompany* blogger, has had a very different experience when it comes to pitches. "I almost never have a brand pitch itself to me, nor would I promote that brand unless I thought the meaningful work that they were doing was using social media in an interesting way or inspiring others to do the same." Instead, Simon relies heavily on Google Reader for articles about brands, nonprofits, or social entrepreneurs doing work that is altruistic. "If that meaningful work happens to be done by a brand, I want to celebrate it as a permission slip for others to do the same."

Strengthening Your Blogger Relationships

When you're pitching to a blogger, consider adding a line with a request. If they're unable to dedicate a post to a particular story, might they help spread the word and tweet about it or post it as a status update? I've gotten bloggers to support campaigns I've worked on simply by asking them nicely if they could support my project in even a minor way. If bloggers are able to help you out in this way, be sure to help strengthen your relationship by thanking them over that social media channel. Also, bear in mind that you don't need to have the most formal of relationships with the bloggers that follow your brand. Planned or impromptu Twitter conversations between brand and blogger are a fun way to encourage your audience to chime in and participate. Having a brand representative comment on a blogger's social presence is a good way to show that, just like they're your fan, the opposite is true as well: You're a fan of theirs.

As you build relationships with bloggers, keep in mind that—as in any relationship—it can take time to build credibility. If you put in the time, though, your blogger contacts will talk to one another, and it will be easier to build subsequent relationships. The same principle applies for nonblogger online personalities and celebrities. Comic book podcast *Word Balloon* saw its audience grow as a result of host John Siuntres's access to top creators like Brian Michael Bendis and Brian Azzarello because his messages were amplified by those connections. John's early success led to continued positive results: The more interviews he did with creators such as Ed Brubaker, Greg Rucka, and Mark Waid, the more he was able to conduct with others. Prospective interviews knew he was serious based on the pedigree of his previous interview subjects. When the late comic artist Mike Wieringo wanted to hear a *Word Balloon* interview with his writer friend Jeff Parker but couldn't get the episode to download, Parker suggested that Wieringo reach out to Siuntres directly. When Wieringo sent him a note, it led not only to a Wieringo interview on *Word Balloon* but also to a major realization: Instead of Siuntres's always having to reach out to comic creators, now they were actually reaching out to him.

"Brands need to develop relationships in order to truly 'pitch'; I respect that so much more than if I just get a random email, tweet, or post," explains Shannon Downey of Pivotal Chicago. Indeed, personal touches can go a long way in making influencers feel special, and they don't always need to involve swag. Just look at how Aveeno treats its brand ambassadors: Over the 2011 holiday season, Johnson & Johnson (Aveeno's parent company) made a donation in the name of each of its Aveeno blogger ambassadors to CEW Cancer and Career, a fund dedicated to empowering and educating women with cancer to thrive in the workplace. Steps that go above and beyond what other brands are doing have the potential of making your blogger contacts feel truly appreciated.

Bloggers as Spokespersons and Collaborators: Good or Bad?

Brands are approaching bloggers and other online influencers to be celebrity spokespersons with increasing frequency. If you're more used to the old media paradigm, this is a pretty jarring change; you would never imagine Bob Woodward formally becoming the spokesperson for a politician while he was still officially covering him as a working journalist, but online personalities don't work the same way as print journalists do.

"Fans connect to bloggers because of their honesty," says Lianne Farbes, a beauty expert who has served as an ambassador for brands such as Aveeno and MAC Cosmetics. "Bloggers are real people who have morphed into experts—some more credible than others, but experts nonetheless. I think that it is up to brands to do what they can to make certain their ambassadors and representatives are worthy of that title."

Koren Zander of Enkore Makeup is just one of many advocates of brands formally compensating bloggers and online personalities. "It's a great tactic for brands, as bloggers and vloggers achieve a bigger reach these days within minutes than a print ad or billboard."

Simon Mainwaring agrees, finding it appropriate for bloggers or vloggers to serve as official brand spokespersons, provided disclosure is in place, so that both the brand and blogger maintain their integrity. Simon has been approached to be a spokesperson for a number of brands but has never seized the opportunity. "I think what people want from the content they read on the web is impartiality, where somebody can provide an honest, third-party perspective," Simon shares. "Ultimately, the most important thing is that all parties involved maintain their integrity. That way, you'll keep your communities' attention and continue to earn their trust, which is critical for any success in the social business marketplace."

"It has to be done really well or it feels inauthentic, and the blogger risks losing their credibility," warns Shannon Downey. "There are so many 'bloggers for hire' that it gets hard to trust any information being pumped out by them because you just aren't sure what's authentic and what's a paid advertisement."

"Legitimacy is such a big thing in the online space," says Ava Scanlan, my former coworker and Vice President of Communications at Temptu. "It's all about objectivity. Bloggers and 'new influencers' have to always be honest with their audiences. Without that, they lose their authenticity." Ava cites Michelle Phan, arguably the matriarch of the self-styled beauty gurus who have developed sizable audiences over the last few years. Since signing a deal with Lancôme, Phan realized she would have to work even harder to preserve authenticity and maintain her status as a trusted source for beauty tips. "J.Lo could lose an endorsement deal if she was caught using other products. Someone like Michelle Phan has to cover other products. Michelle can't be all Lancôme, all the time, because she'll lose her authenticity."

Glen Hellman, a serial entrepreneur and blogger, agrees that transparency is key when an arrangement has been made between a brand and a blogger. "Microsoft offered me a Sony Vaio loaded with software and to increase my Klout, if I'd join their Windows Champions program and blog about them once every other month," explains Glen. "But for this to work, the brand and the blogger have to be transparent and honest. For instance, Microsoft does not demand that I post positive posts, just that I talk about their products and that I mention I'm a Windows blogger and it's a sponsored post."

CASE IN POINT: *Coach Delivers Authenticity Through Stellar Blogger Relations*

Coach has been at the forefront of blogger–brand collaborations since they began. There is a concerted effort to make Coach's blogger relations a focal point of their overall social marketing strategy because the luxury retailer realizes how much authenticity is lent to the company by developing bloggers as brand ambassadors. "Coach knows it's more personal than a brand marketing directly to them," says Katie Rodgers of Paperfashion, an illustrator who has collaborated with Coach. "Bloggers have authenticity. If Coach came out with something that just misses the mark entirely—not that that happens often at all—we wouldn't be singing its praises."

On Coach's MYNY section, 15 bloggers create looks using their favorite products from their favorite New York City spots that inspire them. Bloggers such as Christine Cameron of My Style Pill, Keiko Lynn, and Gemma Rowlands of Fade to Black were featured in pictorials that allowed each blogger to tell viewers about their look in their own words. Bloggers were also interviewed on topics such as their favorite ways to spend a day in New York City, the best backdrops for fashion photos in New York, how art and music inspire their fashion sense, and more, including links to each blogger's blog. The bloggers largely found it rewarding to be featured. "It gave me wonderful exposure to a network and audience of people that I might not ever had the opportunity to share my style—and brand—with otherwise," offers Christine of My Style Pill.

In addition to the MYNY campaign, Coach has had multiple campaigns for its Guest Blogger Search, all eliciting significant interest. This guest-blogger program features bloggers from different geographic locations and life experiences and highlights their product picks.

Coach has also directly partnered with bloggers in order to develop designs for bags, one of which was collaboration with the fashion blog Fashion Foie Gras. Emily Johnston, editor of Fashion Foie Gras, helped design a bag with Coach with the fashionable blogger in mind. The bag has a hidden compartment perfect for storing a camera and flats, and it also includes pockets to hold blogger must-haves like a laptop, iPad, and phone. The limited edition bag started out as an exclusive for London Coach stores and was soon made available exclusively online. "My feet haven't touched the ground!" said Emily, when asked how she felt about being asked to collaborate. "Coach is the pinnacle of luxury and sophistication. Designing a bag with a brand that I have always held in such high regard has been the most nerve-racking, but also the most exhilarating, experience of my life. I couldn't be prouder or more pleased with what we have produced." It's energy like this that Coach's blogger collaborators invest in virally spreading the word about how much they love Coach's brand.

While Coach's PR department "owns" the relationships with bloggers, the company's Mobile and Social team is a major beneficiary of all blogger collaboration content. "We don't want every post to be about selling product, because that's not what our audience wants or needs," says Karen Yung, who manages Social and Mobile at Coach. "Our blogger collaborations give us less promotional messaging and more striking visuals that our audience responds well to."

Coach supports bloggers with products on an ongoing basis but is always looking for opportunities to go one step further. For instance, to celebrate the music festival Coachella, Coach created a Coachella Survival Kit for some of their favorite bloggers. A burst of online buzz ensued after the bloggers posted pictures of their gifts, which were shared many times over.

At Coach, everything that can be tracked is tracked, including the impact of brand–blogger collaborations. The company's cross-functional teams look at metrics for two hours every Monday. As standard practice, all of their Facebook updates link to their .com using bit.ly so that they can better track click data. This back-end analysis is just the icing on the cake for Coach, whose strong blogger relationships and inventive programs have set the tone in terms of how a brand can succeed by working with a blogger.

Celebrities as Influencers

Finding the right celebrity to amplify your social marketing message can go a long way. After all, unlike an everyday fan who's a hardcore supporter of your brand, celebrities tend to have relatively robust built-in audiences and can amplify the conversation surrounding your brand.

popchips considers itself fortunate to be able to count several influential celebrities as fans of the brand, including social media evangelist Ashton Kutcher, who joined popchips as its President of Pop Culture. Kutcher leads the company's social media strategy and creates exciting digital marketing programs, one of which has been a campaign to find his second in command as Vice President of Pop Culture. Of course, part of the excitement comes from the opportunity to interact with Ashton, but, hey, you can't deny that it drives significant attention to popchips.

While we're on the topic of current and former *Two and a Half Men* stars, though most brands might not be able to afford Charlie Sheen (and there are those who might not want to), Internships.com jumped at the opportunity to work with him in early 2011. You know, back when "Winning!" and "dragon's blood" were big. When Sheen requested a social media intern via Twitter on behalf of Internships.com, more than 95,000 people clicked through his tweet and were asked to apply. Within two days, he had received 74,040 applications from 181 countries, largely due to Sheen's direct vocalization of the message—and that was only at the halfway mark of the four-day application window.[1] For a company looking to build an audience rapidly, the Sheen stunt gave Internships.com a chance to showcase its services.

When it comes to building relationships with celebrities, be proactive whenever possible. When my PR team at Kiehl's saw Kim Kardashian blog about a particularly bad case of sunburn, they rushed her a pack of our Anti-Oxidant Skin Preserver, a rich moisturizer perfect for sunburn relief. A day later, Kim posted the following: "This face cream saved my life! It's called Anti-Oxidant Skin Preserver and it's by Kiehl's. It is the only thing that calmed down my sunburn and healed my skin!" Best of all, Kim was kind enough to link back to the product page where we were selling the product, and she gave us a personal thank-you on Twitter as well, mentioning our @KiehlsNYC handle. The result of this celebrity relations coup? Besides a short-term 400 percent sales spike in demand for the product, @KiehlsNYC netted hundreds of additional followers within the hour.

Kim and her Kardashian sisterhood are an excellent example of how the right pairing can pay off for both the celebrity and the brand. Mainly, it's because the marketing is done in a way that makes it feel authentic, as opposed to a hard sell. The girls use their official blogs and social media channels to connect with the fans who use the products they endorse. They also do giveaways of the products on their blogs, leading to incredible brand awareness and a subsequent increase in sales.

I'm sure you can imagine how much exposure your brand could pick up from just one interaction of this nature. Best of all, engagement with a celebrity can open the door to a continued conversation with your audience members, both new and old. Build the right relationships, and you have the potential to see engagement on your social channels rise to new heights.

· · · · · · · **GUEST POST** · · · · · · ·

The Importance of Celebrity on Social Channels

Jennifer Haughton is Director of Celebrity Social Media Strategy and Development at BUZZMEDIA, the web's fastest growing pop culture publishers, managing properties such as Celebuzz, Buzznet, and OKMagazine.com.

There really is no voice louder and more influential online than that of a trusted and prominent celebrity. Twitter and Facebook have given the celebrity a voice in a world jam-packed with consumers. Kids don't look up to their parents; they look up to celebrities. They are highly influenced by what celebrities wear, read, listen to, eat, and drive. Although a celebrity's involvement in a brand's online marketing campaign isn't essential for its success, it can certainly help propel it to a higher level. Of course, the power of celebrity can also be harmful to a brand; it wouldn't be ideal to have Lindsay Lohan endorse Chantix and be spotted smoking two weeks later. So it's vital that the brand find a match that makes sense to the consumer.

It is absolutely essential that brands find a celebrity who "fits" with their product or service. People won't buy a product or pay for a service if they don't believe that that celebrity actually uses it. You can pay a celebrity X amount of dollars to tweet about your product, but if consumers don't believe the celebrity would use that product, why would they click on your link and make a purchase? It's essentially just a random tweet with absolutely no context, and context is everything! Having said that, Justin Bieber could probably sell cat litter to his fans, but you get my point. The pairing has to be authentic and believable for it to be successful and beneficial to the brand.

going further · · · · · · · · · · · · · · · ·

For bonus materials and updates pertaining to this chapter's topics, please visit: *http://goingsocial.jeremygoldman.com/ch10*.

11

increase engagement by turning your employees into marketers

MOST OF YOUR employees have the potential to be stellar social marketers for your organization. Not only are they a captive audience that you have the potential to loyalize, but they're (I hope!) financially incentivized to help your company succeed.

Also, keep in mind that social platforms are a lot more democratic than the physical world. If your vice president of public relations starts talking about a new product launch in the physical world, it's much more likely to start spreading informally than if a lower-level employee raises the topic. However, the way that most social networks are set up, both the head of PR and a junior employee posting the same content at the same time have equal chances of their posts going viral. In fact, lower-level employees may have a better shot at spreading news if they have 1,000 friends on Facebook who tend to be very active; the head of PR may have only 300 friends who are only moderately active. On-line influence doesn't necessarily reflect offline influence.

Now, a lot of people might say, "But I work in accounting. How can I possibly help?" The answer is, first, acknowledge that every employee, whatever their position, can be a brand promoter or detractor. A company needs as many advocates as it can get. A company whose employees assume that it's someone else's job to be the organization's cheerleader is a company that's not going to succeed.

I've worked at Kiehl's, a fantastic L'Oreal brand that has fought through difficult economic times to grow at an incredible pace—and around the world—over the last few years. One of the biggest things Kiehl's has going for it is how much people love it. Its customers love it, sure, but that's not all. Kiehl's employees are typically fanatical about the brand. This gets the rest of L'Oreal excited about the brand, allowing Kiehl's to recruit strong talent from the entire L'Oreal talent pool. All of this leads to getting the whole beauty industry excited about the brand, which leads to positive word of mouth with consumers in general.

Letting Employees Be Your Lead Generation Tool

For most companies lead generation is typically an expensive endeavor. To reduce customer acquisition costs, it's important to develop a virtuous cycle in which your customers are going social on behalf of your brand. In many ways, your employees are a representative microcosm of your consumers. It's easier to study this small group of people, figure out what makes them happy, and give it to them before trying to turn your customers into advocates.

The multiplication effect of going social is huge. Let's say your brand is running a one-day promotion in which customers who share their favorite product on Facebook receive a promo code for their next purchase of that product. This sounds great, but if you're a small brand, many people might not even realize this promotion is happening. Now, let's say your employees are active social marketers. Suppose you have 25 employees, and each of them shares the promotion on Facebook and has 300 friends on average. Your potential reach is now 7,500 people. And don't forget that each of these 7,500 people has friends. Just as important, these are people who are being marketed to by friends and acquaintances, not by a faceless corporation. If you get just 1 percent of those 7,500 people to share with their networks, with their immediate connections totaling 250 on average, you now have an additional potential reach of 18,750.

But if you don't get your employees excited about sharing programs, the picture looks very different. What if only five of those employees shared that promotion? Well, instead of reaching up to 7,500 people as part of that first share, you're now reaching a maximum of 1,500. If 1 percent of those 1,500 people share the promotion, that's 15 people sharing to their 250 friends, or 3,750, a fraction of the people who would have known about your promotion had your employees felt passionately about your brand.

Setting the Tone from the Top

It's going to be a lot easier to turn your employees into advocates if you get the right people in senior leadership positions. Whether or not you agree with trickle-down economics, it's hard to argue against trickle-down moods in organizations. If the leadership of the company has the right passion, belief, and drive, then the entire organization is much more likely to resemble that model. These senior leaders will want people who work for them to buy into that vision.

> **CASE IN POINT: Laura Geller Makeup Uses Founder to Connect with Its Audience**
>
> When deciding to step up their efforts to go social with their audience, Laura Geller Makeup realized it needed someone passionate about the brand—and who would be more passionate than founder Laura Geller herself? As a result, the company decided to use Facebook, Twitter, and video to promote Laura Geller as a brand spokesperson.
>
> In terms of year-over-year performance, Laura Geller Makeup's Facebook presence has grown 29 percent, Twitter has grown 102 percent, and YouTube 44 percent. The brand's fan base has grown 142 percent over the previous year, simply by sticking to organic and viral tactics, as well as authenticity.
>
> A lot of the success can be tracked back to Laura's vibrant personality. Laura Geller Makeup fans love being able to connect with the brand's founder directly. Although they typically enjoy tips and special promotions, engagement is particularly high when Laura posts more whimsical, personal photos. For example, it was recently Laura's turn to serve as a crossing guard at her child's school. Laura posted the picture of herself as a crossing guard, wearing a bright orange vest, on her Facebook page. She has also posted photos of herself at the beach, as well as Halloween photos. Things like this make Laura's audience identify with her so easily.

Laura is also open to customer feedback. Recently she had a name-the-shade contest on her brand Facebook page. Her audience was asked to determine what the next shade of Laura's popular product, Eye Rimz eyeliner, should be. The shade was then created based on her fans' votes. Laura took it one step further by asking her audience what the shade should be named, with Stainless Teal the eventual winner.

Through Laura, the brand makes a concerted effort to connect with brand promoters in other ways. To celebrate Laura's upcoming sale on flash sale site Hautelook, Laura hosted a live chat on Hautelook's Facebook page. The brand also uses UStream, a live video streaming platform, to hold monthly events so that Laura's fans can chat with her in real time and receive professional makeup tips and tricks.

Laura hosts The Geller Girl's Blog on QVC.com's popular Community section, where her average post nets thousands of views and often easily tops 50 comments. Given her QVC popularity, it was a natural fit for Laura Geller Makeup to be included in QVC's Fashion's Night Out event in New York City. Together, QVC and Laura Geller hosted Laura's Tweet Suite, where top celebrities walked through, tweeted directly to Laura, and engaged with fans. Fans could tweet using the hashtag #QVCFNO and tag @LauraGeller to experience the event online even if they weren't in New York.

The keys to Laura's success at going social? Being relatable, authentic, and passionate about her product.

Developing Current Employees Pays Off

One of the best ways to turn your workforce into a vibrant group of social marketers is to develop your existing employees. Many of us are frustrated by the fact that, while we all understand the importance of education, it seems to be among the first things to get cut when federal, state, and city governments need to reduce costs. The same thing happens to companies: when expenses have to be cut; one of the first things to go is training and development, particularly for junior employees who probably need the training most. It doesn't take a genius to realize spending $2,000 to get an employee properly trained is worth it, especially since it's most likely going to lead to that employee's bringing in 20 to 100 times that in new revenues. Plus, it's going to keep that employee engaged and less likely to look for a job elsewhere, decreasing your overall hiring costs. Yet most companies automatically cut training and development expenses when money is tight, regardless of the practicality of these efforts.

There are cost-effective ways to train employees. For example, you can have your community manager teach people how to use social tools. This kind of insider training allows people to become better marketers for your organization.

Sometimes, the best way to accomplish this is to develop better internal cohesion first. Two of the tools that can help you achieve this are Yammer and Rypple.

In a nutshell, Yammer is Facebook but for enterprise use. It lets your organization set up your own private social platform in a matter of minutes. Best of all, it's designed for business collaboration, so you can set up different groups for different departments of your business. Users can share status updates, post polls, ask questions, post events, and award other users badges of praise.

Rypple is a bit like Yammer but more focused on coaching as opposed to internal socializing or collaboration. Instead, it's focused on recognizing employee contributions, offering feedback, and coaching team members. Companies that use Rypple have the advantage of real-time feedback and coaching instead of the typical annual reviews. Hundreds of companies use Rypple to increase productivity, including Facebook, which actually helped Rypple design the platform. Rypple is a great way to help employees boost their careers, improve morale, and put your team on the path toward becoming better brand advocates.

Encouraging Employees to Go Social

Granted, it's not always easy to motivate your internal team to Tweet, share Facebook links, and so on. Before anything else—and this might sound obvious to some—you have to make sure your people like your brand! If they don't know what sets your brand apart in the market or simply don't care, there is a good chance their presence is doing more harm than good. This is lost on many executives. Although they may agree it's a good thing to have employees like the company, very few see how truly important it is.

Noted social marketing advisor Jay Baer puts training "first and foremost" when it comes to turning your employees into the best possible online advocates for your brand. He advocates developing participation guidelines for all employees who want to contribute to your social channels.

"Companies also need to make sure employees know what's going on," Jay stresses. "The era of the monthly newsletter is over. You need real-time news dissemination to all employees. The companies that are best at external social media are usually very good at internal social media."

Needless to say, there is a risk in this brave new world where data can be shared so easily; you need to make sure the right data is being shared. At one of my previous brands, a summer intern posted how excited she was about having just seen the art for the upcoming holiday promotion. The problem was that the holiday promotion was not planned for release for quite a few months. Luckily, a PR executive at the company saw the post and made sure it came down, but this example brings up an important question: How do you make sure the right information is shared and the wrong, or private, data is kept in-house? Being transparent with employees about what is shareable and what is proprietary data is key. Don't assume junior personnel know what's okay to share and what is not. Something that is second nature to you due to your many years in the workforce could be an unknown to a new employee. At the same time, make sure not to talk down to people; you run the risk of demoralizing them.

If someone does share something accidentally and not maliciously, make sure the person is not treated harshly. Keeping secrets in-house is crucial, but so is keeping your workforce engaged and marketing on your behalf. The people more likely to make mistakes and overstep your official policy are often your most fervent internal advocates. If they make an innocent mistake, be sure not to lose them as an advocate by reprimanding them too severely.

It's not a bad idea to think like an economist and incentivize people to like the brand. When I joined Temptu, it was a small brand with a pretty tiny following on Facebook. To ramp up our number of likes, I held an employees-only contest. All employees, from marketing to operations to finance, were encouraged to invite their friends to join the Facebook page; the person who got the most sign-ups would be rewarded with $300 worth of beauty products from my beauty closet, amassed from a number of my brands and colleagues' brands over the course of my career. If you're going to do an internal competition like this, make sure the prize is well thought out and relevant to your audience. In this case, more than 20 beauty lovers competed for free beauty products from high-end brands such as Redken, Bumble & Bumble, Kiehl's, Jurlique, Livingproof, and others. This campaign was also successful because it made sure to combat any employee objections ahead of time. For people unfamiliar with Facebook, there were clearly outlined instructions, with screenshots, on how to participate. For employees who might have missed the contest's launch, multiple e-mails were sent out over the campaign, updating everyone on the results. For those not sure if this competition was serious or not, the CEO's participation was prominently touted.

Recruiting via Social Platforms

Nearly half (48 percent) of all job seekers—and 63 percent of job seekers who are on Facebook—leverage Facebook in their job search. Approximately 16 percent of all job seekers have received a referral to a job from someone whom they count among their Facebook friends.[1] Increasingly, just as your LinkedIn audience may connect with personal connections, your Facebook audience is using that platform for professional purposes. In fact, one in five Facebook users has added professional information to their profiles in the past year.[2]

Given that, you can't overestimate the importance of making sure that your Facebook presence is optimized for potential future star employees who might be researching your brand. Many top brands, such as Starbucks, Red Bull, Sony PlayStation, and McDonald's, have a career page incorporated into their Facebook presence.

To attract prospective candidates, be sure to design a beautiful, uncluttered career page. Also, incorporate authentic employee experiences. No one wants to take your word that you're a great company to work for; they want to hear employee stories! Also, when a prospective hire asks a question via a public social channel, make sure to be responsive and make the candidate feel heard. Even if the candidate isn't right for your organization, you don't want the right candidate to see your exchange and get the wrong impression.

Hiring Social Individuals

The easiest way to make your employees social is to not have to force them to become social. It may sound obvious, but hire social people! I've come across organizations where the individual most in charge of creating a social online presence isn't social in real life. When this occurs, it's much more difficult for the social bug to infect the rest of your staff.

In regard to making your employees passionate about your brand, making the right investments in your workforce can go a long way: Technology is one of the best areas to cultivate. One of the highest-return developments in corporate America's recent history is the rise of smartphones in the workplace. Suddenly, key personnel became tethered to the office even when they were off the clock. For less than $100 a month, companies now had, in effect, electronic leashes on their employees. Maybe that's a pessimistic view, but it's true. If you have an employee making $50 an hour, and he or she works an additional two hours per month due to their company smartphone, you've broken even on that phone plan.

If you're reading this book, there's a pretty good chance you're one of these tethered individuals. I've been tethered for the last decade or so, yet I actually felt quite honored when I received my first company smartphone. Here's my question: Why stop at smartphones? If you're already investing in the smartphones, why not install the latest social "productivity" apps for them? Putting Hootsuite on employees' phones and giving them proper direction on how to use it help them share your content. Making an investment in these employees shows them you care, which only increases the odds that they will share.

> ### CASE IN POINT: Gilt Groupe's Recruiting Evolution
>
> The age of going social has changed human resources functions across the board, and that's certainly the case for Rockman Ha, Director of Technical Recruiting at shopping website Gilt Groupe. Rockman is involved in all aspects of recruiting at Gilt. This includes sorting candidates, speaking with them, and connecting them with the right people at Gilt for the correct positions.
>
> Gilt uses its social media marketing as a recruitment tool because it lets potential recruits understand what the company is all about and what the corporate culture is like. Gilt's social engagement as a recruiting tool is aligned with the brand's audience.
>
> Gilt is engaging on social channels not just because it's the shiny new object in the company's marketing arsenal but also because it makes sense for its business. "If you think about social media, it is primarily for the companies that are pretty up-to-date in terms of technology, which definitely helps me in regards to my job," says Rockman, who is primarily hiring engineers. "If a company doesn't have either a Facebook page or anything in regard to social media, that's always a red flag for engineers who are looking for their new next home. So, just getting that brand awareness out is definitely big."

One of the benefits to Gilt's leveraging social channels in its recruiting process is that it can be more targeted than it would be otherwise. When Gilt posts a job on LinkedIn, for example, it will target people directly.

The social marketing age has changed how Gilt recruits. Although a potential recruit doesn't get knocked out of contention for a role solely because of the lack of social channel prowess, social media aptitude can help. "It's always a bonus if engineers are involved in the social spaces in the sense where they are talking about technology," Rockman told me. "That just really shows they are passionate about it and I would assume that would go across the board." Gilt isn't looking for brand evangelists per se. They are, however, looking at recruits on social channels who are passionate about their roles and responsibilities. For Rockman's group, it is incredibly important that people are passionate about technology and about their careers because everything else will sprout from that. According to Rockman, "If people are making software for Gilt and they are proud of it, they will naturally evangelize Gilt Technology and what they have built."

While social channels are ultimately a boon to Gilt's recruiting efforts, they are by no means all positives and no negatives. Social channels give prospective candidates a good sense of the corporate culture, which is a positive because it increases the odds that candidates who aren't right for Gilt won't apply in the first place. This can lower Gilt's overall recruiting costs. At the same time, this can lead candidates who are more appropriate for the company to apply or become interested in the first place.

On the other hand, there are negatives. Although most Gilt alumni I've spoken to have positive things to say, Gilt could theoretically have a disgruntled worker more easily voice their gripes via social channels and share the worst aspects of their employment. This becomes more of a challenge as a company grows. A company the size of Google could have thousands of reviews online on sites like Glassdoor, analyzing what it's like to work there. Ultimately, social platforms give prospective recruits a better sense of the culture and provide a better inside view of Gilt before joining the company, making the pros outweigh the cons.

With respect to potential recruits, they have greater access to information about the company. Thus, Gilt is getting a higher-quality recruit because they will have done their due diligence and aren't applying if they wouldn't fit into the culture in the first place.

Being a popular company, Gilt has many candidates coming through its doors for interviews. While some are hired, the majority who come for an interview won't walk away with jobs, despite their qualifications. Gilt doesn't have the ability to hire everyone, but they don't want a brand promoter to become a detractor. Much like a customer who goes for pizza, has a bad experience, and leaves a scathing review on Yelp, Gilt has to be mindful that, after being rejected, applicants still have a loud voice via social channels. Says Rockman:

> Our goal, whether or not someone gets hired, is to give them the best possible candidate experience; we

don't want anybody having a poor experience here, regardless of whether they come to work for us or not. They could be a potential customer, or they could be someone we might engage with down the line and become one of the best people we've hired. We always want them to have the best experience during the interviewing process.

Although Gilt was always mindful of giving all applicants a positive experience, in the age of going social it has become that much more important.

Outside of Rockman's more traditional recruiting responsibilities, he must also engage in an ongoing dialogue with Gilt's current employees, so that when a job referral is appropriate, those employees are engaged and excited to send referrals.

Gilt also leverages social media to get the existing employee base excited, encouraging them to like and share content and to talk up the company in general. Rockman's group operates Gilt Tech, a tech blog hosted on Tumblr. Individual members of the technology group share content from the Gilt Tech Tumblr via personal Tumblr, Twitter, and Facebook accounts. The greater Gilt organization participates as well, Liking posts about Gilt in general, which increases the brand's visibility. Employees such as Associate Buyer Caroline Knapp are routinely asked to participate and become part of the brand's content. In Caroline's case, she did a series of Gilt TV episodes where she hosted Shop the Video sales on Facebook and other social media sites. A personal style blogger on the side, Caroline was encouraged by Gilt to include the videos on her blog as well as through her social media channels. Gilt Groupe has also sponsored Caroline with social platform exclusive sales dubbed Caroline's Favorites. Gilt amplifies its messages in a cost-effective manner by recruiting and loyalizing the Carolines on their team, ensuring that the brand has the best chance for success in a competitive market.

going further · · · · · · · · · · · · ·

For bonus materials and updates pertaining to this chapter's topics, please visit: *http://goingsocial.jeremygoldman.com/ch11.*

12

how to engage with ROI in mind

LET'S FACE IT: You have a finite number of resources at your disposal. You don't have enough hours in the day to build all the relationships you need to develop. That's part of why you're promoting conversations with your customers online: If you're good to your customers, they will help you recruit new customers. You're communicating not only with your own network, but also with all your network's contacts. As such, your marketing messages and content are amplified and syndicated to a much greater audience than you possibly could have reached by yourself.

At the same time, even though getting into the social waters is the right thing to do, you need to be thinking about your potential return on investment (ROI). From junior employees to middle managers to executives, I've seen businesspeople skip this step, in businesses large and small. They mean to get around to analyzing a project's ROI, but they get busy with other projects, and they're behind on a few deadlines. Plus, the project they're not measuring ROI for is something they have a gut feeling is important to their business, so they plow ahead without doing any ROI analysis.

Engaging is important, but so is ROI. This principle applies whether you're launching a Facebook page, starting a Twitter campaign, creating a corporate blog, or establishing any other social initiative. While I strongly believe in the power of going social, it's entirely possible that what you're going to do is of little value to your business and might even detract from what you're trying to do as an organization. Yet everybody seems to know that they need to get into social media in one way or another, so they just jump in without a plan.

There isn't really a point to having a presence on a social network unless that presence will improve your business's fortunes. If it's not adding value in some way or another, it's subtracting value. Social media is not free; there's always an opportunity cost involved.

Determining value and ROI in regard to your social media investment is never easy. Although most companies today have an investment in going social, most of these investments are done without any clear way to measure their ROI. This brave new world of social marketing is moving pretty fast, but it's still incredibly important to determine your likely return on investment so that you know how much time, energy, and capital to spend on developing a social relationship with your customers.

In his book *Social Media ROI: Managing and Measuring Social Media Efforts in Your Organization*, Olivier Blanchard offers a critical rule about measuring social media ROI: "Just because you can measure it doesn't mean that it matters." Indeed, many companies spend a significant amount of their hours allocated to analysis-measuring metrics that don't matter to the bottom line. Make sure you pick your metrics carefully and ask, "Is this going to help us assess the true value of our social marketing program?" You need to be focused, and measuring *everything* is a great way to become unfocused. Establish your objectives for going social in order to select the proper metrics to determine whether you're succeeding. Then you need to hypothesize what your ROI is going to be. We'll discuss target ROIs in a bit.

Brands go about determining ROI for their social marketing strategy in many different ways, in large part because different brands are looking to go social for different objectives, including market research, goodwill in the marketplace, and other returns.

The Keys to a Positive ROI

According to research by Alterian, social marketers lack clarity in terms of what they should be measuring, as well as how they should be measuring it. In the poll, 33 percent indicated they have little to no understanding of what conversations pertain to their brand, with 40 percent indicating that they're using a few disconnected tools to track social marketing ROI very loosely. Alterian CEO David Eldridge says the results "show the majority of brands lack direction on what exactly to measure and analyze, how to go about it, and how to utilize that information to continually improve on their marketing efforts . . . . [I]t's crucial for marketers to seek guidance and the right tools in order to develop a strategic plan that allows them to fully engage with customers across channels." Of the marketers surveyed, 80 percent admitted their lack of understanding of ROI as it pertains to social marketing; their disconnected, ad hoc means to track results are placing their companies at a competitive disadvantage. Despite all this, the vast majority of marketers said they will be spending more money on going social in 2013 than they did 2012. This is craziness! This is akin to buying your spouse an extravagant present instead of figuring out why he or she is mad at you. Throwing money at the matter is not likely to help things.

According to the Corporate Executive Board, midsized companies have approximately doubled their social media investments over the last two years, with 74 percent of these companies using Twitter, 71 percent engaging on Facebook, 53 percent on YouTube, and 36 percent posting via company blogs.[1]

Those respondents that indicated that their social marketing tactics actually drove business results—the CEB dubs these Social Media Exemplars (SMEs)—tend to do a few things in common: listen, assign value, track, and extend.

- *Listening:* This is the linchpin of social marketing. Ironically, when many marketers see this word, they don't quite listen to what it means. Listen essentially means to understand—understand what your customers care about, what they need, and what they're looking to you for. All other activities come after doing this well. Southwest Airlines is one example of a brand succeeding in this area because it monitors Twitter, message boards, and blogs to understand how their customers feel, and then it responds appropriately.

- *Assigning Value:* Going social can help an organization in many ways. If your consumer research budget has gone down from $200,000 to $35,000 a year due to focusing on tracking customer sentiment on social media, that's a pretty big deal. The same thing goes for customer service: Many companies have seen a decline in customer service costs and a rise in perceived customer service levels as a result of leveraging social interaction with their customers on social sites. Despite all the ways social marketing can add value to a business, many companies trying to measure ROI purely based on sales figures are missing out on other ways socializing with their customers can help. To fully get the value of social media, you must think of all of the ways it contributes to your business.

• *Tracking:* Track the right metrics. It's all well and good to track the number of fans you have on your Facebook page, but there are better things to track: the number of interactions your fans have over time on your Facebook page; whether they click through to your e-commerce site or store locator; the number of fans you have in your target demographic (i.e., if I could get 15 male fans under 18 to the Kiehl's page, it would be less valuable than three or four women between 35 and 44); and so on.

• *Extending:* The CEB found that one of the things that sets SMEs apart from regular businesses is their ability to think outside the box when it comes to social interactions. SMEs don't think of the different departments of the company as a sales function, PR function, or marketing function. They look at them as all-encompassing entities that can create new business paradigms. One example is Best Buy's Twelpforce, dubbed for its combination of Twitter and help force. Twelpforce extended a competitive differentiator that the brand already had—its tech-savvy retail staff—and a new technology, Twitter, to create an even greater competitive differentiator, one that no competitor could even touch. Best Buy then leveraged new uses for this technology, not just the default functions everyone else was offering.

At the end of the day, it really is all about ROI. That doesn't mean you have to define ROI narrowly; you can take a creative approach in defining both return and investment, but you do have to get to a point where you have a solid ROI.

Determining Your Goals

Before determining ROI, you have to determine what you want to get out of your social marketing efforts. In the strictest definition of the acronym, the *R* in *ROI* should stand for financial returns. If you want to define the *R* more broadly, that's fine by me, provided you think long and hard about what kind of value you're trying to generate from your investment. For example:

- Are you looking for a 25 percent boost in revenue from return users?

- Is your company's objective to increase revenue from customers acquired in the last year from 8 percent to 15 percent of your overall business?

- Is your social marketing meant to push your customer service costs down by 15 percent per year?

- Is your brand looking for its call center costs per customer to drop 15¢ per call as a result of a better social marketing presence?

The best way to determine your return on investment is to create an objective for yourself first and measure success in a way that can be clearly seen in your bottom line. "When it comes to our social media objectives, market research is huge for us," says Beth Doane, founder of Rain Tees. "Social Media gives us an incredible real-time way to gain feedback directly from one customer—or millions of them—all with a simple post and click. For many companies, social media is used mainly as a tool for sales, but for us the market research element is priceless."

As with anything in life, you can't succeed if you don't define what you're trying to accomplish. As such, you should be setting targets to aim for at the beginning of your social campaign. Examples: Is your company trying to inspire a certain reaction from your fans? Are you trying to sell more of an existing product or launch a new one? Without knowing what you're trying to push, you won't know how successful you're being.

It's very important that you clearly outline both your objectives (your company's desired end goal) and targets (the specific quantifiable values you would like to reach). When you're defining goals, it's admirable to want to achieve things like improving the ratio of positive to negative sentiment and increasing your overall number of followers, but these are not specific enough. If your goals are unclear, nonspecific, or unquantifiable, it will be difficult to impossible to know whether your efforts are paying off. Moreover, if you set specific targets, you create accountability; team members know how they're doing in regard to what they're supposed to be accomplishing and can adjust their approach midstream to improve the odds of success.

If your social marketing program is to be effective, you must establish a clear methodology for measuring progress on objectives and targets. If you don't develop a mechanism of gauging success, you won't know how you're doing. Although I've seen businesspeople launch programs and begin to think about their objectives and targets after the launch, it's a better idea to develop a measurement methodology at the outset.

When measuring your social marketing ROI, you'll be focusing on different metrics if you're looking for your ongoing social marketing ROI versus a campaign-specific ROI. It's tricky to calculate return on daily engagement and support programs: "Measuring ROI here is like measuring ROI on your business having a phone line," says Maria Ogneva of Yammer. There is definitely a return on the investment, though it's hard to quantify specifically what the exact return is.

Make sure to develop key performance indicators (KPIs) for your program, which helps you track your campaign's overall effectiveness at reaching the targets that you established at the outset. Your KPIs have to be linked directly to your goals. If your program changes or your goals have morphed into new goals, chances are you need a new set of KPIs.

One KPI I would recommend focusing on is your brand's Conversational Reach, which is simply the average number of replies or comments per post. The engagement that your brand generates on Facebook is a major component of EdgeRank, Facebook's algorithm for determining the odds that your brand posts will be displayed in a fan's feed. Conversational Reach is typically one of the top metrics that separates brands that have successfully gone social from those that just have slews of followers thanks to an advertising blitz. Content Amplification is another very useful KPI because it indicates the number of shares, retweets, and Google +1s per brand post. Shares are implied endorsements and allow your message to extend way beyond your current network.

When developing KPIs, bear in mind that it's a bit silly to focus on your brand's total number of fans or followers. If you encourage somebody to follow you on Twitter or like your page on Facebook, and then they never engage with you again, that's not worth much. Maybe finding ways to artificially inflate your audience helps if you're raising the profile of your start-up while trying to get funded, but that's a rare exception to the rule. You need to tie these easy-to-measure numbers to something that's more substantive and that relates more to the bottom line.

> ### CASE IN POINT: Whistler Blackcomb's Quest to Quantify ROI
>
> While Whistler Blackcomb is garnering many likes and follows, the company realizes that's not enough. One of Amber Turnau's key initiatives, for example, is to figure out how many of the ski resort's 86,000-plus Facebook fans have recommended Whistler Blackcomb to their friends or have been guests themselves. Whistler Blackcomb has tracking mechanisms in place to quantify the number of recommendations as best it can.
>
> One of Amber's mandates has been to start tying revenue to social media. A couple of years ago, many people were saying that there was no ROI on social marketing, only return on engagement (ROE). Amber felt strongly, however, if you have a product to sell, you can tie social engagement to sales. She spent a lot of time working with her interactive marketing team and e-business team to make sure Whistler Blackcomb was, for example, tracking unique links that send people to certain campaigns. Whistler Blackcomb often posts links to the page where

customers can purchase season passes, then tracks how often those links have been shared and visited, as well as the resulting purchases from their website. Since building a clearer relationship between engagement and revenue, Amber has been able to show Whistler Blackcomb's senior leadership team the revenue potential of going social. Consequently, the buy-in has really accelerated, making it easier to request and obtain additional funds and support for future programs.

Although Whistler Blackcomb isn't at the level where it can directly attribute social media to a specific percent increase in sales, that's the next step for the resort. Whistler Blackcomb isn't quite ready to set ROI targets for social media, but Amber envisions that will be part of it in the near future. Right now, Whistler Blackcomb is simply trying to get as many impressions, shares, likes, and comments as possible, and Amber's role is to attempt to track what revenue results from these social interactions. The resort is now focused on the building blocks, knowing that financial targets will most likely be built into the plan in the future.

Estimating Return at the Outset

It's simply not professional to avoid estimating the return on investment before creating a program. After all, how do you know whether the program is even worth engaging? If you think that your program will have a negative ROI, maybe you shouldn't be starting it in the first place.

When you're making the case, focus more on what your desired financial and nonfinancial results should be. Ask management what type of ROI they'd like to achieve from the program. Don't make up a target ROI just to get your program funded, but don't shy away from trying to estimate it beforehand either. You might be somewhat off, but that's the beauty of going social: In many cases, you can tweak elements of your campaign in real time.

If your campaign involves a social ad platform, such as Facebook or LinkedIn Ads, you can tweak elements such as geographic location or age range and see the changes take place almost instantaneously. In addition to tweaking the settings on your social platform of choice, you can make last-minute brand decisions to encourage more engagement. When we developed a 12 Days of Flawless campaign at Temptu, in which we gave a different prize package to a lucky customer every day, we noticed that the sooner we seeded interest for the next day's giveaway on our social channels, the more our audience would engage with us. This allowed us to alter when and how often we posted about the content, which led to a more successful campaign than if we had just set everything up at the start and left it alone.

Understand that if you're estimating the ROI on your social marketing program before your program has begun, it's just that—an estimate. However, even if something isn't a perfect science, that doesn't mean you should avoid it. Think of it this way: Can your organization's head of sales simply decide they're not interested in doing sales forecasting? Your operations team needs that forecast to develop quantities to sell. Although the forecast won't be perfect, you can't avoid the process. The same is true for estimating your ROI on going social.

Target ROIs

Most companies are okay with green-lighting programs that have a positive ROI. In that case, a program requiring an investment of

$25,000 to get back $28,000 would be considered acceptable. After all, it has a 12 percent ROI: ($28,000 − $25,000) ÷ $25,000 = 0.12, or 12 percent. Some companies, however, have much higher ROI requirements for a project to be approved. Sadly, most organizations, particularly small and medium-sized businesses, neither calculate ROI for their projects nor develop a target ROI for their projects. Do your homework, and figure out the culture of your organization to see what type of ROI you need to be proposing in order to get funding for your programs.

Accounting for Costs and External Factors

Every resource that you use on a project has a monetary value. If you don't measure how much your resources are costing you, you're not really going to have a good idea what your investment is, and then you can't determine your ROI. Think about the costs of personnel associated with your project, including both full-time employees and consultants. You want to be thinking about how much time all these people are spending on your project. The other big buckets are your costs and investment in technology products and services. These can include monitoring services, software licenses, costs in creating advertising, and so on. For organizational purposes, I like to break up fixed costs from variable costs. Finally, think about any additional expenses you haven't thought about in regard to these categories: travel expenses to get to social media events, webinar costs, and so on.

When you are trying to track down ROI, don't try to take credit for something where credit isn't due. A social media manager who shall remain nameless calculated that his company's ROI on their social marketing strategy, over a three-month period, was 900 percent. The problem is that another department had put in pretty significant online advertising spending during this time. The social media manager didn't factor in the cost of this advertising in his ROI calculation, nor did he acknowledge the existence of the ad buy in any way. As a result, he overinflated his efforts and gave himself a tremendous ROI to present that wasn't reliable or credible. If you present numbers in this way, you're going to lose credibility—not just as a social marketer, but also as a businessperson.

Developing an ROI Calendar

It's a great idea to create an ROI calendar containing all your data so that you can look at everything that's impacted your campaign simultaneously. Here you can measure all your activities, all your results, the financial impact to your business, and anything else that's important to note. Let's say a key event occurs—such as a new product announcement at an industry conference or the departure of a member of the executive team—that either increases or decreases demand for your product significantly. That event would be something important to put on your ROI Calendar. Obviously, you're trying to prove financial impact, so if you see a downward spiral or even a flat line, you should investigate why the metrics you're focusing on are not improving. Once you identify positive changes in these business metrics, you should spend your efforts explaining how your social marketing program has contributed to these changes. Remember, your social marketing program does not operate in a vacuum, and you won't be able to take all of the credit (or blame) for changes in your brand's financial metrics, given all of the other departments that are contributing to the company's success in one way or another. That being said, if you can't show that what you're doing is contributing to the bottom line, then you don't have much of a shot at proving a positive ROI.

Do you like detective work? Great! Figuring out how to draw correlations between your company's nonfinancial and financial results typically amounts to nothing more than extensive sleuthing.

Conversion Funnel Cake

Have you ever gone to a fair and ordered a funnel cake? They tend to be incredibly tasty and have all those little strings of fried pastry merging into one another. If you follow any single thread, you'll notice that eventually they're connected to the center of the cake—the end point. This is somewhat similar to how you interact with your audience online. They're all taking slightly different approaches, but ultimately you're trying to get them to your end point—the sale.

You've probably heard of the conversion funnel, the e-commerce term used to describe the track a consumer takes through an Internet advertising or search system, navigating a company website, and finally converting to a sale. The metaphor of a funnel describes the decrease in the number of visitors that occurs at each step of the process. What customer wants to be in the middle of a funnel? Being part of a conversion funnel cake is much more rewarding.

When trying to drive true ROI, your mission is to make a conversion funnel cake. This begins with brand awareness, leading to ongoing social conversations with prospects across social networks and online media, which eventually turn those social participants into customers. One of the best ways to drive social marketing ROI is to acquire new prospects online and develop those prospects by guiding them through the funnel cake. This can be done by selling something to a prospect whom you've never sold to before or by selling more to an existing customer than they're currently buying, either by increasing the number of transactions or the average spending per transaction.

Dell baked a strong conversion funnel cake in 2007, when they began promoting their Dell Outlet as @DellOutlet on Twitter. In less than three years, @DellOutlet had generated 1.5 million followers interested in hearing about deals, building reach that led to sales. During this time period, @DellOutlet generated over $6.5 million in incremental sales directly from Twitter engagement.

Tracking ROI Through Promotions and Upselling

One shortcut to determining the ROI of your social marketing program is to develop special promotions that are communicated only within a particular social channel. For instance, you can create an exclusive promo code posted only on your blog and then capture how often that code was used online. Then you would know exactly how much new revenue you brought in as a result of creating that coupon and messaging it out to your customers.

Another way of improving ROI within your online communications (and any channel, for that matter) is to get your customers to want to spend more money on your brand. If you can get one out of every five customers to spend 15 percent more per transaction via the art of the upsell, you've raised revenues by 3 percent. If you keep those upsold customers happy, you increase the odds that they'll talk about their positive experience with your brand, helping you acquire new customers via peer-to-peer recommendations.

If you're a company like Temptu and you're developing a social marketing program touting the benefits of purchasing more makeup up front, your goal might be to move the number of people who were buying blush, foundation, and highlighter as part of their initial purchases. So let's say one-third of initial customers are just buying an airbrush makeup system plus foundation, another third are purchasing a makeup system with foundation and blush, and the final one-third are buying a makeup system, foundation, blush, and highlighter. If so, you might want to develop the key performance indicator (KPI) around getting 50 percent of all initial purchases into that most expensive bracket, that is, purchasing an airbrush makeup system, foundation, blush, and highlighter at the outset.

Keep in mind that a promotion doesn't always have to come in the form of a 30 percent off coupon or a buy-one/get-one-free code. At Kiehl's, we had a get-out-the-vote campaign when our Supremely Gentle Eye Makeup Remover was nominated for a TotalBeauty Award for Best Makeup Remover. Although the typically modest selling product didn't ultimately win, our audience was motivated to vote for it by the hundreds. During the course of the vote mobilization campaign, online sales of the Supremely Gentle Eye Makeup Remover increased about 270 percent as a result of the conversation generated around the product. By using Google Analytics and tagging URLs with parameters so that we could see where traffic was coming from, we were able to attribute this entire sales increase to the social marketing campaign.

Financial Versus Nonfinancial Measures

As mentioned earlier, by definition, ROI is about measuring financial outcomes. You can measure a lot of nonfinancial intangibles as well, but these shouldn't really factor into ROI calculations. For example, goodwill and positive sentiment for your brand are great but pretty much immeasurable. Since it's hard to measure goodwill directly, it makes sense to find a good proxy measure, something that represents what you really want to measure. You may not be able to quantify goodwill to your brand, for instance, but you can use the number of times someone says they love your brand via social channels as a proxy measure.

Likewise, for most brands, social marketing will not be sound, scientific market research; receiving five comments on a status update should not directly lead to a new product innovation. But it can be the catalyst for more primary statistical data analysis.

Don't misunderstand me: It's important to analyze some of the nonfinancial measures, but you should be focusing on the nonfinancial metrics that lead to financial results. There's one pretty simple difference between financial results and nonfinancial results: The former you can put into dollars pretty easily, and the latter you cannot. Just about everything other than making more money and saving more money are nonfinancial results. They might lead to financial results, but they're not worth anything by themselves unless they lead to a financial result. Your goal when measuring nonfinancial results is to see how well they lead to increased conversions. Let's say since you developed an awareness program centered on your Facebook page, your brand has been averaging 1,000 likes a week on your page and your company has had 200 more transactions a week than usual. Are these two facts related? Maybe. It's up to you to show whether they are. The 1,000 likes a week is important only in relation to how much they can be tied directly to the extra conversions.

Many nonfinancial results are important to track because they are precursors to a transaction. These include sign-ups for a snail mail catalog or an e-mail marketing list, subscribing to your RSS feed, and registering for a competition under your Facebook page, to name but a few.

The number of Twitter followers that you gain per week doesn't matter at all to your company's financial results in and of itself. However, let's say you pick up 100 new followers per week, and four of these followers become first-time customers, and each one of those spends $80 on their first transaction. Now you're getting into financial results, and this is the kind of stuff that should be interesting for you to prove. You have to show the relationship between new followers and net new transactions. Though difficult, this is not impossible: Through data analysis, I can dig through my data and figure out how many of these new followers purchased from my company in the last week.

Many social media programs will give you nonfinancial results. But when it comes to something like brand awareness, bear in mind that an increase in brand awareness will not necessarily lead to a short-term increase in revenue. Temptu's primary product is an air-brush makeup system designed for everyday at-home use. During my tenure with the company, the airbrush makeup system alone (makeup sold separately) retailed for $225. As great as going social has been for overall awareness of the product in the marketplace, many consumers are not going to spend that amount of money on a product just because they became more aware of it. However, brand awareness can increase awareness of the product and its value proposition, in turn helping consumers realize that $225 is not that unreasonable if they want to look better than their peers.

That being said, customers often require a number of so-called touches in order to convince them to purchase. Thankfully, the leadership at Temptu was keenly aware that starting a relationship with the new prospect is just that—a start. It's not going to lead to immediate growth in revenue. Temptu was aware that it was part of a longer sales cycle. If you're marketing a product that requires a longer sales cycle, be sure to let your management know that your investment in social marketing will need time to prove its worth.

Measuring Sentiment

You can measure the number of mentions of your brand or of one of your products. Even if you don't have much of a budget, basic monitoring tools, such as Social Mention and Addict-o-Matic, can help you with this. Next, you can measure the overall sentiment of these mentions: How many of these are positive? How many of these are negative? Generally speaking, the more views that are positive, the more likely you are to be able to sell to people. I've seen companies where the ratio of negative comments to positive ones is three to one. If your brand is in a circumstance like that, it will be very hard to convince people to buy from you or even to hear you out. Tools are available to automatically measure sentiment toward your brands, and these are definitely worth a look, but you need to start by manually looking at sentiment. A lot of these automated tools get things wrong. You might be okay living with a tool that automates this work and is wrong 5 percent of the time, but make sure it's just 5 percent of the time. I've seen tools that are wrong 30 percent of the time, and that's simply not reliable enough. You might just have to suck it up and spend the time manually looking at sentiment.

· · · · · · · **GUEST POST** · · · · · · ·

Andrew Grill, CEO of social analytics company PeopleBrowsr UK, on:
Mining Social Data

In many ways, social media is the best piece of market research you never commissioned.

Every company is generating activity on social media networks, and the challenge is how to harness and understand what is being said and why in nearly real time.

This is the first time that the collective consciousness has been recorded in real time, and so the data revolution is just beginning. One of the biggest opportunities is inherent in the richness and real meaning in this data, far beyond what we're accustomed to from the traditional measures.

For example, analyzing social data in real time about television shows lets us know what the audience is feeling about the show, its ads, and its characters where previously we settled for merely knowing that they were watching. By working with this data, the viewer is instantly elevated from the role of an automaton to a thinking, feeling being who is truly engaged with your product and giving useful feedback.

The same is true for marketers in any industry. If they dedicate the resources and patience, the opportunity is there for a deeper relationship and richer engagement with customers than they ever imagined.

Focus on ROI, Not on Tools

One potential social marketing pitfall comes when a company focuses too much on tools and not enough on business objectives. I've been guilty of this many times. Whenever a cool new social media management tool pops up on my radar, I immediately have to sign up and check it out. The vast majority of these tools are distractions, but I'm afraid of missing the one out of every 50 tools that would give me a tremendous competitive advantage. You have to make sure not to fall victim to this tendency, and you have to focus on your business objectives. If your business objective is to increase followers who have tweeted that they wish their toilet paper were softer, you should look for tools that help you find people like that. Don't look for tools to use simply because of their cool factor if they don't support your business objectives. The best tool for you isn't necessarily the flashiest one; it's the one that suits your program's purpose the most.

More important than any tool's cool factor is its ability to do one thing very well. If you don't have much in the way of a budget set aside for tools, that's okay; plenty of free and inexpensive tools are on the market. However, make sure that you get a few tools that each do one thing very well rather than one big, shiny tool that is a jack of all trades but master of none.

Developing a Positive ROI Campaign

Tourism Queensland's 2009 The Best Job in the World campaign is a great example of an initiative generating a strong ROI. Anchored by a simple concept, the campaign involved asking applicants to post a 60-second video on Tourism Queensland's website explaining why they should be selected to be the next caretaker of the Great Barrier Reef's Hamilton Island. The winner could receive a six-month job making roughly US$100,000. The novelty of the contest struck a chord. In less than 48 hours, the contest had received 1,100 television placements in the United States, and the contest's website, www.islandreefjob.com, received 400,000 new visitors in less than a day and a half (400,000 was the goal for the entire one-year campaign). Roughly 35,000 people from around the world applied for the island caretaker position.

Unfortunately, there is no magic formula for creating a successful social marketing campaign. The odds of recreating the success of Tourism Queensland are pretty low. For one thing, a few years have gone by; for every business that tried to develop a viral campaign in 2009, twice that number are trying to have that same type of success now. So the competition is fierce.

Instead of thinking what must be done to guarantee a viral social success, cover your bases by addressing all the things that could stop your campaign from taking off. One thing that can help or hurt you is social integration. If you develop a campaign that is contingent on fans' tweeting your content and you don't make it easy for people to tweet on your behalf, you're decreasing the odds of your campaign taking off.

Another thing that can make or break your campaign is getting the right kind of buy-in at all levels. If you're a marketing VP and the PR team is independent of your department, make sure they're excited about the social marketing campaign you've developed. Allow them to contribute ideas. If they can make it theirs and get excited about it, they will be more likely to fight to seed your campaign online, in print, and on TV. If you might need extra marketing dollars to help the project really take off, get whomever manages your budget to become excited about the project too. If you really feel you need those extra dollars to make a project take off, fight for them.

Make sure your social marketing campaign has stellar content. Get your audience excited about your social marketing campaign and deliver something they haven't seen before. The more you make the campaign stand out in an interesting way without offending people, the more likely you are to get people to participate.

The Highest ROI Social Channels

Facebook is clearly the most popular social network on which to develop your social marketing campaigns, but many companies feel it doesn't have the highest ROI. According to a University of Massachusetts Dartmouth Center for Marketing Research study, 71 percent of the *Inc.* (magazine) 500 companies used Facebook for their social marketing in 2010. That's up from 61 percent the year prior. In other findings, 59 percent of this group used Twitter in 2010. Interestingly enough, old-school blogging was considered to be more successful from a business standpoint. Although marketing on Facebook was considered useful by 85 percent of respondents, the numbers were better for tools like blogging (88 percent) and podcasting (89 percent).[2] Perhaps even more surprising, message boards were considered to be the most helpful tool of all; even though only a third of respondents said that message board monitoring was part of their strategy, 93 percent indicated they were finding success when using some kind of online forum.[3] Foursquare, debuting on the study for the first time, was only used by 5 percent of respondents, yet 75 percent found success with the platform.[4]

Going Social Takes Patience

When it comes to determining ROI on your social marketing, make sure you give yourself a long enough payback period to analyze. Don't expect an immediate payback.

Social marketing success is something built over time; this is an area of your business where patience is a virtue. If you just moved from another city and were trying to make new friends, would you expect to amass a new group of close friends in the first month? Probably not. At least, I hope you wouldn't. Imagine approaching people and saying, "Hi, I need ten good friends. Will you be my good friend?" Chances are people would walk away. It's the same way with social marketing online. At the time of this writing, Temptu has 19,000 Facebook fans. When I joined the brand, we had around 850, with 300 being personal friends of the same employee. Upon my joining the team, we picked up maybe 200 people in the first two weeks. Not bad, but certainly unimpressive on a numbers basis compared to competitors who had over 10,000 at the time. If we had looked at those 200 new recruits and given up building relationships with them, we wouldn't have recruited our next 200 or the 200 after that. But showing that we were a brand worth engaging online (coupled with an innovative product) helped us grow online and build not only our numbers, but also meaningful relationships behind those numbers.

> ### CASE IN POINT: Fab Builds a Social Business Model with ROI in Mind
>
> At the end of 2010, Jason Goldberg had to give his investors some bad news. Fabulis, a social network aimed at gay men he had started a year earlier, was not gaining traction. However, Jason noticed that the site's Big Gay Deal of the Day—a daily deal targeting the gay male lifestyle—had attracted a lot of attention thanks to cofounder Bradford Shellhammer's impeccable, quirky taste. Jason and Bradford made a decision to shutter Fabulis and rebrand Fab.com, a shopping site focused on selling modern, innovative, design-oriented products, often at steep discounts.
>
> Shoppers reacted positively to the new venture. Just one day after the company sent out the initial e-mail touting its first four sales, Fab.com had sold $65,000 of product, leading to $18 million in sales in just the second half of 2011. Products they feature range from Domitalia outdoor furniture to Azra hand-stitched rugs from Pakistan to oversized Oniss and Adee Kaye watches.
>
> One of the secrets to Fab's reinvigoration was that, despite being so creative and design driven at its core, it is also very data driven and ROI focused. When the company decided to raise a round of financing in October 2011, they knew that the numbers were good, but it was

critical to prove the business had a chance at long-term health. Jason and his team developed a forecast for how much capital the company would require. It was easy to see that at its current growth rate, the company would hit $100 million in revenue pretty soon. The hard part, however, was to show how many investments the company would need to get much bigger over the next few years. To do this, an entrepreneur has to be aware of customer acquisition metrics and equations for calculating a customer's lifetime value. Without this, it's impossible to create an accurate model. A start-up's model is dependent on how much it needs to spend in order to acquire new users and what happens to those initial users (such as dropping out or buying more) over time.

Fab sent potential investors a login to their RJ Metrics Dashboard so that they would be able to view the company's data. Jason thinks that this tool is "the best of business intelligence dashboards for start-ups on the market." All a web company has to do is link its database to RJ Metrics, and the tool will generate complex, visually attractive charts and graphs detailing complex data such as changes to customer lifetime value and the relationship between on-site social activity and purchasing behavior. RJ Metrics allowed Fab to do an intense cohort analysis, giving the company great insight into lifetime value, payback periods, and other key metrics of its growth.

"The data is the data is the data. If you can't measure it, it never happened," writes Jason. "If the data is good, it'll speak for itself, and then you need to tell the story of how it gets even better. If the data isn't good, well, then you need to tell a story of how you are going to turn it around. Either way, the data is the data is the data."

The company has been able to engage customers and encourage repeat purchases among those customers through platform innovation.

Companies like Groupon started out strong but ran into trouble when they couldn't develop a model with near wholesale prices that still left enough profit both for the supplier and retailer, but Fab was able to crack this model. Another key component of the business model is built around social discovery via social platforms. Fab offers campaigns on an ongoing basis where existing customers are incentivized to invite friends in exchange for perks such as additional discounts or free shipping. Jason has stated that over half of Fab's members have joined via social sharing, with the company doubling its referrals from Facebook since going live with its Open Graph platform in January, which made it incredibly easy for users to share Fab products via their Facebook feeds and Timelines. Pinterest was also a major source of traffic for the company, doubling within just one month's time and surpassing other strong referral channels such as Twitter.

Another high ROI focus of Fab's has been the Inspiration Wall. Since renamed simply Inspiration, it was originally started as a way to keep people engaged as Fab transitioned from a social networking site to flash sale portal. The Inspiration Wall allowed users to create collages of their design inspiration from things that they find online, have saved on their computer, or are in their Instagram account. Once users find other users with good taste, they can follow them, which is an easy way for the company to increase purchases.

The company has also embraced mobile in a big way. Since launching apps optimized for mobile in October 2011, Fab has seen mobile grow to over 25 percent of its daily orders. Noticing that customers purchasing from iPhones and iPads were buying at two to four times the rate of browser-based customers, the company pushed more resources into these channels.

Fab's founders were smart enough to realize that building affinity toward friends early on would lead to lower marketing costs. Although approximately half its traffic came from daily e-mails in November 2011, direct visits overtook referrals from e-mails just two months later. Jason attributes that to a tipping point in awareness of the brand when it reached about 2 million members, and it's yet another reason that Fab is growing after a less than "Fabulis" start.

going further · · · · · · · · · · · · · ·

For bonus materials and updates pertaining to this chapter's topics, please visit: *http://goingsocial.jeremygoldman.com/ch12*.

13

going social in real life

"SOCIALLY CONNECTING doesn't necessarily mean online, but everyone wants to know that they are heard, that someone else cares about them, and that someone else has similar thoughts and emotions to theirs," says Brandie Feuer, Director of Marketing for Bath & Body Works. "However, at the end of the day, a beer with someone face to face is much more meaningful than a virtual beer."

Engaging with your customers online is great. Don't get me wrong: I've made a living from it. However, the next step for most companies should be taking that online engagement and turning it into offline engagement. If you've already bought a customer a virtual beer, why not make the next round a real-life one? Although this book is largely about going social through digital social platforms, I am in no way saying that online socialization can—or should—replace old-school socialization in real life. The phrase in real life (IRL), for short, implies a face-to-face meeting in the physical world as opposed to a digital meet-up. That phrase will likely become deprecated over time, as younger people hardly consider socializing via digital social platforms to be "fake life." At the same time, humans are hardwired to need in-person, physical socialization. Maybe in the year 2214 someone will read this and laugh at my assertion, but I think that's unlikely.

The rise of social networking platforms reflects the fundamental human need to connect in real life. This need was studied by Ed Keller and Brad Fay, coauthors of *The Face-to-Face Book: Why Real Relationships Rule in a Digital Marketplace*. The authors conducted a six-year study using over 2 million face-to-face, online, and phone conversations. Keller and Fay found that 75 percent of conversations in the United States still happen in person, whereas less than 10 percent take place via the Internet. The rise of social media has led to a reduction in e-mail conversations but not to a decline in personal interaction. In addition, face-to-face conversations tend to be more positive and are perceived as more credible than those that take place online.

Traditional media, including television, radio, print publishing, and online content, motivate far more conversations than online social media does, demonstrating that all media are social, or at least should be. Social media has helped us rediscover the power of sociability. However, the richest social goldmine remains face-to-face conversations.

As Lauren Brenner of creative event production company MKG says, "Marketing has gone beyond radio, TV, and print; it's now engagement face to face, as well as engagement digitally, and with new platforms growing each day, companies are struggling to keep up and continue the brand loyalty they once had." Because it's hard to keep loyalty up, brands need to reach into their bag of tricks and connect IRL too. A brand that engages only online misses out on true personal engagement, which is often a key component of driving sales. For most brands, the overall goal of online or offline interaction is to increase sales. "Online medias increase brand awareness," shares Lauren, "but people at the core still want to see, smell, feel, etc. the product in order to trust it. By dual-engaging consumers on and offline you are creating the number one goal each and every brand wants: loyalty."

Susan Towers, Vice President Marketing and Communications for Material ConneXion, a subsidiary of Sandow Media, acknowledges that "most consumer brands recognize they need to engage both on and offline, although some obviously do it better than others." While it's important to engage in both contexts, it's unlikely that "any brand can decide it's going to either focus online or offline," says Susan. Rather, "It's about integrated marketing campaigns across the board. A good campaign is one that seamlessly integrates into consumers' lives."

Although IRL connections are crucial and can never be completely replaced by digital interactions, social platforms can help build IRL bonds. By going social with your audience before an offline event, you can build buzz, which can, in turn, lead to increased interest, attendance, and press coverage. Use social platforms to host a contest to build interest in an event. For instance, brands have offered highly coveted tickets to events, in some cases making available tickets to an already sold-out event. Encouraging your audience to use a particular hashtag on Twitter or Instagram can also do wonders to build buzz ahead of an event. In this way, your brand leverages your audience's followers and fans so that more prospects are exposed to your brand name, or branded event, through their trusted connections.

Driving IRL Through Foursquare and Other Geoplatforms

As already mentioned, social platforms can be used to enhance the IRL experience for consumers. For instance, Foursquare is a platform that's great at driving real-life socialization, in part because it's almost entirely used by mobile users while they're out and about. Foursquare is a location-based platform that leverages GPS to allow users to share where they are and what they're doing at any given time. The main usage for Foursquare, which is often syndicated to other social platforms such as Twitter and Facebook, is for users to check in at different venues, where they can also leave tips for other users. Most venues on Foursquare offer specials that users can take advantage of. For instance, Apple retailer Tekserve offers a special of a free old-fashioned soda from their vintage Coke machine every third time a user checks in. Foursquare also offers up Flash Specials, where the first x number of users to check in to venue y at time z will receive an ultraexclusive deal. Offering up more unique specials will encourage virality—if they incorporate a visual, even better— because your customers will be more likely to share their experience with their peers.

Users also have the ability to create lists of their favorite places, which are grouped in any number of ways, and they can explore locale-specific features, such as restaurant menus and movie show-times, in their vicinity. Because of these features, Foursquare has become for many a bit of a local, social search engine. Due to its high degree of utility, Foursquare is growing quickly, with over 500,000 merchants on Foursquare and over 2 billion check-ins.[1]

Foursquare isn't useful only to customers; brands can also use Foursquare to connect with their audience. If your brand has multiple brick-and-mortar locations, you can make sure that all of these locations are listed on Foursquare, increasing the odds that they will show up in a search. While many people still search using Google, as Foursquare grows, there is also a pretty good chance that they might open Foursquare and use it to explore as well. Foursquare can also be a great customer acquisition tool; Groupon/LivingSocial deals for your brick-and-mortar locations can be accessed directly from Foursquare. In addition to allowing people to check into fixed locations, Foursquare supports listing events, so your audience can not only check into a venue, they can specify what event they're checking in for. If you're a venue promoter, you can promote specific time-sensitive events through Foursquare.

Brands can also offer their own specific Foursquare badges, which are virtual accolades users can earn based on their check-in habits, such as visiting five different locations of the same retailer, going to the same retail location five times in a month, and so on. These badges can be easy or difficult to unlock depending on the brand's preference. Fashion house Marc Jacobs, for example, has offered the Fashion Victim badge to people who have checked into any Marc Jacobs store in the United States, UK, France, or Italy on a few specific occasions. Daniel Plenge, who heads up digital experience at Marc Jacobs International, explained that by leveraging these badges in addition to their other social channels, "Marc Jacobs fans are able to get a 360-degree perspective of what we're about. Using these connection technologies, we want our fans to be a part of the Marc Jacobs community."[2]

In addition to Foursquare, there are other geo-centric platforms that are on the rise and worth investigating. Highlight, Sonar, Banjo, and Glancee in particular are worth paying attention to, as each lets you know when contacts are in the area and what they're doing. Highlight is a location-based service that alerts you when other Highlight users are nearby. Sonar helps people learn about other users in the immediate vicinity by surveying their Facebook, Twitter, and Foursquare accounts and determining the most appropriate connections to recommend. Banjo alerts its users when their Facebook, Twitter, Foursquare, or Instagram connections are nearby and also informs users about nearby hot activities. Another tool, Glancee, is a radar tool that also helps users learn which of their contacts are nearby and allows people to keep notes in the app's diary about encounters and events.

Although they all work a little differently, the overall premise of connecting people face to face is the same. In addition to facilitating socializing, these apps can also be useful for networking and are built for both personal brands and developing B2B connections. At the same time, it's only a matter of time for businesses of all sizes to find a unique way of using these platforms to connect with their audiences. As a general rule, even if no one else is using a new platform for a certain function, don't be afraid of using features in innovative ways! After all, someone has to be the first.

· · · · · · · **GUEST POST** · · · · · · ·

Why Going Social IRL Is Key

Cecilia Pagkalinawan has managed e-commerce for brands such as Nine West, Burberry, Frette, and La Perla. She is currently the CEO of StyleTrek.

Whether you run a small company or work for a large one, you cannot ignore the most important aspect of social networking: networking in real life. Building social connections online with those you admire as well as those with whom you've gone to school is not a true relationship unless you've made an effort to meet them face-to-face.

What I love most about conversing with those whom I'm connected with via social media is that we get to circumvent small talk and actually go straight to the point. Meeting with a venture capitalist, for instance, without having followed him on Twitter and being familiar with his posts is akin to going on a date without Googling someone. Online social ties make real-world conversations richer and more interesting. I once ran into Bijan Sabet of Spark Capital in line at a deli in New York's SoHo. I introduced myself and asked how his trip with his kids to Brooklyn went (a week earlier he had asked on Twitter where to take his children in Brooklyn while visiting from Boston).

Between start-ups, I worked for larger brands and was not aware how well my social network would benefit me until I was starting my company StyleTrek. I was not familiar with to what degree my random posts about my work at Burberry, Frette, and La Perla were being read until I updated that "I was pondering my next gig" on Facebook and LinkedIn. Not only was I inundated with job offers, but also friends who were angel investors and VCs [venture capitalists] were proactive about reaching out to me and communicated that they wanted to back my next idea. In six months, I was able to raise $1.5 million in my seed round and was oversubscribed.

It has been said that most of us are separated from one another by six degrees; I actually think it's less than two. I've discovered in random ways that people I've known as college roommates, neighbors, or Little League parents were connected with a potential investor or business partner. It also made me more conscious of the importance of my own reputation management. It's a fine line between perceptions and what is real.

As more and more of our "real" value is based on our social connections and is being measured by companies such as Klout, the lines between online and offline personas are being blurred. Once a female entrepreneur was complaining to me that VCs were not investing in her company. I responded, "Perhaps you've been too honest when you've felt overwhelmed, unprepared, and resentful on Twitter." Her honest and vulnerable posts were helpful in gaining her many female followers but may have backfired with male venture capitalists that were already wary of women CEOs.

In social media, I try to communicate my best self—the most interesting, intelligent, entertaining, and well-rounded person I can be. It's still me, but minus the bad, lazy, and cranky days.

Going Social with Meet-Ups

Setting up a meet-up so that you can engage with your best customers is a great way to strengthen connections. B2B companies in particular can generate tremendous value by bringing together a few potential prospects from their social audience for drinks or another informal meeting. Not only do meet-ups like this have a chance to turn prospects into paying customers, but they can generate long-term industry goodwill as well.

Meet-ups don't have to be only for strengthening corporate brands; personal brands can benefit as well. To get to know better my professional connections with whom I tend to spend more time online than offline, I set up a networking group called Professionals in E-commerce, E-marketing, and Digital. I realize this made the acronym PEED—not very classy, I know—but I wanted it to be memorable. PEED's mission is to help my colleagues informally network and make new friends simultaneously. To be a member, you simply need to be introduced by a current member of the group and be someone who loves to help others whenever possible. While Google Groups helps everyone stay in touch between meetings, the bond that gets built over a few rum and cokes strengthens the relationship in a way our digital relationships can't. Either directly or indirectly as a result of the group, I know multiple people who have found new, more rewarding jobs, discovered new vendors, and picked up skills and knowledge to help them in their careers.

Hosting Your Own Events

Hosting events at your offices is a cost-effective way of furthering your relationships with customers. Although bringing your entire social audience into your offices is not feasible, you can at least bring in some of your MVCs or blogger friends. When I was at Temptu, we invited some of the top bloggers and YouTube gurus in our audience to our offices for a sneak peak at some of our upcoming products, taking turns to interview each in our makeup studio. These videos netted nearly 100,000 views on YouTube, introducing our small airbrush makeup brand to new prospects we would never have been able to engage had we not ever extended the invite.

When I managed global e-commerce and social media at Kiehl's, we often held parties at our flagship store, which has been operating at 13th Street and 3rd Avenue in New York's East Village neighbor-hood since 1851. The historic nature of the store and the tremen-dous party-planning abilities of our PR team made admission to these parties much sought after. While most of the guest list was naturally comprised of celebrities, influencers, and employees, we always made sure to invite as many of our most hardcore fans as we could. Not only do these events elicit live tweeting by fans who have the opportunity to participate in person, we experienced halo effects as well. Fans who attend these parties often post pictures the next day on Facebook sharing their experiences and tagging the brand as well as any celebrities or influencers they ran into at the event. Photos of exclusive events tend to elicit high levels of engagement from the poster's connections, often raising brand awareness and affinity.

If you're not ready to host a full-fledged event at your offices, you can still encourage engagement by allowing visits. Clothing company Bonobos, featured earlier, allows customers to schedule appoint-ments to visit their offices so that fans can engage with guides, get sized, feel fabrics, and try on clothes in a relaxed environment. If you're looking for a no-hassle scheduling app to replicate the Bonobos approach, Setster is one app I'd recommend looking into.

Developing and Attending Conferences

Conferences are a good way of building connections with your audience IRL. If your business is large enough to support one, con-sider hosting a conference yourself. Mashable, the popular social media and technology news outlet discussed earlier, has held multi-ple conferences to strengthen the relationships the brand has devel-oped online. Its signature conference, Mashable Connect, brings together members of the news portal's social audience for three days, according to the Mashable site, "in a unique and intimate setting to share, inspire and really connect with each other offline." Leaders from esteemed brands such as Unilever, MTV, Discovery, Klout, CNN, Victoria's Secret, and many more attend content sessions, connect with Mashable editorial, and discuss the future of digital communication and technology. Speakers range from Harvard Law professor Lawrence Lessig to Mashable CEO and founder Pete Cashmore, to Leslie Berland, who heads up Digital Partnerships and Development at American Express. It's the kind of event that attracts not just representatives from larger brands, but agencies, entrepreneurs, and solo strategists as well.

Having your brand host a conference by itself tends to be high-risk/high-reward, and doing so won't be right for most companies. If you're looking to go social with conferences and your brand operates in or touches on the social media/communication/mobile/technology categories, Lanyrd is a great app and website I'd recommend checking out. Lanyrd offers a pretty robust directory of conferences and includes user-powered event details, as well as transcripts and videos of the previous year's content, so you'll know what to expect. Even better, Lanyrd lets you see what conferences your online connections will be attending, which I've found to be a great way for me to build my personal brand. If you're managing any consumer or B2B brand, however, a tool like Lanyrd is great for figuring out where your customers will be and what topics they're interested in building IRL connections around.

A Virtuous Circle: Use Events to Boost Your Social Audience

"If a brand is engaging offline—and by that I mean really connecting with customers, being authentic and inspiring people—they will naturally connect online," says Susan Towers of Material ConneXion. One company that used their IRL strategy to bolster their online communications is mineral water brand Evian. Through so-called activations at events such as the South Beach Wine & Food Festival and sponsoring the world's longest roller skating conga line in honor of World Health Day, Evian has developed a powerful IRL following. Without a robust online presence, however, the brand realized they were only reaching those at their events and then only for short periods of time. Evian reacted by incorporating a dedicated social team responding to all @replies on Twitter, posting content tying into the brand's "live young" ethos on Facebook, and pinning inspiration to Pinterest. Through social platforms, Evian has identified influencers and sent them care packages with handwritten notes to build relationships.

To receive the best consumer engagement, going social online and offline go hand in hand. Once you're at an event and face-to-face with your social audience, your brand should be pushing to your social platforms in order to further develop relationships and maintain momentum past your two-hour cocktail event or four-day conference.

During an IRL event, make sure to promote your brand's presences on social platforms. After all, by getting members of your social audience to interact with your social channels while physically on-site, you raise the odds that they will continue to engage with you long after the event ends.

I've gone to many conferences where all tweets involving the conference's hashtag are syndicated onto large flat screen monitors, often including the host brand's Twitter handle. Beauty giant Avon includes their Twitter handle @AvonInsider as well as the hashtag #buggard as part of their presentations to bloggers, to encourage live tweeting and allowing Avon to reach many more people than are physically present. John Frieda Hair Care did the same when hosting a dinner with their creative consultant and celebrity stylist,

Harry Josh. The hair brand included their handle @JohnFriedaUS and hashtag #expertperfect and then continued to display the handles at each of the tables as well as tweetable facts, making it easy for guests to tweet some of the main highlights of the event. Some brands will print out cards with their social media handles to pass out as guests come in at their events, and I've seen more than one include their Twitter handle on cocktail napkins. Other brands, such as Ideeli, have even taken their events one step further. At their Spring Fling preview, the flash sale retailer allowed all their guests at the event to host live giveaways for certain products via Twitter to build buzz. All guests had to do was choose one item from a selection at the event, take a picture, and tweet including the #springfling hashtag and @ideeli handle. As a result, Ideeli's Spring Fling preview garnered many more impressions and allowed the brand to expand its social following.

CASE IN POINT: charity: water Blends Digital + IRL for Optimum Engagement

Dedicated to bringing people in developing nations' clean, safe drinking water, nonprofit charity: water blends both online and offline engagement to maximize its potential impact. At the core of charity: water's online marketing is driving offline activations. "We take our story and make it their story," says Paull Young, Director of Digital for charity: water. The main way the brand accomplishes this is by building word-of-mouth sentiment.

charity: water's founder Scott Harrison speaks to brand advocates regularly and, as such, he is a powerful force in developing word-of-mouth communications. Seeing

Scott speak is at the core of activating new charity: water advocates. It also has a multiplication-type effect because going social IRL leads to a lot of online chatter.

charity: water fosters such high levels of loyalty offline that they often turn into content opportunities for the brand. One example is the recent Campaign to watch: Get them engaged! on their blog, which featured a young couple, William and Tori, on the way to the altar. Rather than settle for a typical engagement story, William and Tori tasked themselves with raising $5,000 for charity: water to build a well before they would allow themselves to get engaged. William created a YouTube video of his race to propose to Tori, which gave charity: water another opportunity to spread its message to its audience. William and Tori's story is just one of many because a high number of brand advocates will create offline content independent of charity: water that charity: water can repurpose to build advocacy.

Although charity: water leads the way with most of its offline engagement, it elicits so much passion that it creates advocates at other brands. Zappos did not have a formal partnership with charity: water, but it gave out tattoos that read "charity: water" for World Water Day. Zappos celebrated by raising money for charity: water and holding water-themed events. The online retailer raised awareness and money, donating enough money for 85 individuals to have access to clean drinking water.

charity: water is a master at going social to foster offline activity, as evidenced by its campaign to get brand promoters to pledge their birthdays to the cause. Instead of accepting birthday gifts, participants ask their friends and family to donate to clean water projects in honor of their big day. charity: water then takes 100 percent of the money raised to build clean water projects in developing countries. For World Water Day 2012, more than 5,400 charity: water advocates pledged to give up their next birthday for clean water. As word of the pledges began to grow across social platforms, the total number of pledges swelled to over 12,000 in the following weeks.

Every year, the organization holds the charity: ball, a huge event that represents another way for people to experience the brand in person. Last year's event had 2,200 guests and raised over $2.2 million. A constant at each charity: ball is the Waterwalk, in which guests symbolically walk a smidgen of the distance "an average person in Africa might walk each day to provide water for their families. Each time a person walks, a group of sponsors donate towards a well." Participants carry Jerry Cans—containers used by many people in developing countries to haul and store drinking water—filled with water on their Waterwalk, making the reality of many in Third World countries that much more real to them and building further passion for the cause.

Part of charity: water's success at blending going social online and IRL is that they don't think too much about the distinctions; rather, the brand focuses on building advocacy however it can. "We don't see the online and offline as separate entities," shares Paull. Many see this view as responsible for charity: water's ability to build and maintain lasting relationships with its audience. Some businesses look to hold onto a customer for four or five years before they churn; charity: water's aggressive goal is to build relationships that last over a decade. With the passion it elicits, the organization just might succeed.

going further . . . .

For bonus materials and updates pertaining to this chapter's topics, please visit: *http://goingsocial.jeremygoldman.com/ch13*.

14

final word

I HOPE THIS book was helpful—at least some of it. If every single word was helpful, I'd get a swelled head, so I'm glad some of this was filler. I'm joking, of course. Or am I?

If you have any questions about anything in the book, I'd love to help you out. Or if you're having a specific business issue relating to anything whatsoever remotely related to anything I know, I'd love to help with that too.

Just go to jeremygoldman.com and click on the contact link, send your message, and I'll do my best to answer any or all of your questions. Or look on my homepage for links to my presences on

Facebook, Twitter, Google+, Pinterest—you name it—and reach out to me that way. I'd love to hear from you.

Now, as I mentioned at the beginning of the book, I enjoy helping people, and one of the best things you can do to thank me is to go social with me! That being said, if you want to buy me a miniature pot-bellied pig, I might have to take you up on that.

Good luck! Engage away.

NOTES

CHAPTER 1

1. Caroline McCarthy, Quote of the Day: "Social Media Is Like Teen Sex," *CNET*, March 2, 2009, http://news.cnet.com/8301-13577_3-10185477-36.html.

2. Robert Vitale, "How the 'Golden Voice' Went Viral," *The Columbus Dispatch*, January 28, 2011, http://www.dispatch.com/content/stories/local/2011/01/08/how-the-golden-voice-video-went-viral.html.

3. Brandon Keim, "Babies Want to Be Social, Even Before They're Born," *Wired Science*, October 8, 2010, http://www.wired.com/ wiredscience/2010/10/social-babies/.

4. Statistics, YouTube. http://www.youtube.com/t/press_statistics.

5. Boaz Berkowitz, "Cha-Ching: Microsoft Pays Users to Search with Bing," *Seeking Alpha*, August 10, 2009, http://seekingalpha.com/article/155148-cha-ching-microsoft-pays-users-to-search-with-bing.

6. Ibid.

7. "Facebook 2010 Growth Stats: Infographic," *Digital Buzz Blog*, February 14, 2011, http://www.digitalbuzzblog.com/Facebook-2010-growth-stats-infographic/.

8. Melissa Miller, "Twitter's Population Growth: Where Is Everyone Coming From?" *Hubspot Blog*, January 28, 2011, http://blog.hubspot.com/blog/tabid/6307/bid/8642/Twitter-s-Population-Growth-Where-is-everyone-coming-from.aspx.

9. Retrieved from http://www.facebook.com/press/info.php?statistics.

10. Jacques Bughin, et al., "A New Way to Measure Word-of-Mouth Marketing," McKinsey & Company, April 2010, http://www.mckinseyquarterly.com/A_new_way_to_measure_word-of-mouth_marketing_2567.

11. Josh Bernoff, "Introducing Peer Influence Analysis: 500 Billion Peer Impressions per Year," *Empowered*, April 20, 2010, http://forrester.typepad.com/groundswell/2010/04/introducing-peer-influence-analysis.html.

12. "Two Biggest ebook Sales Days Ever for Random House in December 25 and 26," *EzineMark.com*, December 29, 2010, http://business.ezinemark.com/two-biggest-ebook-sales-days-ever-for-random-house-in-december-25-and-26-172122efe8b.html.

13. Ibid.

14. Report released January 2012 by Flurry Analytics.

15. "ComScore Reports $43.4 Bln in Q4 2010 U.S. Retail E-Commerce Spending," *RTT News*, February 4, 2011, http://www.rttnews.com/Content/ QuickFacts.aspx? Node=B1&Id=1545137

16. Retrieved from http://techcrunch.com/2011/11/09/comscore-u-s-Ecommerce-spending-up-13-percent-in-q3-to-36-3-billion/.

17. "E-commerce hits record $161.5B in 2011," *VatorNews*, http://vator.tv/news/2012-02-06-e-commerce-hits-record-1615b-in-2011.

18. "Social Media Agency Umpf Creates Lucrative Foursquare Check In," *PR Newswire*, January 28, 2011, http://www.prnewswire. com/news-releases/social-media-agency-umpf-creates-lucrative-foursquare-check-in-114787179.html.

CHAPTER 2

1. Margaret Rock, "Half of U.S. Use Social Networks, Older Population Catching Up," Mobiledia. August 29, 2011, http://www.mobiledia.com/news/105257.html.

2. Retrieved from http://mashable.com/2012/02/25/pinterest-user-demographics/.

3. Retrieved from http://www.radian6.com/blog/tag/foursquare-day/.

CHAPTER 3

1. "Twitter Patter:@bergdorfs," *The New York Times*, February 4, 2011, http://www.nytimes.com/2011/02/06/nyregion/06patter.html.

2. "Personal Recommendations and Consumer Opinions Posted Online Are the Most Trusted Forms of Advertising Globally," Nielsen, July 7, 2009, http://blog.nielsen.com/nielsenwire/wp-content/uploads/2009/07/pr_global-study_07709.pdf.

3. "What Makes Social Media Trustworthy?" *eMarketer*, August 12, 2010, http://www.emarketer.com/%28X%281%29S%28rdmlydnoekbmhvv1oww-pevbc%29%29/Article.aspx?R=1007863.

CHAPTER 4

1. Amy Porterfield, "9 Companies Doing Social Media Right and Why," *Social Media Examiner*, April 12, 2011, http://www.socialmediaexaminer.com/9-companies-doing-social-media-right-and-why/.

2. Zachary Rodgers, "Ford Jumps into Google+ With All Wheels," *ClickZ*, July 5, 2011, http://www.clickz.com/clickz/news/2084288/ ford-jumps-google-wheels.

3. "The ROI of Social Media," *MDG Advertising*, August 2011, http://www.mdgadvertising.com/blog/wpcontent/uploads/2011/08/the_roi_of_social_media_mdg_advertising_infographic.png.

4. Shea Bennett, "Twitter Users Better Educated Than Facebook Users, But Both Dumb Compared to LinkedIn [STUDY]," *Mediabistro*, July 19, 2011, http://www.mediabistro.com/alltwitter/pew-social-network-education_b11653.

5. Zoe Fox, "Pinterest Drives More Traffic Than Google+, YouTube and LinkedIn Combined [STUDY], http://mashable.com/2012/ 02/01/pinterest-traffic-study/.

6. "Engagement Unleashed: Gamification for Business, Brands, and Loyalty," June 2011, http://www.slideshare.net/Saatchi_S/gamification-study.

7. Scott Galloway, "L2 Prestige 100 Facebook IQ," *CMO.com*, June 1, 2011, http://www.cmo.com/social-media/l2-prestige-100-facebook-iq.

CHAPTER 6

1. Kashmir Hill, "Penn State Scandal Teaches Ashton Kutcher a 'Google Before You Tweet' Lesson," *Forbes.com*, November 11, 2011, http://www.forbes.com/sites/kashmirhill/2011/11/11/penn-state-scandal-teaches-ashton-kutcher-a-google-before-you-tweet-lesson/.

2. Better Business Bureau, "Complaint Handling—An Advantage for Businesses," *SME Toolkit*, http://us.smetoolkit.org/us/en/content/en/2855/Complaint-Handling-%E2%80%93-An-Advantage-for-Businesses.

3. Robert Scoble, "Apology to Twitter," *Google Plus*, August 20, 2011, https://plus.google.com/111091089527727420853/posts/ birhHh9jWfK.

CHAPTER 7

1. "Strategies for Effective Facebook Wall Posts: A Statistical Review," *Buddy Media*, April 6, 2011, http://forms.buddymedia.com/rs/buddymedia/images/review-strategies-for-effective-facebook-wall-posts.pdf.

2. Ibid.

3. Ibid.

4. Lauren Drell, "HOW TO: Improve Engagement on Your Brand's Facebook Page [STATS]," *Mashable Business*, April 6, 2011, http://mashable.com/2011/04/06/facebook-engagement-data/.

5. Jim Tobin, "Analysis: How Often Brands Post to Facebook, and the Impressions They Generate," *Ignite Social Media*, August 26, 2011, http://www.ignitesocialmedia.com/social-media-measurement/analysis-how-often-brands-post-to-Facebook-and-the-impressions-they-generate/.

CHAPTER 8

1. Jessie Jafet, "Tapping into the Benefits of Social Media," *Bedford-Katonah Patch*, January 28, 2011, http://bedford.patch.com/articles/tapping-into-the-benefits-of-social-media.

2. Retrieved from http://www.forbes.com/sites/tomiogeron/2012/02/27/gigya-now-reaches-1-billion-users-per-month/.

3. Retrieved from http://www.socialmediaexaminer.com/facebook-geotargeting-draws-500000-fans-for-small-biz/.

CHAPTER 9

1. Ben Straley, "HOW TO: Activate Your Brand's Super Influencers," *Mashable Business*, November 12, 2010, http://mashable.com/2010/11/12/activate-super-influencers/.

2. Drew Grant, "Updated: FourSquare Allows New Yorkers to 'Treat Yo' Self,'" *New York Observer*, November 4, 2011, http://www.observer.com/2011/11/foursquare-allows-new-yorkers-to-treat-yo-self/.

3. Nick Bunkley, "Joseph Juran, 103, Pioneer in Quality Control, Dies," *The New York Times*, March 3, 2008, http://www.nytimes .com/2008/03/03/business/03juran.html.

4. Josh Bernoff, "Introducing Peer Influence Analysis: 500 Billion Peer Impressions per Year," *Empowered*, April 20, 2010, http://forrester.typepad.com/groundswell/2010/04/introducing-peer-influence-analysis.html.

5. Jeffrey Grau, "Are You Able to Identify Your Influential Customers?" *eMarketer*, October 5, 2009, http://www.emarketer.com/ blog/index.php/identify-influential-customers/.

6. Bernoff.

7. "North American Technographics Empowerment Online Survey, Q4 2009 (US)," *Forrester Research*, December 2009, http://www.forrester.com/North+American+Technographics+Empowerment+Online+Survey+Q4+2009+US/-/E-SUS762?objectid=SUS762.

8. Jay Baer, "The Science of Inequality—Finding Your Influential Customers," *Convince and Convert*, April 28, 2010, http://www.convinceandconvert.com/social-media-marketing/finding-your-mass-influencers-customers/.

9. Ryan Flinn, "Sephora, Best Buy Enlist Social-Media Consultants to Attract 'Super Users,'" *Bloomberg*, December 9, 2010, http://www.bloomberg.com/news/2010-12-09/sephora-best-buy-snag-super-users-with-social-media-tools.html.

10. Ibid.

11. Ibid.

12. Ibid.

13. Ibid.

14. Joe Fernandez, "A New Era for Klout Scores," *The Official Klout Blog*, October 19, 2011, http://corp.klout.com/blog/2011/10/a-new-era-for-klout-scores/.

15. Drew Olanoff, "Klout to Update Algorithm, Launch Score Insights Tomorrow," *The Next Web*, October 26, 2011, http://thenextweb.com/apps/2011/10/26/klout-to-update-algorithm-launch-score-insights-tomorrow/.

16. Cotton Delo, "Social-Influence Site Klout Partners with Brands to Distribute Freebies," *Ad Age Digital*, November 2, 2011, http://adage.com/article/digital/freebies-klout-brand-partnerships-ftc/230756/.

17. Helen Leggatt, "Affluent Social Media Users Loyal, Not Seeking Discounts," *Biz Report*, May 11, 2011, http://www.bizreport.com/2011/05/wealthy-social-media-users-arent.html.

CHAPTER 10

1. Mark Pasetsky, "Charlie Sheen: How Many People Applied for His Social Media Intership?" *Forbes*, March 9, 2011, http://blogs.forbes.com/markpasetsky/2011/03/09charlie-sheen-how-many-interns-applied-for-his-social-media-internship/.

CHAPTER 11

1. Lauren Hockenson, "How to Recruit with Facebook [INFOGRAPHIC]," *Mashable*, February 5, 2012, http://mashable.com/ 2012/02/05/facebook-recruiting-infographic/.

2. Ibid.

CHAPTER 12

1. Corporate Executive Board, "Driving Business Results with Social Media," *Bloomberg Businessweek*, January 21, 2011, http://www.businessweek.com/managing/content/jan2011/ca20110120_489176.htm.

2. Helen Leggatt, "Facebook Most Popular, Not Most Successful, Social Media Tool," *BizReport*, February 2, 2011, http://www.bizreport.com/2011/02/facebook-most-popular-not-most-successful-social-media-tool.html#.

3. Ibid.

4. Ibid.

CHAPTER 13

1. Dusan Belic, "Foursquare Surpasses 20 Million Users, 2 Billion Check-Ins," *IntoMobile*, April 21, http://www.intomobile.com/2012/04/21/foursquare-surpasses-20-million-users-2-billion-checkins/.

2. Macala Wright Lee, "How Premium Fashion Brands Are Maximizing Their Social Media ROI," *Mashable Business*, February 11, 2011, http://mashable.com/2011/02/11/fashion-brands-social-media-roi/.

INDEX